My Liverpool Home

KENNY DALGLISH

My Liverpool Home

with Henry Winter

HODDER &
STOUGHTON

First published in Great Britain in 2010 by Hodder & Stoughton
An Hachette UK company

This edition first published in 2011

2

Copyright © Kenny Dalglish 2011

The right of Kenny Dalglish to be identified as the Author of the
Work has been asserted by him in accordance with the Copyright, Designs
and Patents Act 1988.

A CIP catalogue record for this title is available from the British Library

Trade Paperback ISBN 978 1 444 70420 4
Ebook ISBN 978 1 848 94691 0

Typeset in Galliard by Palimpsest Book Production Limited,
Falkirk, Stirlingshire

Printed and bound by CPI Group (UK) Ltd, Croydon, CR0 4YY

Hodder & Stoughton policy is to use papers that are natural,
renewable and recyclable products and made from wood grown
in sustainable forests. The logging and manufacturing processes are expected
to conform to the environmental regulations of the country of origin.

Hodder & Stoughton Ltd
338 Euston Road
London NW1 3BH

www.hodder.co.uk

To Liverpool FC and the people of Liverpool for adopting me, Marina and all the kids, and for everything they've done for the family.

To Marina, Kelly, Paul, Lynsey and Lauren – the best team I've ever represented. Many might think it would be great to be the son or daughter of a person in the public eye, but that's not always the case. Sometimes, other people's reactions have made it difficult for the kids, and all four have been a credit to themselves. We're really proud of them. The way they've grown up and conducted themselves is a tribute to their mother, who was there to bring them up. I didn't mind one bit playing the role of Assistant Manager in that team.

Contents

Acknowledgements

First of all, thanks are due, as ever, to my mum Cathy and my dad Bill for all the sacrifices they made for my benefit and for giving me a sense of discipline. Thanks are also due to my sister Carol, whose support, like my parents', was unfailing, and to Marina's dad Pat, mother Martha and sister Catherine. I'd like to thank everyone who has helped me throughout my career, but most of all I want to thank my wife Marina and my children Kelly, Paul, Lynsey and Lauren just for always being there. I will never forget what they have all done for me.

My thanks to Henry Winter, Football Correspondent of the *Daily Telegraph*, for recording my story; Roddy Bloomfield, my publisher at Hodder & Stoughton; assistant editor Sarah Hammond; copy-editor Marion Paull; and John Keith for the statistics at the back of this book.

Photographic acknowledgements

The author and publisher would like to thank the following for permission to reproduce photographs:

Action Images, AFP/Getty Images, Clive Brunskill/Getty Images, Peter Byrne/Press Association Images, Central Press/Getty Images, John Cocks/Getty Images, Colorsport, Andrew Cowie/Colorsport, Daily Mail/Rex Features, Paul Ellis/AFP/Getty Images, L'Equipe/Offside, Evening Standard/Getty Images, Stewart Fraser/Colorsport, Johnny Green/Press Association Images, Mark Leech/Offside, Liverpool FC via Getty Images, Tony Marshall/Sporting Pictures/Action Images, Mirrorpix, MSI/Action Images, Eddie Mulholland/Rex Features, Michael Regan/Getty Images, Mike Powell/Allsport, Press Association Images, Andrew Powell/Getty Images, John Powell/Getty Images, Rex Features, Neal Simpson/Empics Sport, SMG/Press Association Images, Chris Smith/Getty Images, Dan Smith/Allsport, Sporting Pictures/Action Images, Simon Stacpoole/Offside, Michael Steele/Getty Images, Bob Thomas/Getty Images, John Varley/Offside, Witters/Press Association Images, Andrew Yates/Getty Images.

Glossary of nicknames

Barney – Alan Kennedy
Belly – Alan Kennedy
Big Al – Alan Hansen
Billy – Alan Kennedy
Bugsy – Ronnie Moran
Bumper – Steve Nicol
Cally – Ian Callaghan
(Champagne) Charlie – Graeme Souness
Clem – Ray Clemence
Digger – John Barnes
Doc – David Johnson
Dogs – Kenny Dalglish
Dugs – Kenny Dalglish
Dusty – Ronnie Whelan
Fergie – Alex Ferguson
Golden Bollocks – Kenny Dalglish
Hodgy – David Hodgson
Howie – Howard Gayle
Jinky – Jimmy Johnstone
Jocky – Alan Hansen
Lawro – Mark Lawrenson
Nealy – Phil Neal
Nico – Steve Nicol
Old Bob – Bob Paisley
Omar – Ian Rush
PBR – Peter Robinson

Robbo – Michael Robinson
Rushie – Ian Rush
Smithy – Tommy Smith
Souey – Graeme Souness
Super – Kenny Dalglish
Super Sub – David Fairclough
Terry Mac – Terry McDermott
The Incredible Turning Man – Frank McGarvey
Tosh – Ian Rush
Tosh – John Toshack
Vitch – Ronnie Whelan
Wee Tam – Tommy Craig
Whip – David Fairclough

1

HOME IS WHERE THE HEART IS

Tʜɪs is Anfield, this is home and this is 2010. When I settle into my Main Stand seat on match-day, my eyes instinctively swivel right towards my favourite sight in football – the Kop. I feel Anfield sway as the Liverpool supporters sing their songs, wave their flags and their many colourful banners, showing their undying love for Stevie Gerrard and the team. Listening to this massed terrace choir, my heart fills with regret as well as awe. For all the hundreds of times I performed in front of the Kop, I never got to stand on it. I never experienced life among that great community nor the surge of emotion as the goalscorer turns to salute them. I wanted to be in among the Liverpool fans, thanking them for being there, for keeping the faith and always reminding the players that, as the anthem says, 'You'll Never Walk Alone'. A strange feeling runs through me. For those standing on the Kop, I lived a dream they craved. Pulling on the No. 7 shirt of Liverpool was an honour I felt hugely yet I envied the fans on the Kop for living the dream I desired. If only I could have joined them to share the atmosphere, jokes, stories and camaraderie. Just once.

The people of Liverpool have always been in my heart. From the moment Bill Shankly invited me down from Scotland for a trial in 1966, the first stirrings of a love affair began. When Bob Paisley signed me from Celtic in 1977, giving me a chance to perform in front of the Kop, that passion deepened. Even when

I moved away, finding employment at Blackburn Rovers, Newcastle United and briefly back up at Celtic, memories of special times drifted through my mind. I remembered the European Cups, FA Cups and Championships, the friendship of special team-mates, the unquestioning backing of the Kop and then the challenge of management after 1985. The darkest of hours, brought on by Heysel and Hillsborough, were never forgotten, never will be and never should be. Those deaths still haunt me. I think of the 96 who fell on the Leppings Lane End, and of how the Kop became a shrine with flowers and tributes spreading across the terrace and then the pitch, a beautiful demonstration of the depth of emotion. I wished the club had left the Kop covered in all those wreaths, scarves and mementos as a monument to people's love for the 96. During Hillsborough, we stood shoulder to shoulder with the families of those who died, helping them as they grieved. I still share their anger towards the Football Association and particularly South Yorkshire Police, who took twenty years to admit their part in a disaster that could have been avoided. I totally understand the families' distaste for a particular newspaper, which caused such distress with its vile allegations about Liverpool fans. Neither the newspaper nor the authorities have ever said sorry. That one word would mean so much, bringing closure for many of the families. The Kop wants justice and so do I.

As a man with Liverpool in my heart, the trauma of Hillsborough stayed with me. I'll never forget the stress counsellor who came into my Anfield office after the tragedy, telling me I needed to talk about the stresses and strains I was going through. I sent her packing. How could anyone help me deal with the pressure? This lady was, I'm sure, highly qualified and well intentioned but I wouldn't dream of opening up to her, a stranger, about a matter so intensely private. I never even spoke to my wife Marina about Hillsborough. Having talked to the families all day, I just couldn't discuss my own feelings, which seemed insignificant compared with their grief. The Kop was in mourning and I focused all my energies and emotion on helping the people of Liverpool. Anyway, I just couldn't comprehend how some counsellor could cure heartache. She'd leave my office but the numbness would remain. Only on the twentieth anniversary in 2009, when everybody was talking about Hillsborough, did I feel I could properly open up. Even so, recalling the events of 15 April 1989 proved a painful experience in these pages.

Hillsborough changed me, changed the sport I love and changed my Anfield home. It was a sad day when they ended standing on the Kop, sad but inevitable. Liverpool had to comply with the Taylor Report's requirements for all-seater stadia after the crushing on the Leppings Lane End. Sadly, the atmosphere has altered – you can't ask the fans to sit in orderly rows and then expect a completely raucous crowd. But when I hear people propose the return of standing, I shake my head, knowing how present legislation would prevent that and how it would be disrespectful to those who lost loved ones.

For all the changes, the Kop still retains much of its old power, rolling back the years for a big match, particularly in Europe or if Manchester United are in town. As I sit and admire the Kop, my mind rewinds to my playing days – like in May 1982 when I scored against Ray Clemence, an old friend returning with his new Spurs team-mates. The fans came spilling down the Kop, right down to the railings at the front and if I could have leapt into the crowd, I'd have thrown myself into their embrace. Leaning over the railings, I celebrated with them as they poured forward. This wave of humanity then fell back, and people returned to their starting positions. The crowd's ebb and flow has always fascinated me. Really, I should have known, having spent my youth watching Rangers at Ibrox with my dad. Every game, Dad led me down the same passageway, heading for the same barrier, meeting his same mates from work. Liverpool fans flooding on to the Kop in the hour before kick-off had the same ritual, all with their own set places. After Hillsborough, I understood the

Kop more as I walked on the terrace and saw all the keepsakes left in the spot where that person once stood. The Kop was so much more than an uncoordinated congregation – 25,000 individuals formed that mass and all had their own separate place almost reserved for them.

During my time managing Liverpool, my son Paul enjoyed the privilege of life on the Kop. Paul came in through the front door, walked past the dressing rooms and went out along the track. Stewards led him on to the Kop and left him with a boy from Edinburgh called Jim Gardiner, a huge fan who came to all our games, home and away. Of course, I worried about Paul going on the Kop but I knew Jim would take care of him. As a thank you to Jim, I gave him directors' box tickets for my testimonial, and Jim was so excited he got there at six, sitting in his seat for an hour and a half before kick-off. That's the type of people they are on the Kop, passionate about Liverpool. Jim would stand with Paul just in front of a pillar, protecting him in case fans pushed forward. As Paul headed on to the Kop one day, a photographer overheard one steward saying to another, 'This is Kenny's boy. Any trouble, get him out at once.' Waiting until Paul took up his position with Jim, the photographer snapped away. I admit the picture that appeared in the papers was wonderful, capturing the passion of a young fan watching the team he adored but I was still annoyed. I feared people might believe the picture was stage-managed, because it was taken in the wake of Heysel, when 39 mainly Juventus fans died, and Paul wore a Juventus shirt out of solidarity for the Italians. So there was Paul on the Kop, in that black-and-white top and Liverpool scarf, giving it plenty, singing his heart out and I must confess to a twinge of jealousy.

After every game, I drove home with Paul, quizzing him about the experience. 'What was it like singing the songs? Did one person start them? Which players got stick? Tell me the jokes you heard.' I was full of questions for Paul. Standing among the fans was a great thrill for Paul, helping him appreciate even more how much Liverpool meant to people.

What made the Kop unique was the amazing number of characters who congregated there, and I genuinely believe no other terrace in English football contained as many witty souls. One day, I tried to curl a free-kick into the Kop goal and it was a shocker, veering away for a throw-in. 'What a waste of money,' the Kop sang about me, their sense of irony a joy to hear. Then they started chanting 'Dalglish!' as if to remind me of my place in their hearts. Hearing them sing my name always lifted me. One of their favourites was 'I'd walk a million miles for one of your goals, oh Kenny . . .' and one season they almost had to travel that far before I scored. The beauty of the Kop is that people can laugh at themselves. When Manchester United visited in 2009 after the beach-ball goal at Sunderland, everybody knew the United fans would throw inflatable beach-balls on to the pitch, so the Kop beat them to it, kicking hundreds on to the pitch, claiming ownership of the joke. The stewards all had pins to burst the United balls anyway. I'll never forget back in 1980 when Liverpool faced Grimsby Town in the FA Cup and the fans changed all the players' names to fish to reflect Grimsby's major industry. Phil Neal became 'Phil Seal', Jimmy Case was 'Jimmy Plaice' and there was 'Sting Ray Kennedy' while I was 'Kenny Dogfish'.

As I sit in the Main Stand, I think of what Liverpool fans have done for the team. I think about Istanbul with the team trailing 3–0 at half-time and the fans defiantly singing 'You'll Never Walk Alone'. Down in the dressing room, holding their heads in despair at being outplayed by AC Milan, Stevie, Carra and the boys must have felt the return of hope on hearing the fans. They learned then, as I did, how much Liverpool means to the people. Fans obsess about the club, going to work and talking about Liverpool and then going to the pub and talking about Liverpool. As a professional, it's humbling to witness how they live and breathe Liverpool FC. It's helpful for players to understand how much the club means to people. If that dedication and love for Liverpool is matched by the players on the pitch, it will go a long way to bringing success.

When I wore the shirt, the dressing room's connection with the Kop was incredibly strong. Nowadays, I don't know if the players are allowed to be in touch with what the club means, especially those coming in from abroad, although Carra and Stevie explain to the foreigners the importance of the Kop, the history of Liverpool, and Fernando Torres, for one, became immersed in the tradition. Now that I'm working at the Academy, I know the Spanish coaches here at Kirkby are adopting the Liverpool philosophy. They've gone online, picked up the songs, know about fan culture and have come to understand the Kop. They share my love for the home I found in the Liverpool dressing room.

MOVING HOME

WHEN I first stepped into the dressing room at my future Liverpool home, none of the players knew who I was and, to be honest, I hardly knew who I was. Only 15, I'd never travelled away from Glasgow before. Suddenly, there I was, blushing as red as the shirts of the players in front of me, asking some of Bill Shankly's legendary players for their autograph. It was August 1966 and my love affair with Liverpool was under way. When Liverpool's scout in Scotland spotted me up front for Glasgow United, Bill Shankly invited me down for a trial. Also on the train south was another Scot with a kitbag full of dreams, George Adams, now Ross County's director of football. Emerging from Lime Street Station, George and I walked across to the YMCA where Liverpool booked us in for 10 nights. In the morning, a car took us to Anfield, making us feel incredibly grown up, particularly when we saw Shanks waiting to greet us.

'Right lads,' he said, 'get changed.' Liverpool's training gear was amazing, far removed from the sleek kit Stevie and Carra wear now. Hardly the most strapping of teenagers, I almost got lost pulling this polo-neck jumper over my head, a big, knitted affair better suited to an Aberdeen trawlerman.

'Now get on the bus,' Shanks smiled, 'and I'll see you at Melwood.'

Climbing the steps, I glanced nervously down the aisle and stretching out in front of me was a *Who's Who* of British football.

George and I nudged each other almost in disbelief. England had just won the World Cup and there was Roger Hunt, so close I could almost reach out and touch him. Nearby sat Ian Callaghan, another of Alf Ramsey's famous players. Then I saw Ian St John. The Saint! I'd seen the Saint play many times, for Motherwell at Ibrox and for Scotland at Hampden Park, but never this close. For any young Scot, the goalscoring Saint was an idol. My reverential gaze strayed further down the bus, encountering the familiar figure of Willie Stevenson, such a stylish left-half and a particular favourite of my father's during Willie's Rangers days. Strong characters left an impression on every seat, real men including Tommy Smith and Ron Yeats, tough centre-halves who could stop a striker with a stare. I felt like I was walking among giants of the game.

'Sit anywhere, lads,' Shanks shouted. Anywhere! Stopping our star-gazing, George and I threw ourselves into the nearest available seats. Simply being on the bus felt good enough but then the banter began, jokes flying through the air, coming thick and fast. Rolling down the aisle came the Saint's laughter. Even now, 44 years on, I always smile on hearing the unmistakable sound of the Saint around Anfield. The years disappear and I'm a teenager again, listening respectfully as a bus full of happy pros set off from Anfield to Melwood. All this chatter made me begin to realise Liverpool's special nature. Even on retiring, players never fully leave Anfield, many choosing to put down roots locally and always returning for matches, functions and dinners. Attending an old players' AGM in 2009, I looked around the room and there was Yeatsy, Saint, Cally and Willie. These famous men on the bus to Melwood were responsible for setting down Liverpool's traditions: camaraderie, banter, hard work and a passion for the shirt. Liverpool's DNA.

The man inspiring most awe in my impressionable mind was the manager who set Liverpool on the road to greatness. Coming down from Scotland and meeting Shanks, being greeted by this legend, was an emotional experience and I quickly understood why players ran through brick walls for Shanks. Like Jock Stein, whom I would play for at Celtic before coming south, Shanks exuded an unbelievable presence. If I stood in a mobbed room with my back to the door and Shanks walked in, I'd know instantly. Everybody would. 'Shanks is here.' An electric charge would shoot through the room and people would move and strain to get a look at the Great Man.

Like Big Jock, Shanks was very approachable. No starry airs or graces could be detected in the man on the bus to Melwood in 1966, although I soon appreciated Shanks's sharp wit. As we boarded the bus one day, Shanks was accosted by a boy in a Rangers scarf.

'Go on, Mr Shankly, gees us a game, a trial,' said the lad, juggling a ball. 'I'm good.'

'OK,' said Shanks. 'There's a trial on tonight.' Shanks gave him details and the lad ran off, happy as Larry. The following morning, we were all intrigued to know how he'd done. As Shanks strode towards the bus, the lad appeared out of nowhere.

'Mr Shankly, how did I do?'

'Drive on,' Shanks shouted at the driver. All the players looked at him.

'How did he do?' the Saint asked.

'Him! The next trial he'll get will be at the Old Bailey.'

A demanding manager, Shanks worked George and me hard. One day, Liverpool's first team played a closed-door game at Anfield against Wrexham because Shanks was thinking of buying their full-backs, Stuart Mason and Peter Wall. Shanks told George and me to fag balls off the terraces. No fans were watching, so we hared around, collecting any stray shots or passes, mainly from Wrexham, not that they saw much of the ball. Liverpool won 9–0.

I got a chance to play when Shanks put me in against Southport and as I ran on to the pitch, wearing a Liverpool shirt for the first time, I never felt on a mission to impress anyone. I was just me, desperate to win as always. When we were losing 1–0, I had a simple chance to equalise but as I was about to roll the ball into the Southport net with my left foot, a wee guy called Jimmy Bowman nicked it off my toes and bloody missed. The anger that raged through me then I can still feel now. I hated Jimmy Bowman for ruining my chance. I would have scored. I'd a better chance with my weaker foot than Jimmy Bowman did with his stronger foot. Afterwards, I trudged off the Melwood pitch, still seething at the incident and at losing.

On 13 August, I savoured my first taste of a local rivalry that would stoke my competitive fire over many years. It was time to meet Everton, Liverpool's neighbours and enemies, with the Charity Shield at stake. Adding to the excitement of my first Merseyside Derby was the thrill of jumping on the Soccer Bus, a shuttle service from the city centre, and sitting alongside all the fans heading to Goodison. After the Soccer Bus dropped us off near where the Dixie Dean statue stands now, George and I strode into Goodison, swept along on a tide of local fervour. Liverpool's line-up remains etched in my memory: Lawrence, Lawler, Byrne, Smith, Yeats, Stevenson, Callaghan, Hunt, St John, Strong, Thompson. When Hunt got the winner, Goodison fell silent, if only temporarily.

At Anfield on Monday, I told George, 'I'm going back to Glasgow soon and this is my last chance to get Willie Stevenson's autograph.' I said, 'Dad will kill me if I don't.' Willie and all the first-team players were in the dressing room, preparing for training. I hesitated outside the door.

'Go on, get in,' urged George. Too many of my idols were inside and I hated the thought of making a fool of myself in front of them. Encouraged again by George, I finally plucked up courage, opened the door and inched my way in. Seeing Willie Stevenson, I walked across, clutching a piece of paper and a pen.

'Will you sign this please, Willie?'

'No.' His answer was short and brutal, stunning me. My hero

had refused. Just as I turned away, my heart broken, Willie said, 'Oh, all right!' Then Hunt, Cally, the Saint and all the players laughed. Their behaviour gave me a glimpse of the Liverpool way. This teasing was how the dressing room worked and how they made people feel at ease. As Willie signed, I felt even more that this could be home. My reverie was disrupted by Shanks beckoning me over.

'Kenny, we want you to play in a trial on Tuesday.' I should have been overjoyed but I wasn't for a very simple reason. Rangers were due to face Celtic that night and I desperately wanted to go to Ibrox with Dad.

'Sorry, Mr Shankly, but I can't.'

'What?'

Thinking quickly, I remembered that there was a trial for Under-16s on the Monday. I could play that and get to Lime Street first thing in the morning.

'Mr Shankly, can't I play in the 16s game?'

'They're older than you!'

'Doesn't bother me.'

After the Under-16s game, Shanks offered me a lift back into Liverpool. He could have chosen any of the 11 players but picked me, so I knew this was an honour. His kindness stayed with me. So did his words that day. As his assistant Reuben Bennett drove us to the YMCA, Shanks sat in the back with me. After chatting about Rangers, Shanks suddenly said, 'Kenny, we like you. We think you'll make a good player at Liverpool. We'd like to sign you. We'll send our Scottish representative to see your mum and dad.' Here was my chance.

'Thank you,' I muttered. 'Thank you for the lift and thank you for the trial.' On the train north, I thought over Liverpool's offer but knew I was really too young to leave my parents, and I loved my football at my wee club, Glasgow United. Signing for Liverpool would mean missing watching Rangers every week, and I struggled to imagine a world without visits to Ibrox. Maybe

Rangers might even want to sign me, although they'd shown no
interest. Rangers were my team and when they got beaten that
Tuesday night by Celtic, it hurt bad. The following morning,
Shanks's scout came to the house and explained Liverpool's
interest. The conversation proved a brief one as my parents and
I had already made up our minds.

'Kenny's too young to leave home,' said Dad.

I was also chased by West Ham. A fortnight after my Liverpool
trip, I flew down to London and was put up in a bed and breakfast near Upton Park, rooming with Jimmy Mullen, who came
down from Scotland with me. Another Glaswegian, Jimmy
Lindsay, a pro at West Ham who went on to Watford, met us
and took us to the B & B. Yet another Glaswegian, George
Andrew, a centre-half who eventually moved to Crystal Palace,
was there as well. A real buzz surrounded West Ham because of
the World Cup, and even as a Scot, I appreciated that Bobby
Moore, Martin Peters and Geoff Hurst were gods in claret and
blue. West Ham's manager, Ron Greenwood, was very welcoming,
even inviting us to his house.

'That's a touch of class,' I said to Jimmy Lindsay after
Greenwood talked passionately about what a great club West
Ham were and how well I'd fit in.

'Go see the kit man and get yourself a pair of boots,'
Greenwood told me at the end of the week. For a young player
who'd never worn boots from a recognised manufacturer before,
to own a pair of Pumas felt like a rite of passage. I'd always
worn copies of the main brands. The Co-op did a version of
Puma boots with the stripe going from ankle to instep – the
real one went ankle to toes. Timpsons, the shoemakers, did a
boot with four stripes instead of the adidas three. To receive a
pair of real boots, which I cleaned with a religious zeal after
each game, was a truly special moment in my coming of age as
a footballer.

The generosity of Ron Greenwood, one of football's gentlemen, extended to my stomach as well as my feet. After we'd spent Friday morning doing sprints by the side of the Upton Park pitch, the players were handed luncheon vouchers for the greasy spoon around the corner. A stranger to East End customs, I carefully avoided the jellied eels. Greenwood also gave me tickets for West Ham's home match the next day, 3 September. As I walked up the tunnel before kick-off, I realised to my horror the identity of the visitors. Liverpool. Oh God! Turning into the dressing-room corridor, I spotted Shanks and his players marching towards me and I was gripped with embarrassment. What would Shanks think if he saw me at West Ham? I didn't want Liverpool's great manager to feel I'd betrayed him. I had too much respect for him. So I kept my head down, hoping Shanks and the players wouldn't spot me. As I flattened myself against the wall, the players came past, familiar faces I'd spent time with a fortnight before, including my idols Willie, Cally and the Saint.

'Kenny!' shouted Shanks. I kept walking, too scared to acknowledge him, praying he'd think he was mistaken. Escaping into the crowd, I breathed a sigh of relief.

Liverpool never forgot me and I never forgot them. Even during my working days in Glasgow, packing goods in a warehouse, toiling as a van-boy and then an apprentice joiner, an image of the boys on the bus to Melwood floated before my eyes. My parents were right, though; 15 was no age to leave home. So my footballing education took place at Celtic, mainly because they came in for me and Rangers, disappointingly, showed no interest, but Liverpool remained in my thoughts. I was given a refresher course on their quality when Liverpool visited Celtic Park for Billy McNeill's testimonial on 12 August, 1974. Shanks had just announced he was standing down and the Celtic fans gave him a wonderful reception. Celtic Park also appreciated that Shanks brought a fine team to town: Clemence, Lindsay, Smith, Thompson, Hughes, Heighway, Hall, Callaghan, Cormack, Toshack, Keegan. We held them 1–1 but Liverpool were really a class apart. Playing up front on my own, I just couldn't get near Tommo and Emlyn, who were passing the ball around the back, playing it into midfield, showing the style that was to become Liverpool's hallmark. Only a philistine would have failed to be impressed.

As the shadows began lengthening across the Seventies, the day loomed when I had to leave Scotland. Crystal Palace and Spurs were sniffing around me. Malky Macdonald, Spurs' scout north of the border, took Bill Nicholson to a Scotland game when I was playing. Malky knew my dad and by chance they ran into each other outside Hampden.

'Mr Nicholson, this is Kenny Dalglish's father,' said Malky.

'When's your boy coming down to England?' asked Nicholson.

'You'll need to ask him that,' Dad replied. The decision was mine. Celtic were great to me and I loved my time there but the desire for a new challenge grew inexorably. Craving a move in 1975 and 1976, I was persuaded to stay. Big Jock could convince anybody that his path was the right one but by the summer of 1977 I was adamant.

'It's right to go,' I told my wife, Marina. 'It's the perfect time for us with two wee ones.' Short of school age, Kelly and Paul could easily be moved to a new area. Marina and I never really mentioned Liverpool but she knew my dream. Memories of 1966, of Shanks and the Saint, stayed strong. Annoyingly, Celtic had other ideas and on 2 May 1977, five days before the Scottish Cup final with Rangers, Jock called me into his office at Celtic Park.

'Kenny, we want you to sign another contract,' he announced.

'I'm not signing, Boss. You know I want to go.'

'Kenny, if you don't sign, we have to register it with the SFA. Somebody will leak it to the papers that you've not agreed to stay and that will destabilise us before the Cup final.' Stein was so clever, trying to pull at my heart-strings. He knew I'd never do anything to undermine the team going into such a big match. My respect for my Celtic colleagues was too strong.

'The last thing I want to do is lose the Cup final,' I said. 'OK. Get the contract.'

Having signed under duress, the contract was worthless in my eyes. I was just playing fair by Jock and Celtic, but my plans hadn't changed simply because of a splash of ink on paper. First thing Monday morning I drove to Celtic Park. We'd beaten Rangers so everybody was in a good mood, but I didn't share the jollity because I knew the time had come to force the move. Entering Jock's office, I came straight to the point.

'I still want to go,' I said.

'But Kenny, you've signed a contract.'

'I know I have, and you know why I did. We've won the Cup. You'll no be keeping me. I've been loyal to Celtic Football Club. You know I stayed two years ago when you got injured. I wanted away but I stayed.' Stein knew it was true. In 1975, Jock was hurt in a car crash and Sean Fallon took over while he recuperated. The temperature in the room rose a couple of degrees. Charging into Jock Stein's office and standing up to such a fearsome man, a manager who had been so good to me, was tough but I had no choice. 'Life is no rehearsal' was Dad's mantra and I could never live with regrets, with thoughts of what might have been. In my mind, my bags were packed, and Stein wasn't happy.

Leaving the tension behind, I reported for Scotland duty in Chester. The Home Internationals fixture-list pitted us against Wales at Wrexham on Saturday, 28 May, giving us a five-day build-up. On the Tuesday night, relaxing in the hotel, I turned on the television and caught a documentary about Liverpool, who were taking on Borussia Moenchengladbach in the European Cup final in Rome the following night. Eloquently capturing the team's camaraderie, the film crew were on the bus with the Liverpool players on their way back from Wembley. Even losing the FA Cup final to Manchester United couldn't diminish the team spirit so clearly bonding Bob Paisley's players. I knew what I wanted. I wanted to be on that bus, sitting with those Liverpool players again, enjoying the special atmosphere I'd experienced as a 15-year-old. All the players were stars, household names, but they came across as humble, genuine and utterly determined to win the European Cup. The documentary couldn't have been a better advertisement for the attractions of Liverpool FC if the club had produced it themselves.

I was aware that echoes of Celtic Park could be heard at Anfield. As cities, Liverpool and Glasgow share many similarities, such as the great humour permeating both sprawling conurbations. Driving into Liverpool from Glasgow on one of my first forays south, I noticed somebody had painted a message on a bridge. 'Free George Davis' it read, referring to somebody in prison for armed robbery. Some Scouse wag got the paint-pot out and embellished the sign: 'Free George Davis – with every four gallons of petrol'. I laughed and laughed. I became so curious about it that I asked the chief of police when I met him at Anfield.

Anybody from Liverpool or Glasgow also knew the cities had intertwined roots across the water in Ireland. The Potato Famine brought hundreds of thousands to Merseyside and Clydeside in search of work before the two cities' traditional industries took a hit, forcing them to make the painful change from shipyards to other businesses. As clubs, Liverpool and Celtic are worldwide brands yet have remained entrenched in the local community. Feeling comfortable in my working environment was vital to me and Liverpool, brimming with parallels to Glasgow, just felt right. Anfield's dressing room had long rung to the sound of Scottish accents, from Billy Liddell and Bill Shankly to Yeatsy and the Saint. Anfield was used to accents like mine. I wanted to move there but Jock was obstructing my path.

After the Wrexham game, Scotland beat England 2–1 at Wembley on 4 June, a victory made even more memorable by my scoring against Clem. The previous year, I'd even nutmegged Clem to score. In the middle of June, my hopes of a transfer sinking, I was touring South America with Scotland when the phone rang in my Rio hotel room.

'There's something in the paper about Liverpool and you,' Marina said.

'Well, nobody's spoken to me.' It was true and I reported back for Celtic training a frustrated man. All the guys were talking about the pre-season tour to Singapore and Sydney, starting on 12 July, and I could see how prestigious the tournament was with games against Arsenal and Red Star Belgrade. More significantly, the clock was ticking down to the start of the English season and I knew, the moment I boarded the plane, that would be the rest of July written off.

'I'm not going to Australia,' I told Stein. 'I want to leave.'

'If you go to Australia, I'll make a call to someone who's interested,' said Jock.

I came back later and said no.

'Go home,' said Jock. 'Your career's just taken a backward step.'

I never knew who Jock was going to call but I hoped it would be Liverpool. I knew Jock had talked to Shanks about me before Shanks stepped down as Liverpool manager, and Jock also enjoyed a great relationship with Bob Paisley.

'We'd like Kenny if you are ever selling him,' Paisley had told Jock.

'OK, you can have first hit at him,' Jock had replied. Now the time had come for Stein to honour his word to Liverpool.

While these discussions were going on, I was sent to train with the reserves. One of our games, ironically, was at Annfield, the home of Stirling Albion. I hoped it was an omen. When Jock returned from the tour of Australia, he came up to me in training.

'How you doing?'

'Fine.'

'Do you still want to go?'

'Yes.'

I felt this was now getting ridiculous, but Jock kept his word. On 9 August, Paisley came to watch me in a pre-season game at Dunfermline. Stein stripped me of the Celtic captaincy, handing the armband to Danny McGrain, which was pretty humiliating but I bit my lip, knowing the end-game was being played out. Later that evening, Stein rang my father-in-law's pub, the Dart Inn, where I was having a Coke.

'Do you still want to leave?' Stein asked.

'Yes.'

'Well, Liverpool want you. Come up to the club.' First, I phoned home to talk to Marina.

'We're going to Liverpool,' I told Marina. 'Liverpool's perfect and if it doesn't work out, we can come back up here. I'm sure I'll get a game somewhere.'

'Not a problem,' Marina said. 'It's your job. Right? If you want to go and play in England, I've got to come with you.' So that discussion was quick and simple. Now for Big Jock.

When I reached Celtic Park at midnight, I found Jock waiting impatiently. Jock knew any final plea was pointless and it quickly became apparent to me that Celtic and Liverpool had done the deal anyway. With Jock was John Smith, the Liverpool chairman.

'Would you like to come to Liverpool?' said Smith.

'Yes.' I was so keen to join that our meeting lasted scarcely five minutes. After a bit of small talk, John Smith and Bob Paisley got into their car and headed south.

'Bob and the chairman will meet us in Moffat in the morning,' Jock explained. To keep reporters off the scent, Paisley and Smith had booked into a hotel in Moffat under the name of the Smith brothers. It seemed a clever plan. As Bob got out of the car outside the hotel, the doorman said, 'Hello, Mr Paisley, how are you?' Some secret!

At the hotel, Jock shook my hand and cuddled me. 'Good luck, you wee bastard,' Jock said affectionately and he meant it.

It must have hurt Jock's pride that I wanted to go, but managers can't have it both ways. Is the player not hurt when he wants to stay and the manager shows him the door? Jock knew I never let him down in terms of effort for Celtic Football Club. I went through a full year as captain when I was desperate to go and we still won the Double. I conducted myself honourably, bringing trophies to Celtic Park. Europe was a disappointment but we'd gone close, reaching the semis of the European Cup and Cup-Winners' Cup. Moving to Liverpool, I was convinced, would mean taking a step further, making a final and winning it. My blood boiled when some people in Scotland claimed I was going to Liverpool for the money. Of course, I'd gain financially, but I've never been driven by cash, just the glory and the quality of people I work with. My heart and head told me Liverpool, and even if they'd lost the final in Rome, I'd have gone. Even if Kevin Keegan had stayed and held on to the No. 7 shirt, I'd have joined.

On my arrival at Anfield that afternoon, I had a very brief medical, did the official signing and press conference, and then Bob dropped me at my new home, the Holiday Inn in the city centre.

'Emlyn might call by later,' said Bob before driving off. I soon had a call to my room.

'Kenny, it's Emlyn. I'm in the bar downstairs.' I hurried down and shook hands with my smiling visitor, Emlyn Hughes, Liverpool's captain.

'Do you want a drink?' Emlyn asked.

'I'll have a Coke.'

'Go on, Kenny, have a drink.'

'Emlyn, I had a game last night, I travelled up early, just signed, I'm not up for anything. I appreciate you coming to see me but I need to get to my bed and get to work in the morning.' Emlyn shrugged. He wasn't disappointed as he quickly found someone else to go out with. As Emlyn headed off into the night, I was just impressed that the Liverpool captain had taken time out to come and welcome me.

The following morning, Liverpool sent a car to drive me to Anfield and I was as nervous as if it were my first day at school. There would be nobody I knew in the dressing room, barring Emlyn and I'd met him only briefly. Fortunately, Emlyn was waiting for me and took me around the players, introducing me. Even after 11 years, I was delighted to discover little had changed in the way Liverpool did things. Get stripped at Anfield, have a laugh and a joke, get on the bus, have a bit more banter and train at Melwood. As we ran out of the pavilion, I noticed some kids sitting up on the wall, pushing the barbed wire to one side.

'Hey Terry,' one of the kids shouted at Terry McDermott. 'That was my sister you pissed on!' What the hell was going on?

'What did he say?' I asked Terry.

'He said I pissed on his sister.'

'You're joking!'

'When we won the European Cup, we came back to the Town Hall. We were all out on the balcony with the Cup and I needed the toilet.'

'You didn't!'

'I did.'

'You peed off the balcony?'

'Yes.'

Terry and some of the players then whispered to me I should wind up Clem over the goal at Hampden in '76, when I knocked the ball through his legs.

'You've got to mention it,' Terry Mac said.

'Give me some time to settle in,' I told Terry. 'Wait for tomorrow!' First, I had a more pressing duty. John Toshack took me to see Shanks. Even in retirement, Shanks still had the same aura I remembered from 1966. After reminiscing about my trial, Shanks said, 'Look son, I've two pieces of advice for you. Don't over-eat in that hotel and don't lose your accent.' I kept one of the promises.

The following morning at Melwood, we finished off our Charity Shield preparations and the boys egged me on again to wind up Clem.

'Don't worry about that goal, Clem,' I told him. 'You've always been weak between your legs!'

As we headed to London, I knew I'd have to deliver at Wembley. Some people questioned whether Liverpool were right to buy me, mentioning other Scots who had come south and not worked out – Joe Harper at Everton, Jim Baxter at Sunderland and Nottingham Forest, and Peter Marinello at Arsenal. I always felt that Marinello was naive, which is probably what made him a half-decent player, but he never settled at Highbury. 'I've come here and I'll do my very best,' I told local reporters. 'If it's not good enough, I'm sorry, but it won't be for lack of effort. Hopefully, it will be good enough.' I couldn't concern myself about those Scots who'd not really made the adjustment. Anyway, around Anfield there were enough pictures of Scots who *had* done well.

I also realised that I had to tackle the Keegan issue. Although I was an established player, with 47 international caps, I was still following a Kop legend. All the comparisons made in the papers were unfair – seeking to emulate somebody else was not my style. Kevin was quicker than I was, although I smiled when reading Tommy Docherty's verdict that 'Kenny's ten yards faster upstairs'. Kevin was a very effective player but completely different. He ran on to flicks while I went about my work slightly deeper.

'You two could have played together,' Bob told me one day. Paisley genuinely believed Liverpool could have accommodated me, Kevin and John Toshack in the same attack, but the simple reality was that Kevin wanted to leave. Liverpool sold him to Hamburg for £500,000 and got me for £440,000, so they were in profit. The whole Keegan business created a lot of fuss but didn't really bother me. I never felt I was pushing somebody

out of the side. I was simply picking up the No. 7 shirt left behind
by Kevin. He did brilliantly in Germany, twice becoming
European Footballer of the Year, and I was delighted for him.
Liverpool carried on being Liverpool, collecting trophies. Liverpool
were always bigger than any one player.

One day, I read with interest Tommy Smith's column in the
Football Echo. 'You can't take a world-class player out of your
side and not suffer for it,' Tommy wrote. 'It is essential that
Liverpool win something this year to take the pressure off Dalglish
– and off Liverpool for selling Keegan.' I understood Tommy's
point, but the pressure was always on Liverpool to accumulate
silverware. That was the Liverpool philosophy, the reason why
we worked hard. Winning was everything. Tommy was central
to the success of that creed, as Kevin had been, and I was determined to be. I just had to make the move work. Just before
Liverpool were due at Parkhead for Jock's testimonial in 1978,
my father-in-law, Pat, called.

'What are you doing about the game?' he said.

'What do you mean?'

'You're going to get some stick.'

'What?'

'Honestly, the Celtic fans have been practising.'

'You're winding me up.'

'No.'

I hadn't realised Celtic fans would be that angry. I thought
they might have simmered down by now.

'Is your dad going?' Pat said.

'Of course.'

'Right. I'll tell you what we'll do. We'll put him in the middle
of us. I'll sit one side and we'll get some of the boys from the
pub to sit the other side, make sure he's all right.'

After thanking Pat, I put the phone down, seething. After all
I'd done for Celtic, didn't I have a right to decide where my
career went?

Bob made me captain for the occasion, giving me the honour of leading Liverpool out at Celtic Park. As I ran out on to the pitch, there was a pipe band straight ahead that I had to skirt around. Engrossed in making sure I didn't bump into any of the musicians, I failed to realise I was alone as the rest of the Liverpool boys stopped in the tunnel, leaving me to face the wrath of Celtic Park. Amid the thunderous reaction from the 62,000 present, I'm sure I heard a few fans clapping me. Otherwise, my ears were assailed with boos.

'Thanks, boys,' I shouted at the Liverpool players when they finally came out of the tunnel, laughing their heads off.

'Hey, Kenny,' Tommo said, 'they love you up here. You must have done them a great turn as a player.'

Celtic supporters were entitled to be angry but they should also have remembered what I did for them. Celtic received £440,000 for a player who cost nothing and who left them with the Double – not a bad return. I never betrayed Celtic, as some claimed I had. Celtic Park's unpleasant reception made me angry, so I took great joy in scoring twice. Surely the Celtic fans could understand my celebrations? I was only doing for Liverpool what I'd done for them. Celtic had been my home. Now it was Liverpool.

3

ANFIELD

RELISHING the new start, I confided to Marina, 'I will not be superstitious this year. I'm just going to get up on the day of the game and see what happens.' Marina smiled. She knew how obsessed I was with ritual. Fans see the player for 90 minutes but never know how complicated match-day preparation can be, particularly for somebody as superstitious as I am. At the start of every season at Liverpool, I promised myself I'd relax, relinquish my usual customs and just go with the flow. Every August I tried, I honestly did, but I couldn't shake the habits. Call it superstition, call it pre-match routine, but everything had to be done in the same order – otherwise, Liverpool would lose and I'd consider myself responsible.

The established procedure started the day before the game when we'd meet at Anfield and hop on the bus to Melwood for a team meeting with Bob. Arriving with my own superstitions, I soon realised Liverpool had their own long-running convention, a tradition passed down from generation to generation. I not only got Kevin's shirt, I inherited his seat. In the dressing room, all the fixed benches were shaped in a U around the treatment table and Liverpool had an unspoken rule that nobody took anybody else's place. Before Bob took his place at the tactics board, I'd enact the first stage of my pre-match schedule. I'd always bring packets of biscuits from Anfield, and open the milk chocolate packet. One superstition that began under Joe Fagan

was that Steve McMahon had the solemn honour of opening the
plain. Of all the plain openers, 'Macca' had the best technique,
so good the players once pleaded with him to drive into Melwood
when he was absent injured simply to perform his biscuit duties.

I'd conceal three packets of biscuits down my tracksuit top,
although hiding them was unnecessary because Bob or Joe would
never dream of pulling us up for eating biscuits. Such astute
readers of footballers' minds knew what the biscuits meant to
our ritual. Holding a cup of tea in my left hand, I'd slip my right
into my tracksuit and extract the biscuits one by one. The rotation of the biscuits was carefully orchestrated. If I'd eaten two
milk chocolates followed by a plain the week before and Liverpool had won, it was obviously the same order again: milk, milk,
plain. If we lost, the sequence would obviously change. Rotation
was a staple of Liverpool life long before Rafa Benitez.

As the hours ticked down to kick-off, the routine intensified.
If the game was a Saturday one at Anfield, I'd have the same
dinner on the Friday night: tomato soup, steak pie with boiled
potatoes and peas followed by apple pie and custard, a menu that
never deviated.

'Never change a winning menu!' I told Marina. Alan Hansen
would come over and eat with us. If Marina was away, I'd cook
dinner and Al would still visit. I always felt this was brave of Al,
and a sign of our strong friendship, because I'm a liability in the
kitchen. Fortunately, we had a tin-opener for the soup and peas
and an oven for the pie, so we got by. Just. For a drink, I'd pour
myself a glass of American cream soda. Al and I often debated
whether the stuff sold in Merseyside was different from the version
we grew up with in Scotland.

'It can't be the same,' I insisted. 'For a start, it's green instead
of white, and it doesn't taste the same.' One day, I mentioned
my concerns over American cream soda to John Keith, one of
football's most respected writers, and he wrote about this great
puzzle in the *Daily Express*. Shortly afterwards, I received a call

from Barr's, the manufacturers, inviting me to visit their factory situated between Liverpool and Manchester.

'How do you get *green* cream soda?', I asked the people at Barr's. 'I've never seen it in my life before.' Having dressed me in overalls, the Barr's people took me around the plant and explained that the English prefer their cream soda green.

'But it doesn't taste as good,' I replied. 'The white cream soda is far better.' I knew I was right, and Big Al backed me up, but Barr's replied that it was the way the English liked it. Bizarre. After extensive research, I concluded it was to do with the water. Al and I noticed Irn Bru tasted different down here as well. On my visits north, I always made sure I returned with the Scottish originals, but otherwise I put up with the English cream soda and Irn Bru.

Dinner over, we'd drive to the Cherry Tree Hotel in Kirkby where we'd be picked up by the coach, which took the team to our pre-match base, the Lord Daresbury Hotel near Warrington. Al and I took it in turns driving to the Cherry Tree from South-port. One day, Al was rolling along the M57 with me and defender Richard Money when a terrible racket erupted.

'Al,' I said. 'Can't you hear that?'

'What?' replied Al.

'You've got a puncture. Pull over.' So Al parked up on the hard shoulder and the three of us got out to take a look.

'Have you got a spare wheel?' I asked Al.

'Don't know,' he replied. It was fair to say that Big Hansen was not known as the practical type.

'Where's the jack?' I asked.

'Don't know.'

'Come on, Al, you need to open the boot.'

'How do you open the boot?'

'You're hopeless. Leave it to me.' Having managed the straight-forward task of opening the boot, I removed the spare and jack and began changing the wheel.

'By the way, you'd better flag somebody down because we're going to be late,' I said, crouching down by the wheel. A car soon stopped, Richard hopped in and dashed to Kirkby where he explained the situation.

'Big Al's got a puncture,' said Richard. 'He and Kenny won't be long.' Graeme Souness was never sluggish in spotting a sporting challenge, so he immediately said, 'Let's have a bet on whose hands are dirtiest when they get in.' When Al and I finally arrived, Graeme made us present our hands for inspection and, sure enough, as everybody predicted, Al's were spotless.

Settled into the Daresbury, I'd climb into bed and watch whatever was on the television at nine, whether *Bouquet of Barbed Wire* or *Budgie*. I'd lie back and run through the match in my mind, thinking about whom I was facing, goalkeeper and defenders, and how I'd react to any situation. Would I chip the keeper if one-on-one? Would I lay the ball off? More rituals. At 10 sharp, I'd fall asleep for 11 hours.

Having woken at nine on the dot, I'd read the papers in bed, do the concise crossword and then conduct one of the important steps in my ritual – the pre-match shave. Superstition again dictated the format. If Liverpool had won the previous week, I'd move the blade in exactly the same direction as before. If we'd lost, I'd change direction. It sounds trivial, and I should really have been locked up, but it was a ritual and so deserved respect. Getting dressed, I'd never wear clothes that I'd worn when we lost. Shirts, underpants, ties and socks all got binned if they hadn't brought the right result. No mercy, out they went. I'll admit I had to address my lucky suit addiction. If I wore a new suit, and Liverpool won, I thought I'd better buy another to keep up the momentum. That was getting serious, and expensive, so I compromised on keeping the same suit during a winning run. After breakfast of tea and toast, it was time to get the coach to Anfield.

By now, with kick-off approaching, the superstitious nature of the whole squad would begin to show. When the bus turned into

Utting Avenue, the long straight up towards Anfield, we'd try to work out from how many cars were parked along the road what the total crowd would be – '38,000,' I'd predict, '35,000,' Souey would shout, '36,000,' said Big Al. The Tannoy announcer would give out the crowd figure, and there'd be some crowing in the dressing room from the ones who'd been closest. Ronnie Moran, nicknamed 'Bugsy' after Bugsy Malone, often got it right. Money never changed hands, so Bugsy never profited. Such silly little games were important, not just to pass the time during a period inevitably strained with nerves for many players, but also because the banter bonded us even closer.

The Daresbury routine lasted until 1983 when Joe took charge and we were allowed to spend Friday nights at home. My routine expanded then. I'd be in my bed at eight sharp, clutching a bottle of Irn Bru and a big bar of Dairy Milk chocolate – always the same combination, always the same respect for tradition. Marina broke off the same two squares from the bar and if she ever took more than two, or a different two, there was a riot. Marina's naturally of a mischievous disposition but she would never, ever tamper with my chocolate. I'd always eaten chocolate because it gave me extra energy and it became habit. Marina would be out on the landing on patrol, making sure the kids kept quiet. Usually, little disturbed my sleep and if I was struggling, I'd just swallow a tablet supplied by the Liverpool doctor.

Even the route from my home in Southport to Anfield was decided by superstition. If Liverpool got beaten, it was out with the map and change the route. If I saw a wedding while driving in, I knew that spelled good luck, so I was always hoping to spot a wedding car before every game. Funerals meant bad luck, and so it went on. Magpies caused endless problems. If I saw one magpie, I'd scan the garden, hunting for a second one because of the old saying, 'one for sorrow, two for joy'.

Entering the Liverpool dressing room, I continued my preparations while taking care not to interrupt anybody else's routine.

At home, I decided what clothes to wear, depending on results. At Anfield, I went about taking them off in the right order. First move – jacket off; second – unknot tie; third – remove shirt. And then I worked south. The kit was simple – jock-strap and then shirt. The shorts had to wait.

When I brandished a pair of nail-clippers, Liverpool tried to stop one of my routines. 'Don't be cutting your nails,' Paisley said. 'You'll cut them too short and give yourself a sore toe.' Nail-clipping had been a beloved tradition of mine at Celtic but Bob didn't like it. My nails probably didn't require attention but I needed to give it to them because of my superstition, so I carried on clipping.

My routine then became complicated, descending into real detail, starting with strapping up my ankles and picking up my socks – the correct way was right first then left. Even in an era of tough tacklers, I hated shin-pads and never wore them because they cramped up my shin. Climbing on the treatment table, I had a massage and then it was on with the shorts. Boots came next, adidas before I switched to Puma. When I first got free boots off adidas, I thought it was Christmas. Then Puma came along offering financial attractions and I started wearing Puma Kings and Puma Royals. I felt I'd arrived when they stitched my name into the boots – Dalglish Silver and Dalglish Gold. I really appreciated my good fortune. Kids were wearing boots with my name on them when I couldn't afford proper boots at their age. My boots were my fortune and I tended them lovingly. Even on elevation to the ranks of professional, I inspected everything the ground-staff did with my boots, particularly when they put them in the drying room. They'd be like crisps in the morning. I had two pairs, one for training and one for matches, and I was obsessed with these boots, running them under a tap to soften the leather and remove any flecks of mud, often imaginary, and checking that the studs were tightened just right. When I look at the boots worn by Stevie and Fernando, even some of the kids in the

Academy, I feel a twinge of envy, which might also be a touch of arthritis in my toes. Players now don't need to break boots in. They can wear them fresh from the box, but the trend for blades, rather than round studs, worries me because when the player turns, he encounters resistance that can damage cruciates.

Studs ruled back then. Continuing my routine, I put the right boot on first, then left, before the vital visit to the toilet, always the right-hand cubicle of the two at Anfield. That was the one I used for my first game, against Newcastle United, and since I scored that was me sorted trap-wise for my Liverpool career. If another player was in my cubicle, and the other stood empty, I'd still wait. Each player had his set time with the toilet and any new boy accidentally jumping the queue would be stopped by a shout of, 'You can't go now. It's my turn.'

To the untrained eye, Liverpool's dressing room might have appeared a jumble of players weaving in and out of each other, but method underpinned the seemingly chaotic movement. More routine was provided by the chairman, John Smith, who would visit the dressing room, going around each player, saying a few words. 'How are you, Kenny?' he'd ask. 'Fine, chairman,' I'd reply, and he'd move on.

'How's Headquarters, Terry?' John Smith would ask Terry Mac. John was in the pub game so he knew Headquarters was the social club Terry frequented at Quarry Green. 'Good, chairman,' Terry would reply. 'Fine.' Move on. Liverpool's chairman never got in the way. If John Smith had ever felt he was, he'd never have come down from the boardroom.

Kit donned, chairman sorted, I'd flick a ball up into my hands and head into the showers with Terry Mac for a further routine. Terry and I knocked the ball off the walls, warming up the Liverpool way – by passing. Every time, I'd say the same thing to Terry Mac – 'Right, competition time.' Terry and I played our little game, trying to hit the shower handle. Within a minute, Bob would call us back for a few final words. He was so calm, just walking around, worrying more about the 2.10 at Aintree than the 3 o'clock at Anfield.

'All the best,' Bob would say. He never mentioned anything especially pertinent to the game because he'd done all that the day before. Bugsy, Roy Evans, Tom Saunders and Joe Fagan would be wandering around, making sure we were fully motivated and making observations about the opposition. I'd be sitting in my place, always next to Al. He was No. 6, I was No. 7, and I'd have Jimmy Case or Sammy Lee on the other side at No. 8. Al would be absolutely silent, legs crossed, reading the programme, lost in reflection. That was the Hansen warm-up. Others stretched, got strapped up or rubbed down by Ronnie or Roy. Each player dealt with his nerves in different ways. Some chattered, some never said a word, but each person in that dressing room had supreme confidence in everybody around him. People talk about the secret to Liverpool's success as if it were some great mystery but I never felt it was particularly complicated. It was just good players trusting implicitly in each other. Merely looking around the room filled me with belief. I knew we'd win. Graeme Souness would crunch into somebody or hit a wonder pass. Rushie would score, or Clem or Bruce would make a save.

I find it hard to believe any team could possibly have matched Liverpool's comradeship. If I was taking a kicking, Souey would drop by to sort out the defender. 'Leave it,' I'd say. 'I can sort it.' Graeme was always there, a friend in need. Souey was the most elegant enforcer in football, a commanding midfielder with so many qualities that his price-tag nowadays would run to many millions. Jimmy Case and later Ronnie Whelan were fantastic footballers who could also put their foot in. We looked after each other. We knew the Kop would always be there for us, supporting us, singing our praises. Inside the dressing room, we couldn't hear them. Being cut off made the journey towards the pitch so special, heading towards the noise and the bright lights outside.

Just before heading out, my routine demanded I make a journey around the room. 'All the best,' I'd say to each player. Nothing special, nothing Churchillian, but each player knew from the look in my eye and the strength of my handshake they could rely on me. I'd occasionally have a few words with Rushie, talking to him about the importance of closing down defenders, but we all knew what we had to do. Bob had us well prepared.

Then a few shouts would go up, triggering responses off each other. 'Come on, lads, right from the off,' somebody would yell. 'Let's go,' resounded as the door opened. First out would be the captain, Phil Neal, then the goalie, Clem or Bruce, then me. I'd touch the 'This Is Anfield' sign, a practice so embedded in every Liverpool player's routine that the sign became worn by eager fingers. Some touched it with one hand but I was always two-handed, believing more luck rubbed off on me. 'Just as well you've got your long studs on, Dugs,' Souness laughed when he joined, watching me stretching up to the sign. Another Liverpool custom was the proliferation of nicknames and Souness called me 'Dogs' as in the Dog's Bollocks, but the way he said it, it sounded like 'Dugs'. Terry Mac named me 'Super' after some extravagant headline, but as he had a lisp, this came out as 'Thuper'.

I'll never forget my home debut on 23 August 1977, pausing at the top of the stairs and seeing the 'This Is Anfield' sign lit by a single strip of lighting. Similarly enraptured was Tommy Craig, the Newcastle midfielder. Having played together all the way through Glasgow and Scotland schools, wee Tam and I were good friends.

'This sign is supposed to frighten you,' I whispered to Tam. 'But it terrifies me!' Not for long. 'This Is Anfield' always inspired me. Running out on the pitch, I felt six feet tall, lifted by the sign and the noise of the Kop, knowing the fans were on my side.

My warm-up ritual on the pitch was quickly established. I'd sprint down to the Kop end and drill a ball into the net before doing some stretching and ball-work, hitting four crosses from either side. I hated it if I missed that first shot. 'I'm going to have a bad game,' I'd tell myself if the ball went wide. The Kop would always let me know, nicely of course. They were always supportive. Before that home debut against Newcastle, Liverpool fans gave me a great reception and I'd not even kicked a ball. It helped that I then scored just after half-time, after Ray Kennedy gave me a pass so inviting it came with a compliments slip. Running in behind the Newcastle centre-half, John Bird, I guided the ball past the keeper, Steve Hardwick, with my left foot. My momentum swept me towards the Kop and I loved seeing and hearing that explosion of joy. Turning back, I swiftly found Ray to show my appreciation for the quality of the pass. The morning headlines were kind to me, one of them saying 'Kenny's From Heaven', but we all knew Liverpool were a team. Everybody contributed. I took as much pleasure playing the pass to Steve Heighway that brought Terry Mac's goal, making it 2–0 and sending the Kop wild.

Back in the dressing room, I noticed my new team-mates producing sleek leather bags. 'What have you got there?' I inquired suspiciously. They smiled. Out of those bags spilled shampoos, hairdryers, all manner of toiletries and after-shaves. Anfield's dressing room was transformed into a fancy hair salon, fragrances filling the air. I couldn't believe my eyes or nose, and it got worse when that king of fashion Graeme Souness strode in from Middlesbrough that January. The aura that surrounded Souey on the pitch was more than matched by his style off it. His moustache was a work of art, lovingly clipped and groomed. With the looks and confidence of a Scottish Tom Selleck, Souey walked in one day, wearing a full-length wolf's skin coat, which stopped every conversation in the dressing room and probably for miles around.

'What is that?!' I asked as the other lads started howling like wolves at a full moon. Graeme calmly took off the coat and proudly showed us his initials GS stitched inside – not that anybody was likely to forget who this half-coat, half-animal belonged to. Graeme never wore the coat again in front of the boys, but he soon joined them in front of the mirror after matches, plugging in the hairdryer and styling away.

'What have I done here?' I thought to myself as they preened away like peacocks. 'How can you be football players with hairdryers?' I asked. 'I've never seen football players coiffeur themselves before.' Terry Mac laughed.

'What did you do at Celtic?' he asked.

'We didn't have any of this nonsense. We washed our hair with soap. Look at you with your shampoos and deodorants. Unbelievable.'

When Terry Mac and Souey got perms, the coiffeur sessions lasted even longer. Terry and Souey had these fork-like contraptions they'd stick in their hair, blowing it with their hairdryers.

If that was part of their routine, mine involved the blackest of moods if Liverpool failed to win. I'd be silent in the dressing room, even in the car on the way home, even the next day. Even if I had a couple of glasses of wine to remove the edge, I'd still feel bad, not wanting to see the papers, knowing the weekend was ruined. I trained all week to win and felt sick if we slipped up. When Liverpool lost away from Anfield, the trip back was murder. I'd sit there, staring disconsolately out the window, desperate to get back in the old routine – winning. Fortunately, the legendary Boot Room ensured we did.

4

OLD BOB AND THE BOOT ROOM

JUST A CRAMPED area, 10 foot by 10 foot off a corridor near the dressing rooms, the Boot Room made an unlikely nerve centre for Liverpool operations. Match boots hung from pegs and a carpenter's bench provided space for working on studs. Adorning one wall was a newspaper photograph of Joe Fagan talking to Ronnie Moran in the Boot Room. A calendar reminded everybody what year it was.

Running along the left-hand wall was metal shelving, leaving room at the end for a chair, traditionally occupied by Old Tom Saunders, who liked that seat because he could hide his whisky behind one of the uprights in the shelving if somebody walked in. For the life of me, I don't know why Tom feared discovery. Everybody knew what went on in the Boot Room. Up against the right wall stood two wooden cupboards, housing ledgers and a few bottles of whisky. A crate of Guinness Export stood in one corner, a present from friends at the brewers, who received tickets in return. After matches, Bugsy and Joe would sit on metal skips, holding court. When visiting managers and coaches were invited in for a drink, they usually accepted gratefully, aware of the honour. They'd perch on a skip, sipping whisky from an old glass, totally unaware they had walked into an ambush. Joe, Ronnie and Tom should have worn masks they staged so many hold-ups in the Boot Room. Information was their target and it was extracted with great subtlety. Unassuming and respectful people, never gloating over a victory, Liverpool's coaching staff were masters at making guests relax.

'That's us got a job for another week,' Ronnie said if Liverpool won.

'Oh no, it's not,' Joe piped up. 'We've got a game on Tuesday. Christ, we could be under pressure Tuesday.' The visiting manager felt he was being taken into their confidence when he was actually being led very skilfully into a trap. Gradually, waiting until his guard was down, Ronnie, Joe and Old Tom would quietly grill him.

'You're building a good team there. Got any good kids coming through?' Joe asked. Responding to such flattery, the visiting manager would talk about some real promising teenager on the books of his club. Within days, Liverpool scouts would be checking him out. They were so crafty. All the time in that Boot Room, they were weighing people up, finding out tiny details about what made their team tick, building up a mental dossier on opponents' strengths and weaknesses. Most managers fell for it. Brian Clough didn't. He visited just a couple of times, leading me to suspect Cloughie knew what the Boot Room boys were up to.

Shanks set up the Boot Room and it proved to be a breeding ground for future managers – Bob, Joe and Roy Evans. It was the heart and soul of Liverpool's footballing operation, a centre for research and strategy.

'Many a battle has been won in here,' Bugsy kept telling us players. The Boot Room was mainly the coaches' domain, and players were discouraged from entering. Sometimes I'd knock on the door, checking on timing for training, but on the whole I avoided the place. The Boot Room's history intimidated me. I never went in unless they shouted down the corridor for me.

'It's the officers' mess,' Liverpool's chief executive, Peter Robinson, remarked to me one day.

'Peter,' I replied, 'they are generals, not officers.' And they were, brilliant generals with Bob a field marshal, an amazing man, unpretentious and shrewd.

'Bob's so self-effacing if he wrote an autobiography, he'd only mention himself twice,' Hansen laughed one day, and Al was right. When Shanks left in 1974, Bob didn't want to become Liverpool manager. He enjoyed being part of the coaching staff, loving his work preparing the team and spending his day in the Boot Room. When he did take the job, everybody fell in love with him. People watched Bob on the television and thought, 'He's a nice old man.' With his knitted polo shirt and tie, Bob was like everyone's favourite granddad. You knew if you went over to his house, he'd dish out tea, biscuits and good advice. Everybody could relate to this truly modest man, a simple straightforward guy possessing all the right virtues for success in life. For all his brief doubts, Bob took to management easily and was never shy in solving a problem. When Shanks kept turning up at Melwood, unable to tear himself away, the boys told me how cleverly Bob handled a sensitive situation. Bob loved Shanks but this couldn't go on.

'Look, Bill, I can't do my job because you're still here. The boys still think you're the Boss,' Bob said. 'You're confusing them.' Bob was straight with Shanks, who took the hint. The best managers are decisive and Bob Paisley was certainly that. When he dropped a player, Bob did it unhesitatingly but kindly, recalling what happened to him in the 1950 FA Cup final.

'I scored the winner in the semi against Everton but George Kay dropped me for the final,' Bob told us one day. 'Laurie Hughes played and the decision was right.' Bob never complained.

That final was five years after the war and people still looked up to their superiors, never questioning decisions, but it must have hurt Bob. A caring man, Bob had a heavy heart when he left somebody out. Man-management was a skill of his demanding trade that came effortlessly to Bob Paisley. He'd have a shout, and the outburst carried more impact because of its rarity. On 26 December 1981, we fell to twelfth in the League after losing 3–1 to Manchester City at Anfield, and we were confronted by a seething Bob in the dressing room afterwards.

'It's not good enough,' Bob shouted at us. 'We don't accept that at Liverpool Football Club. If that happens again, you'll not be here.' He tweaked the button, giving us a warning, so we thrashed Swansea 4–0 four days later. Bob's reaction worked.

He was a proud football man, who always demanded pride in the performance. A year later, we were leading Notts County, Rushie grabbed a hat-trick and we eased up. Rather than a 'well done, lads', Bob went ballistic.

'After the fourth goal, you played as if it were a testimonial,' he stormed. 'I never want to see that again. This is Liverpool.' This was Bob simply keeping us on an even keel, stressing that even what may seem like a resounding victory could be improved upon. The game finished 5–1.

Anyone getting carried away, or giving the opposition ammunition with a silly quote to the papers, often earned a summons to Bob's office and an appointment with his wrath. In April 1982 when Liverpool were closing in on the title, Alan Kennedy said something to the Press that led to the headline: 'WE ARE THE CHAMPIONS'. Alan was called in to Bob's office, which, superficially, never seemed the scariest place, with three china ducks rising gently up the wall. On Bob's desk was an ornament of some piglets fighting for a teat with the caption: 'It's easy to stay on top'. So Alan went in and was duly ticked off. Careless talk costs points was the gist of Bob's reprimand.

Having witnessed Bob's methods at first hand, I can readily testify that this man was a master of psychology. After 90 minutes of the League Cup final on 13 March 1982, Liverpool were drawing 1–1 with Tottenham. Before extra time got under way, some of the players sat on the ground, catching their breath.

'Get up,' Bob barked. 'Don't let them see you're tired.' Nobody quibbled. We trusted Bob implicitly so up we stood. The message Bob wanted transmitted to the drained Spurs team was that Liverpool were strong, fresh and ready for another 30 minutes. I glanced across at the Spurs players, some of whom were lying on the grass. Seeing us all standing, ready for action, their remaining energy must have ebbed away. Psychologically, Bob's order not only shattered Spurs but lifted us. Ronnie Whelan and Rushie duly put them out of their misery.

Tactically, Bob was incredibly sharp. In a League Cup replay against Arsenal on 8 December 1982, Bob noted a vulnerability in the Londoners' defence, so he took off Sammy Lee and sent on Craig Johnston. 'Run at them,' Bob instructed Craig. David O'Leary and Chris Whyte couldn't cope with Johnston's pace and movement and Arsenal soon folded.

Bob was very proud of his background in the mining village of Hetton-le-Hole, near Durham. One day, Liverpool were travelling to Sunderland and Bob made the driver take us on a detour to Hetton-le-Hole. There was a monument in the hills and Bob wanted us to see it. We never quite knew why. It was just Bob's pride in the area really. He never lost his roots, never changed, always remembered the tough upbringing, the years as Gunner Paisley in the Army, driving a tank through Italy, fighting the Germans. At Liverpool, Bob kept to a well-rehearsed daily routine. Up, out of the house, drive to a friend's garage, sit in the back, place a few bets and on to Anfield.

'I'm only a modest Geordie,' Bob said to us, 'but back me into a corner and I'm a vicious bastard.'

As a modest Geordie, Bob never got the recognition he deserved. Bob Paisley is the greatest manager in the history of British football and I have no hesitation in saying that. His relentless amassing of silverware justifies such a statement. In nine years, Bob won six titles, three League Cups, the Uefa Cup and three European Cups. Three! In Rome in 1977, at Wembley in 1978 and in Paris in 1981. Some record – and, remember, that was in the days when if you lost in the first round of the European Cup, you were out. There were no second chances, no group stages providing a nice safety net. The Champions League protects the big clubs against a fatal shock by a smaller team. Bob masterminded three European Cup triumphs in a more demanding era yet never got any recognition from the country. Three European Cups and he can't get a knighthood! Matt Busby was knighted. Alex Ferguson was knighted. Bobby Robson, God bless him, was knighted. So why was Bob missed out? I believe it was because he never promoted himself. Bob let the results speak for themselves, but obviously they didn't speak loud enough for somebody to be listening in Westminster.

If he'd been offered a knighthood, Bob would have accepted reluctantly, because that was the nature of the man – humble – but he'd have been down to the Palace, beaming inside and joking on the outside. A man who loved a quip, Bob would have celebrated the honour with some special words. 'Never mind the European Cup final in Rome,' Bob would have said, 'I should have got this award for when I was there in my tank.' For all his one-liners and self-deprecation, Bob would have been the proudest man in Britain to be knighted. Sir Bob Paisley would have sounded good. Such awards are supposed to reward role models and they didn't come much better than Bob, whose conduct was always exemplary. He was a man who lived his life by sound principles.

As players, we didn't bother about not receiving any respect from the country. We were just sitting there with another European Cup medal, another League Championship medal, another League Cup medal. Manchester United attracted all the publicity. But why did Bobby Charlton get a knighthood and not Roger Hunt, another World Cup winner? Why should United set the criteria? Manchester was a bigger city, a magnet to most of the media, who were obsessed with United. So what? Never bothered me. But I always felt for Bob. He deserved better.

The players loved him and it was a painful moment when he stepped down in 1983. Searching for a fitting tribute to a great manager, Graeme came up with a brilliant idea before the Milk Cup final, as the League Cup was known then.

'If we win, we'll send Bob up,' said Graeme. Bob was incredibly reticent, needing persuasion to climb the 39 steps to receive the trophy and the acclaim of the Wembley crowd. A deeply unassuming man, Bob took off his white mac and cap before ascending to meet royalty, but I considered the honour was theirs.

Full of endearing characteristics, Bob had some unique phrases that peppered his talk in the dressing room. 'Champagne only comes along if you get the bread-and-butter values right,' Bob told us. 'He's alekeefie,' Bob said of any player he considered a bit doolally. He had a language to himself.

'The opposition will do a Huddy,' Bob announced in one team-talk.

'Boss?' I asked. 'What's a Huddy?'

'Alan Hudson,' Bob explained. 'Hudson does it. I hate it when a midfielder goes in among the back-four to get a pass. Don't you be doing a Huddy.'

Another day, Bob said, 'Don't be giving it a slow roll across the back.' Looks of bemusement spread across our faces and Tommy Smith burst out laughing.

'What's a slow roll, Boss?' Tommy asked. Bob looked at Tommy and the rest of us as if we'd just taken up football.

'It's when the full-back passes the ball across the back-four,' Bob said. 'Don't hit it slowly. Get pace on it. I'm not having the slow roll.'

When Bob couldn't remember somebody's name, he'd call him 'Dougie Doins'. A team-talk could easily contain the instruction from Bob to Big Al: 'Alan, at corners, you pick up Dougie Doins.'

Bob loathed the long pass, warning us against it with: 'Don't be hitting the far-flung one.'

On one occasion, we'd agreed to pick Alan up on our way to a game down south. 'We'll lift you at Crewe, Alan,' Bob said.

Bob had a wonderful sense of humour, a real wry touch. Brian Kettle, a ginger-haired left-back, went in to speak to Bob one day. Bob was writing at his desk, and in front of him was a huge

Sesame Street puppet. Seeing the puppet, Brian forgot what he'd come in for. Bob just carried on writing and eventually Brian managed to focus.

'Boss, can I have a word with you about my future?' Brian said. 'I need to look ahead.'

'Who do you think you are, son, Patrick Moore?'

One year, Terry Mac didn't turn up to collect a sports writers award, but Bob accepted it for him.

'You've given Terry this award,' said Bob, 'and one of the things you probably recognise in Terry is that he makes some great blind-side runs – but not normally as good as this!'

Having been a physio, Bob had an unbelievable eye for picking out injuries from the way we were walking. Within months of my arriving at Anfield, I was fully informed about how, in the past, Bob used this cannily to exploit the subs system. Liverpool were chasing the game at Upton Park in 1968 when Tony Hateley went down. Bob, then a trainer under Shanks, ran on and signalled for the stretcher.

'No, no, Bob, I'm all right,' said Hateley, who was only winded.

'No, you need it, your legs,' replied Bob, starting to tie Tony's legs together.

'I'm fine!'

'You're bloody well coming off.' A player needed to be injured to be subbed, so strapping Tony's legs up kidded everybody he had a problem. Liverpool then brought Doug Livermore on for his debut.

Assisting Bob was a real brain's trust. Ronnie was always incredibly loyal to Bob, and to his successor, Joe Fagan. Bugsy knew his position but still voiced his opinion, screaming and shouting at us when we needed it. Bugsy was so competitive. If Liverpool were leading and the ball came out of play, landing close to Ronnie, he'd either knock it down the track or jam his fingers into it, checking the pressure before passing it back, just wasting time. If Ronnie picked up the ball, he'd throw it against the wooden edging of the pitch so it bounced back into the crowd, killing a few more precious seconds. It looked so real. 'Sorry,' Ronnie said to the opposition manager, although any tears were very much of the crocodile variety. We knew Bugsy would do all he could to help us to victory.

In pre-season, he worked us incredibly hard, building up our fitness for the long marathon of matches ahead. 'Get yourself early to bed tonight, lads,' he'd say. 'Big Picture tomorrow.' This horror came a week into pre-season and was a gruelling running session. Ronnie made us lap Melwood throughout the morning, giving us the power to last the season. Terry Mac was up at the front with Ray Kennedy, and Mark Lawrenson, better known as 'Lawro', tucked in just behind. I stayed in the pack while the back was brought up by Clem and David Fairclough. At the end, as we struggled to stand up, sweat pouring from us, Bob announced, 'You've been good this week, so we'll give you a game in the morning.' Thank you. We knew we were getting one anyway. When people claimed Liverpool acquired their fitness simply from playing five-a-sides, I always thought of those brutal runs under Bugsy and winced. Those sessions underpinned the season's success, allowing us to play 70 games and never think about it. If a modern player starts two games a week, he complains, in an era when the footballer is supposed to be faster, fitter, stronger! During the season, Ronnie threatened more running.

'You're not training properly,' Bugsy yelled if anybody mucked about during pattern-of-play work. 'If you don't want to do it properly with the ball, we can just set the cones out and do some running. It's up to yourselves.' That threat, and the stern manner in which Bugsy delivered it, usually worked. The Boot Room boys were tough, quick to spot any slacking off.

'Some of you think we've never played,' Bugsy shouted at us. I noted with quiet pleasure that Joey Jones or Alan Kennedy got most stick off Ronnie because they played left-back, his old position, and he followed their movements like CCTV. During matches, Ronnie barked instructions.

'I have the best break of my life – not hearing too well out of my right ear,' Jimmy Case told me. 'Whatever Bugsy's saying, I haven't a clue.'

After games, Ronnie always left us with the same message – 'Any injuries, see you tomorrow. Straight home. Don't go boozing or gallivanting with girls. Rest up, no messing about.'

Bugsy influenced life at Anfield and Melwood in so many ways, and particularly assisted the education of Roy Evans, a man similarly steeped in Liverpool tradition. When Roy represented Liverpool and England Schoolboys, the world and his dog fought battles to sign him. When Anfield beckoned, Roy came running to the club he loved, and he certainly started promisingly. Sadly, Roy was just short of top quality, so Shanks called him into his office.

'You can leave, or I'll give you a job here, taking the reserves,' Shanks said. As a local lad who adored Liverpool, Roy stayed and did brilliantly with the reserves, winning loads of titles. Roy's diplomatic skills were often deployed to good effect as some first-teamers felt reserve games beneath them, even if they needed some playing time after injury. Roy persuaded them of the game's importance. I played once for the reserves, and I knew how much it meant for younger players to rub shoulders with first-teamers.

A coach I respected greatly, Roy worked us hard at Melwood, making sure we did the stretching right, joining in the running, everything to sharpen us up. 'Golden Bollocks' was Roy's nickname for me, and he often shouted at me in training. 'Come on, Golden Bollocks, harder,' he'd yell. He was never the type to rant like Bugsy, but Roy made sure he got his point over.

The sheer cast of characters in the Boot Room was unbelievable. Tom Saunders never played professionally but I soon became aware of his great experience of football. He coached Liverpool and England Schoolboys. 'I went to the university of life,' he told me one day, and I bet he graduated with honours. Tom was very wise, sprucing up Bob's scripts before he gave a presentation or after-dinner speech. Tom's immersion in Anfield life began when he arrived as the first Youth Development Officer in England and he gradually became a fixture in the Boot Room, sitting in his chair, discreetly sipping his whisky and floating perceptive ideas. If the coaches wrestled with a problem, Tom said, 'Step back and reflect on it. Let's come in tomorrow and sort it out.' Under Bob and Joe, Tom was used as a European scout, sussing out hotels and the opposition, compiling detailed reports. Tom was incredibly valued by Liverpool, whom he served loyally from Boot Room to boardroom, eventually becoming a director.

A less restrained member of the Boot Room fraternity was Reuben Bennett. He came from Aberdeen and was a real character, very close to Emlyn and Terry Mac. Totally committed to Liverpool, Reuben was usually first in, making tea, hurrying the players on to the bus to Melwood, getting things ready for training, and quick to bawl people out in training. 'Useless,' he'd shout. We just looked at him in amazement. Reuben fascinated us because he was a complete contradiction. If it was frozen outside, Reuben wore a T-shirt. If the weather was roasting, Reuben would don this thick fisherman's polo neck.

'It's normal,' he said.

'Your metabolism's not,' I replied.

We adored the stories from his days as a goalkeeper. 'Lads, I still hold the record for the longest throw out,' Reuben told us. 'We were playing at Crewe and one my throws went out of the ground. Landed on a train! Ended up in Southampton!' I'm sure half of his stories were fairy tales, football life rewritten by Hans Christian Andersen. Reuben banged on about how much tougher players were when he was younger, claiming he used to clean cuts to his legs with a brush.

'It's a toothbrush,' I explained to the non-Scots when Reuben was out of earshot. 'It's got iodine on it. If you go down on the gravel pitches in Glasgow, you use a toothbrush to scrub the dirt out.'

Reuben became very animated when reliving his anecdotes, painfully so at times. One day, I was sitting in a hotel sauna, listening to Reuben recall some injury suffered at Dundee.

'They put me in the dressing room but I recovered and went back on. I came for a cross and saw this Dundee boy going to hit me. I leapt with my knees up to protect myself. I punched the ball that hard it flew right over the grandstand and into the street.' Mimicking the action of hitting the ball, Reuben's nail caught his forehead and blood poured down his face. I never knew where to look I was laughing so much.

Entry to the Boot Room's exclusive club clearly demanded distinct traits. The man who took the kids' A and B teams, John Bennison, was another character. One of his jobs before Anfield was emptying gas-meters and I'm sure Benno's still got bags of shillings at home. You certainly got little change out of him on the training pitch, where Benno had a well-earned reputation for meting out punishment. After the 1977 Charity Shield, I was building up my fitness by playing for the staff against the kids at Melwood. Benno just booted them hard.

'Is that why they call it the Boot Room?' I asked Benno. If one of the youths tried to go past Benno, he'd nail him. Anything below knee level was acceptable.

'Play on,' shouted Bob while some poor kid writhed on the grass as Benno stalked away.

At Celtic, Jock Stein never allowed matches like this in training, but I took quickly to this Liverpool tradition. The kids loved it, because it made them feel really involved, and it allowed first-teamers who'd been out injured to regain some sharpness. In Liverpool's constant pursuit of excellence, the staff led the way, rarely losing many games at Melwood. I swiftly learned that the Boot Room boys' one-eyed style of refereeing would never have been found on any Football Association course. Not that they ever needed a course.

Nobody could teach the Boot Room anything about football. Bob and Joe, Ronnie and Roy were professors of the game and their paperwork was the very best. The two dusty cupboards in the Boot Room contained loads of books, detailing every training session, every match. Every day, Ronnie and Roy made entries in the books with all the gravitas of clerks filling in ledgers, inscribing notes about the weather, the numbers, any injuries, who'd trained well or who'd been off the pace. Liverpool understood better than any club that football was a science and these training books reflected that professional approach. Stretching back to 1966 under Shanks, they grew into great reference books, shaping football operations. One year, the club was plagued with cartilage problems, so Ronnie and Roy flicked back through the books, analysing previous outbreaks. They'd tweak training, maybe give certain players a breather, and the crisis would be resolved. Ronnie and Roy watched us like hawks, scrutinising every move and word. I know modern-day clubs use technology to chart performances in training, but I'd back the eyes of Ronnie and Roy ahead of anyone's computer.

I resented the suggestion that trophies fell into Liverpool's lap. People outside Melwood's high walls and metal gates couldn't grasp the sophistication of the work going on inside. 'All Liverpool do in training is just play five-a-sides' was an ill-informed critique I heard and read countless times, but such ignorance never bothered me. If Liverpool seemed a mystery, that just made it more difficult for other teams as our aura grew. Before Graeme joined us, I was away with Scotland when we talked about Liverpool, and the five-a-side issue was raised.

'Yes, we play five-a-sides but not ordinary ones,' I explained. 'Everything has a purpose. We're not strolling about – it's all conditioned. If there's something specific Bob wants to work on, it's incorporated into the five-a-sides. It's so simple and effective.' Bob's small-sided games were designed to correct faults from Liverpool's last game and prepare us tactically for the next.

'A team like Everton play with a high defensive line, trying to catch us offside,' I said to Graeme. 'Before we play them, Ronnie and Joe introduce a high line in the five-a-sides. So we get into the habit of not running offside. Sometimes, Ronnie and Joe don't tell us. They just whisper to the other team to play a high line. They make us think, react, take control. If we've not scored many for a couple of weeks, we move from small goals to big ones, just to get us back into the scoring habit. Whatever condition the staff place on the five-a-side has value. One touch, two touch, pass and move.'

Pass and move obsessed Ronnie and Joe, who considered standing still a crime worthy of a lengthy custodial sentence. 'Pass and don't move is a foul,' Ronnie warned us before every training session. 'Free-kick,' he shouted if the conditions weren't met, making sure the message got through quickly.

Liverpool's secret could be found in one of the staff's mantras: 'Get it. Keep it.' I loved how Ronnie and Joe preached the importance of cherishing the ball's company. Guided by such heavy-weight football men, Liverpool stayed ahead of the game for years. Nowadays, it makes me laugh when people bang on about diets, warming up and down, stretching properly and getting enough sleep, as if this was some fancy, new-wave thinking. We did all that under Bob. We never had the technology, the rooms full of computers and conditioning labs, but we appreciated the value of preparation, although at times our warm-down was nothing more scientific than a cup of tea. Nothing happened at Liverpool by chance. In the team meeting before the game, Ronnie ran through set-pieces, telling which players to pick up which opponents. Researching the opposition was a given for me, such as studying the keeper. How far would he come out for crosses? Did he go down early? Watching games on the television, I logged all this information in my head, so when the crunch came in a match, I was ready.

A tried and tested formula dictated how Liverpool's day unfolded. Every morning, we arrived at Anfield at 9.30, changed and hopped on the bus at 10.15 for the 15-minute ride to Melwood. I loved a tradition punctuated only by the arrival of a new driver after the last one got fed up with being hit by mud or banter. They always did. As I remembered from my trial in 1966, that journey was vital for team camaraderie. I always believed this routine gave the club a feeling of warmth. Big Hansen would be in the back seat with Stevie Nicol close by so Al could give him stick. The A and B teams got on the bus, and the senior players had the opportunity to inquire how their matches had gone.

'How did you do Saturday?' I'd ask.

'We won,' they'd chorus, faces reddening.

'Well done,' we'd respond.

It was great for the younger boys to feel part of the football club. The facilities at Melwood and Anfield now are so fantastic that there's no need for a bus and I believe that the kids lose out a bit. They don't see Stevie, Carra, Fernando and Pepe Reina now and that's a pity because these players are role models for the boys to aspire to.

Back then, having got off the bus at Melwood, we walked into the pavilion, put our boots on, went out and loosened up and trained. Back in the pavilion after training, there was a cup of tea waiting. Back at Anfield, there was a three-course lunch spread out on tables in the players' lounge: soup, steak pie and a dessert. With single boys on the books, Liverpool knew they'd have one good meal inside them each day. The players loved those lunches and trouble almost broke out when the board, deciding to cut back on overheads, stopped the meals one year. This affront occurred one pre-season when David Hodgson had just arrived, and he got terrible stick.

'Hodgy, it's your fault the lunches have been scrubbed,' I told him. 'Liverpool spent the money on you. I've had a wee conversation with the other players and we've decided we'd rather have the lunches than you.' Hodgy laughed, slightly nervously.

The food was made by May and Theresa, who became family for the players, as all the staff at Anfield did. Liverpool players of that era being impish by inclination, we'd wind up some of the staff, especially Ken Myers, who ran the maintenance side. A wee bit of a grumpy man, Ken was easy to provoke.

'Ken, the showers are too hot,' we'd tell him. So Ken got the wrench out, attacking the plumbing in the dressing room, grumbling away as he wrestled with the pipes. When he'd finished, we'd announce, 'Ken, the showers are too cold.' Ken just glowered.

Anfield teemed with characters. Friends of players, particularly of local lads such as Sammy or Tommo, wandered in and out, providing services, boys who ran about town and knew everyone. Liverpool now have a player liaison officer but back then the older players helped the new ones, taking them into Southport or the Wirral and showing them houses. John Toshack took me round.

A man often appeared at Anfield trying to sell us cars – legit ones, of course. A pal of mine in the rag-trade popped into the club, selling trousers and shirts to the boys. The clothes weren't snide, they were genuine. Another guy sold fruit and pies, and every Friday, George the Fish came up to Anfield. Another bloke had a contact in the meat market who got us great steaks. A mate of Roy's, Wee Charlie, came to the ground to cut hair. When I came out of the shower, Charlie would say, 'Sit down. How do you want it?'

'Just a touch, Charlie, don't take it all off.'

'No problem. If it's not right, I'll be back in a fortnight.'

I enjoyed having Roy's mates around. Like Roy and Ronnie, they were real Liverpool people. I loved Anfield's community spirit, everyone mucking in. 'Everyone at Liverpool is the greatest,' said Bob. 'The tea-ladies are the greatest tea-ladies.' And they *were* great. They were Liverpool people, who worshipped the club and were just so proud to spend their day at Anfield. Working for Liverpool filled them with a sense of importance. Liverpool's secret was that they employed the best – the best tea-ladies, the best players and the best administrator in Peter Robinson, known as PBR and renowned for looking after the players brilliantly. Most years, a message would come from upstairs: 'There's a new contract for everybody upstairs and you all have a rise, if you want to go up and sign.'

'It's happened to me ten out of the eleven seasons I've been here,' Stevie Heighway told me. Famed for being fair with employees, Liverpool showed similar generosity to me. In that pre-Bosman age, Liverpool's board was under no requirement or pressure to give me a rise. I was tied to Liverpool, yet they always showed their appreciation with a rise nearly every year. In those days, everybody wanted to play at Liverpool but the board never took advantage of that. Silverware was rewarded financially. No wonder the camaraderie was so strong. No wonder, with the Boot Room and a manager of Old Bob's quality, Liverpool dominated England and Europe.

5

ANFIELD SOUTH

IT WAS the afternoon of 10 May 1978, a momentous day in the history of Liverpool Football Club and I was a bag of nerves. As I lay on my bed at Sopwell House Hotel, near St Albans, waiting there until the coach came to transport us to Wembley for the European Cup final against Bruges, I felt the walls closing in on me. All it needed was for the curtains to be replaced by bars on the window. Impatiently, I watched the hands of the clock inch towards my moment with destiny, willing them to hurry up. God, they were moving slowly. A couple of feet away, Stevie Heighway stretched out on his bed, book in hand, a picture of tranquillity. Nothing fazed Liverpool's languid winger, who turned the pages, oblivious of my nerves. How I envied Stevie. Reading never featured high on my list of interests, or abilities, but at that moment I craved any means of distraction. Of course, Stevie had been to a European Cup final before, but he was naturally laid-back, unperturbed by the scale of the assignment. For me, freshly arrived from Celtic, a European final was new territory.

Sleep usually came easy in the build-up to matches but not this time, not before my first European Cup final. I leapt up, desperate to escape the confines of the room, looking for anything to take my mind off time's reluctant passage. Bob Paisley was not a manager for organising games, like the carpet bowls Don Revie staged with England. Even Liverpool's card school had closed down for the afternoon. The only activity available seemed a tour of Sopwell's corridors. After pacing around for a while, I returned to the room. Stevie was still reading, still untroubled by the thought of what lay ahead. Throwing myself down on my bed, I closed my eyes, knowing sleep would not rescue me. Instead, I found my mind rewinding through the season, recalling the events that guided Liverpool here. I found the reflections soothing, reminding me that this was the journey I had craved at Celtic but never managed.

When I'd looked around the Anfield dressing room seven months earlier, I'd realised I was now rubbing shoulders with players who would help me fulfil my European dream. That was the start of Liverpool's European road to Wembley, a venue known as Anfield South because of the club's frequent visits, and I was getting ready for our second-round tie against Dynamo Dresden on 19 October. Liverpool's XI was packed with strong characters you'd want alongside you in a fight, let alone a sporting confrontation. I sat between Emlyn Hughes and Jimmy Case, men not short of commitment. To Emlyn's right were Ray Clemence, Phil Neal, Joey Jones, Alan Hansen and Ray Kennedy. To Jimmy's left were Stevie Heighway, John Toshack and Ian Callaghan. Bob Paisley had built a formidable team and Dresden shattered like old porcelain.

Tosh was an outstanding target-man of the old school, brilliant at the powerful flicks Kevin Keegan had revelled in running on to. Tosh's game was more suited to Kevin than to me. I preferred to do my work slightly deeper at times, not running through like Kevin, but Tosh and I still managed to link up. Dresden man-marked me but that simply created space for others. Alan Hansen scored with a header, taking a smack in the face for his troubles as he leapt for the ball. Once Al scored, Dresden crumbled. Nealy, Ray and Jimmy, twice, added to the scoreline. Over at the Rudolf Harbig Stadium, in the second leg, Dresden were brilliant, scoring twice and threatening to get all four back, but fortunately Stevie Heighway struck and that killed them off. Liverpool's defence was too strong for Dresden to break through again.

In Ray Clemence, Liverpool had a man between the posts who could easily be numbered as one of the best goalkeepers in the world. Strangely, Clem thought he was one of the best left-wingers in the world, a ludicrous point he tried to prove in training. At Melwood, I laughed as Clem looked for opportunities to come out of goal, joining in the Friday five-a-sides. He flew into tackles, nothing deliberately nasty, but we knew Clem was about. He moved the ball slowly – touch, touch, touch – like a rugby scrum inching forward. The players loved it when Clem scored, partly for the rarity value and also because he celebrated as if he'd just settled a Cup final from 30 yards.

The four men charged with protecting Clem on match-day were of similar high quality. Tommy Smith was coming to the end of his distinguished career at Anfield but remained as fearsome as ever. At Melwood one day, I nutmegged Smithy and went after the ball.

'Ohhhhh,' went Terry Mac.

'What?' I replied.

'Smithy doesn't like that.'

'That's not my fault.' Terry Mac stared at me as if I had some kind of death wish.

I survived the wrath of Smithy, which is more than can be said for some of Liverpool's rasher opponents. Part of Smithy's unwritten match-day duties were as Ian Callaghan's enforcer. If somebody gave Cally a hard time . . . BANG. Smithy was in there, a vigilante with studs, leaving a little reminder to show some respect. Against Coventry, Smithy nailed Terry Yorath, hardly a shrinking violet himself. What a challenge that was! Yorath had just 'done' Cally and Smithy came storming out of defence, charging towards Yorath, absolutely clattering him. I was 30 yards away and even my bones juddered. How Yorath picked himself up I'll never know. In another game, against Coventry, Smithy played full-back against Tommy Hutchison, the Scottish winger. Hutch jinked past Smithy, pushed the ball on, ran and crossed. Jogging back past Smithy, Hutch said, 'I was quick there. I'll race you for your wages.'

'All right,' said Smithy. 'Let's go double or quits – I'll fight you for your wages.' Hutch was terrified.

Like Smithy, Emlyn's time was almost up at Anfield. I soon became aware Emlyn had some enemies, and 'selfish' was the usual accusation thrown at the Liverpool captain. Emlyn was always good to me, helping me settle in when I was his room-mate. My admiration grew when I realised what an accomplished defender he was – two-footed, unbelievably enthusiastic, strong, pacey and a brilliant reader of the game. Not many attackers got the better of Emlyn. He loved a goal as well. When Emlyn scored, the whole place lit up because his face was a picture. Banter came easily to Emlyn. When Scotland played England in a Home International at Hampden Park in 1978, we'd qualified for the World Cup but, much to my delight, Emlyn and the English boys were staying at home. Scotland were doing badly in the Home Internationals and Emlyn was determined to rub it in, particularly when England won in Glasgow.

'Hey, wee man, you only got one point,' Emlyn shouted as we walked off the pitch.

'Emlyn, just think, if you'd got one more point, you'd be going where we're going. Argentina. World Cup. Brilliant.'

'Piss off!'

'I'll send you a postcard, Emlyn.'

Liverpool had another top centre-half not going to Argentina after England's embarrassing failure. Long before I arrived at Anfield, Phil Thompson had come to my attention on *Football Focus*. The BBC profiled this rising young talent from Kirkby, filming Tommo with his pride and joy, a new Ford Capri. The cameras followed him into his house for some more filming. I'm sure they got some decent footage inside but it was pure TV gold when Tommo came back outside. His Capri was up on bricks. Somebody had nicked the wheels.

Tommo was a great character, a good leader as well as a fantastic defender. The uneducated looked at the stick-thin Tommo and wondered, 'How can he play?' He was wiry, more a sapling than an oak like Smithy. Shanks famously remarked that Tommo looked like he'd 'tossed with a sparrow for a pair of legs and lost' but he turned tackling into an art form, sliding in to nick the ball at a time when many centre-halves piled in blindly, taking man and ball. When Scotland faced England, I knew the difficulties in store. Tommo was as stealthy as a pickpocket, the king of anticipation, but if the game got dirty, he'd have a kick. Nobody bossed Tommo around. He loved playing the Scots. Sitting next to him on the coach to Jock Stein's testimonial at Celtic Park, I laughed at Tommo's running commentary on all the fans outside.

'Look at that daft Jock there,' Tommo said, pointing out one supporter. 'He'll be butting a bus in a minute.' Tommo was convinced all Scots spent their waking hours head-butting vehicles. 'It's butt-a-bus time,' Tommo shouted whenever we travelled to Scotland.

Noisy and irrepressible, Tommo was steeped in the passion of the Kop. Having stood on the terrace as a kid, he brought the hunger of a Liverpool supporter to his every thought and movement. I soon understood how profoundly Tommo hated the idea of his Liverpool, his friends' Liverpool, his family's club, ever losing. He gave everything for Liverpool, including four cartilages. Few players touched the 'This Is Anfield' sign with such tenderness. Rising up those final steps on to the pitch, Tommo charged straight to the Kop, waving to his brother Owen, standing where Tommo himself once stood. That showed the bond between terrace and dressing room, fans and players belonging to the same family, fighting for the same cause. Tommo was a Kirkby boy through and through and even at his height with Liverpool, he'd help out with the pub team at The Falcon. He even took the European Cup in to the bar there one night.

Like Tommo, Joey Jones was another diehard Liverpool fan. He used to run towards the Kop, shaking his forearm to show off his Liverpool tattoo. Joey was tough and unyielding, a real defender. A lot of defenders don't actually enjoy their duties but Joey took great pride in forcing opponents back, protecting Liverpool's goalmouth with all the commitment of a guard dog. This suited Emlyn, who liked to go forward.

Although far from a classic patsy, Joey was pleasingly vulnerable to our wind-ups. Under Bob, we did a particular heading practice at Melwood, running along and jumping up, an exercise that proved fertile territory for bouts of tomfoolery. On one occasion, I was running alongside Joey and when we landed I said, 'Christ, Joey, did you see that car the other side of those flats?'

'What car?'

'The other side of the flats. Come on Joey, you're not jumping high enough.'

When Wales played Scotland in an October World Cup qualifier at Anfield, on 12 October 1977, Joey was pumped up for weeks in advance.

'The Kop's going to be full of Wales boys, Kenny, just you wait and see. Anfield's going to belong to Wales.'

'Is that right, Joey?'

'Yes, you'll see. I'm going to run straight to the Kop and give it that.' Joey punched the air.

'You'd better be careful, Joey,' I advised.

'Why? I can't wait to see all the Welsh punters on the Kop.'

'All right, Joey.'

When Joey ran out, he sprinted straight to the Kop but stopped in his tracks. The Kop was a sea of blue, swaying with Saltires. Tucked away in the corner of the Tartan Army's home for the night was a wee pocket of Welsh supporters.

'The Kop looks good tonight,' I remarked to Joey as we lined up.

Even under the fiercest pressure, no weak link could be detected in Liverpool's defence. In the eight years I played with Phil Neal, I never saw anybody give Liverpool's right-back a hard time. For a defender, Nealy was really composed in front of goal. It sometimes seemed to me that ice filled Nealy's veins when he ventured forward because he never panicked, particularly when tucking away penalties. Nealy's first job was defending and he was Mr Reliable but anybody heaping praise on Nealy must also acknowledge the contribution of Jimmy Case, who often doubled up on the opposition winger, helping Nealy out. When Nealy went cantering forward, Jimmy slotted in to cover and keep Liverpool's shape.

The Kop loved Jimmy because he was one of them, a proud south Liverpool lad, and their affection deepened because he worked his socks off. A player's player, Jimmy contributed far more than he was given credit for. He could pick people out with a pass and score as well as steam into tackles. Jimmy was a quiet, genuine character, but I upset him when we were returning on the train after the 1977 Charity Shield.

'Kenny, have a drink.'

'I don't drink, Jimmy.' He seemed shocked.

'You must drink.'

'Jimmy, I don't.'

'You're winding me up.' But I wasn't. This wasn't Puritanism on my part; this was just about taste. I can't stand lager for a start, and unless it was Champagne or a glass of wine after a win, my limit would be sweet Martini with lemonade. Any time, any place, anywhere, it was certainly the right one for me. Back at the Holiday Inn, I stuck to the local version of Irn Bru and cream soda.

One day, 5 December 1977, I was relaxing in the foyer of the hotel with my daughter, Kelly, when I spotted a familiar face –

and haircut. Kevin Keegan was in town with Hamburg for the second leg of the European Super Cup. We'd drawn 1–1 in Germany. These were useful occasions to keep us in tune for Europe. The quarter-finals of the European Cup were not until March so Hamburg's visit was welcome, as was seeing Kevin. Cynics in the Press believed tension churned between us, as if we were still fighting over the red No. 7 shirt, a suggestion rooted firmly in the realm of fantasy. Kevin and I had a good chat about Hamburg and Liverpool, about how each other was settling in. Nobody would describe it as the longest conversation ever but everybody could see the friendliness on both sides, putting an end to the lie that we didn't get on. Kevin was brand new.

Mind you, Kevin's mood was better in the Holiday Inn than at Anfield the following night when he played on his own up front and saw little of the ball. I cannot believe Kevin was surprised by the sight of his old team enjoying so much possession. That was the Liverpool way, and Kevin had once been a valued part of that machine. Liverpool duly won 6–0, Terry Mac collecting three goals and a Man of the Match trophy almost as big as himself. Kevin didn't take many great memories from his visit to Anfield – the Kop's reaction was reserved rather than raucous. Liverpool fans respected Kevin but were disappointed with his decision to leave.

When European Cup combat resumed, Liverpool were ready. Our quarter-final assignment was Benfica, and we kicked off in the lashing rain at the Stadium of Light. In goal for the Portuguese champions was Bento, as mad as a brush and an early version of Rene Higuita, the Colombian who lit up Wembley with that scorpion kick against England in 1995. When Jimmy Case lifted a free-kick towards goal, Bento approached the ball like a man emerging from the shower trying to control a bar of soap. The ball slipped into the goal and Bento's night went from farce to worse when Emlyn beat him with a misdirected effort.

'That was a cross!' I told Emlyn.

'I meant it. I meant it.'

'Well, you should be embarrassed if you meant it!' Nothing could prick Emlyn's bravado.

Benfica visited a fortnight later to discover snow blanketing Anfield. They ran into another storm on the pitch when Cally scored within six minutes, leaving the Portuguese requiring snookers. By 1978, the clock was ticking on Cally's career but he was still important, still hugely respected for the experience acquired since making his debut 18 years earlier. The best compliment I can pay Cally is that it took someone of the exceptional calibre of Graeme Souness to divest him of the No. 11 shirt. Cally embodied the Liverpool way, keeping the game nice and simple, just tackling, passing and moving – win it, give it. Cally was Mr Dependable and Mr Versatility, moving effortlessly from right-wing to the holding role in midfield, happily sitting back to release Terry Mac, who also struck that night against Benfica.

What a player Terry was, blessed with unbelievable stamina. 'You've got two pairs of lungs,' I said to Terry and I'm sure he did. Terry could run and run and his mind shifted as quickly. As a footballer, Terry was a creature of instinct and intelligence, a killer mix. If I even hinted at darting into a particular area, Terry read my mind. The ball was waiting for me, almost smiling at me. Not only could Terry see a great pass, he could deliver it. Vision and execution are qualities found in only the very best players and Terry had those strengths. Along with his keen eye for goal, what made Terry even more special was his full-on, committed attitude. Surrender was for cowards, not for men like Terry, who'd never give up.

During my long association with Terry Mac, it has been a constant frustration that people never really appreciated what a sharp footballing brain he had. To many people, Terry was the village idiot because of the lisp, his constant refrain of 'all right, son' and a diet that never strayed far from soup and sandwiches. We used to get taken to the Bryn Awel Hotel, in Wales, with fine wine and wonderful food. It was top dollar and we'd be choosing from the à la carte menu. When it came to Terry's turn to order, he'd ask for 'chicken sarnies and a pint of lager'. You can take the boy out of Kirkby! If that was what Terry liked, fine. Terry's not stupid, far from it, although his personal grooming didn't exactly bestow an air of gravitas. 'Why does your hair look as if somebody has just parted it with an axe?' I asked him one time.

He loved the banter. Terry was self-confident, knowing how much he contributed to Liverpool, and those who considered Terry thick were pretty daft themselves. Whatever Bob said, Terry absorbed. One of the favourite stories to be recounted in the dressing room, about Terry Mac's famous ability to follow Bob's advice, centred around an incident 10 minutes into the 1977 FA Cup replay against Everton at Maine Road.

'Their keeper comes off his line,' Bob said. He was right. David Lawson, who was not to last much longer at Everton, tended to stray a bit. Sure enough, Terry Mac feinted to shoot but checked, exposing Lawson, and confidently chipped him. Terry scored because he'd listened to Bob. In the dressing room, Terry was loved as a great character.

'I drink at Headquarters,' he told me the first time we met, as if I knew where Headquarters was. Along with Anfield, Terry's life revolved around Headquarters, more formally known as the Quarry Green Social Club, a working men's institution in Kirkby.

'Very exclusive,' Terry insisted. 'We're going racing. You can't come. Single boys only.'

Terry's goal against Benfica helped usher Liverpool into a semi-final with Borussia Moenchengladbach, whom the boys had beaten in the 1977 final. At the Rheinstadion on 29 March, Liverpool were caught out by a blast from Rainer Bonhof and I felt the England lads should really have seen it coming. A month earlier in Munich, the West German international lashed one past Clem. God, he could hit the ball hard. Bonhof just connected and it stayed hit, the ball lifting and lifting like a rocket, flying up over the top of Clem's shoulder. Poor Clem had no chance and would have risked losing a limb if he'd managed to intercept it. Clem's blamelessness didn't stop the lads winding him up at Melwood. Whenever anyone lined up a free-kick or long-ranger at Clem, we all screamed: 'BONHOF!' Clem had the good grace to laugh.

We all had the last laugh over Borussia, who were, apparently, 'petrified' of Anfield, according to their defender Berti Vogts. If some of Berti's team-mates were scared at the thought of stepping out in front of the Kop, Borussia also ran into the intimidating Souness, making his first European start and bossing midfield. This unbeatable blend of steel, silk and self-belief arrived just after we'd lost 4–2 to Chelsea in the FA Cup in early January. Bob saw we needed stiffening in midfield and had been given a timely reminder of Souness's qualities the week before. Playing for Middlesbrough, Graeme kicked me in the arm, and I felt relieved because that was one of his lower tackles. Bob acted decisively, spending £325,000 to bring Souey to Liverpool. It was a match made in heaven, and the rest, as they say in the movies, is history. Liverpool's pass-and-move style suited Souey, whose touch and toughness fitted us perfectly. Souey was the sort of all-round, all-terrain midfielder that every manager coveted.

Graeme Souness was the most fearless footballer I've ever known, a talent I respected from the day I met him as a 15-year-old training at Celtic before he joined Spurs and then Boro. He exuded too arrogant an air for some tastes but never among his team-mates, and particularly never with me, his Liverpool and Scotland room-mate. Souey was fantastic company. If you wanted a satisfaction-guaranteed top night out, the man I christened 'Champagne Charlie' wouldn't disappoint. For one of my birthdays, Charlie gave me a caricature – a picture of me holding a big glass of Champagne, which was tongue in cheek. Much was made of Graeme's lifestyle but it never impinged on his football.

He was a single boy, out enjoying himself, and there was no problem. Charlie prepared himself brilliantly. He trained hard and, at the right time, partied hard. Anyway, Charlie's often misunderstood. He's funny and intelligent, right up there as the dream dinner guest, and I'm not surprised to find him such a sought-after television pundit. Graeme doesn't just fire from the hip, he's constructive in his comments. Most of the time.

Like Charlie, Ray Kennedy could also pick out my runs. Ray arrived at Anfield in 1974 as a striker, having scored a bundle of goals up front for Arsenal. When Shanks stepped down shortly after that, Old Bob had different ideas, switching Ray to midfield. Since Ray had played in attack, he tended to look forward instantly, so this was heaven for a striker, knowing that if you moved, Ray would find you. Ray also sneaked in and scored a lot of goals himself, including the first in the 3–0 Anfield win over Borussia in 1978 that swept us into the final. The thought of it brought me back to the Sopwell House Hotel, the quiet and classy establishment where we had set up camp.

Glancing across at Stevie Heighway, I was reminded of the quality in Liverpool's team. Stevie was educated, a graduate with a BSc, but that never bothered me. For me, the only numbers that mattered were 1–11. On the pitch, everyone was equal. The journey each individual made to reach Liverpool's dressing room was of no interest to me. Stevie was there on merit and as committed to the cause as anyone. Wherever Shanks and then Bob asked him to play, Stevie slotted in willingly. Left wing was his natural habitat but Stevie posed an equal threat through the middle. He was a good crosser of the ball, although I could hardly be called upon as a reliable witness, since heading was never a forte of mine. Stevie was ideal for the big guys because he could race past right-backs and whip in crosses. Even on major occasions like this, when he was starting on the bench, nothing troubled the implacable Heighway. If Bob felt he should be a sub, he accepted it for the good of Liverpool Football Club.

Informing the players of the line-up, Bob named David Fairclough at No. 9. Known in the dressing room as 'Whip' because of his shooting action, David scored some vital goals for Liverpool. He was primarily known to punters as 'Super Sub' for his uncanny ability to rise from the bench and rescue situations, such as against St Etienne the year before. For all its heroic attributes, the 'Super Sub' label is one I'm sure David would have preferred to relinquish. Frustratingly for him, and Liverpool, Whip's desire to start games was too often tempered by injury. Just as he got a good run, he would turn lame, so others started up front, and when Whip returned from injury, he had to bide his time in the dug-out. For Liverpool, having a sub who could run on, pick up the threads of the match plot immediately and make an impact was a fantastic asset, but I felt Whip should have had more starts. If he was considered good enough to start a European Cup final, he clearly had qualities.

'I can't wait to get on the bus,' I remarked to Stevie, and when we finally did, I was stunned by the number of Liverpool fans heading towards Wembley. Our ticket allocation was supposedly only 20,000, but Liverpool fans always get tickets, always want to be there to show their support. Liverpool supporters needed no road map to find the way to Anfield South. Shanks and then Old Bob gave them plenty of experience in making the journey. Liverpool fans knew all the short-cuts and all the pubs, because Wembley was a second home. I watched them laughing and joking, standing on the pavements, enjoying a pint before striding up to the Twin Towers. I saw them clutching their banners and waving their scarves. I heard them chanting 'Liverpool', their voices revealing complete faith in our mission against Bruges.

'It'd be horrible to lose,' I said to Stevie, who threw me a look of mild surprise. Clearly, the thought never crossed his mind. That was the Liverpool way, confident but not complacent. Inside the dressing room at Wembley, many emotions were present but I could see they were all positive ones – hunger, belief and impatience for the first whistle. Fear was nowhere to be found. All of the Liverpool players assembling in the tunnel, ready to walk up that incline and out into the noise and lights, trusted each other. Looking up and down the line, seeing Clem, Nealy, Tommo, Big Al, Ray, Emlyn, Jimmy, Whip, Terry Mac and Charlie, I knew we had a chance against Bruges.

The Belgian champions were surprise European Cup finalists, having beaten Juventus in the semis, probably surprising themselves. I was aware that victory came at a cost, suspension and injury depriving Bruges of the creative services of their better players, individuals such as Paul Courant and Raoul Lambert, and their ambition also seemed to be badly missing at Wembley. Bruges were very cautious, I guess understandably, because when they came out and saw Liverpool red everywhere in the 92,000 crowd, it must have felt like an away game. It was certainly never a classic game. Bruges rarely troubled Tommo and Al, who was playing because Smithy had unfortunately incapacitated himself attempting some DIY – a hammer fell on to his foot.

Liverpool kept looking for a way past Birger Jensen, Bruges' keeper, who did well. Watching Jensen closely, searching for a weakness, I noted he went down early in one-on-one situations. When Terry Mac went through on goal, I clocked Jensen committing himself early and I knew what I had to do. Twenty minutes into the second half, the ball was bouncing around next to the Bruges box. I hooked it over my head but it was cleared to Graeme. The Belgian defence froze, not knowing whether to push out or re-form the barricades. As Bruges pondered their options, Graeme worked the ball through to me. Jensen rushed out, trying to force me to shoot early but I held my nerve for a split-second, waiting until he committed himself before dinking the ball over him. The goal was hailed later as a triumph of instinct but it was all planned. I'd done my homework on Jensen. My thirtieth goal of the season was the most special, worthy of a major celebration, so I took off towards the fans, leaping the hoardings, a smile filling my face. This was why I'd moved from Glasgow. Surely the Celtic fans could understand it now.

Bruges stirred after that and Tommo cleared one off the line, which was as important as me scoring, but that was the limit of the Belgians' ambition. At the final whistle, Bruges were very magnanimous in defeat. Their left-winger, Jan Sorensen, came round every player, shaking hands and congratulating us. We discovered later that Sorensen was a Liverpool fan, so the day wasn't a complete disaster for the Dane.

That night, I was introduced to one of Liverpool's great traditions – partying with the trophy.

'Make sure you're on the train in the morning,' said Bob. 'Eleven o'clock from Euston.'

We'd moved from Sopwell into town, setting up base-camp at the Holiday Inn at Swiss Cottage, where the wives were. By the time the players arrived, the bar was heaving with Liverpool supporters, and it was a minor miracle supplies of alcohol had not already run dry. A raging thirst was upon us and we soon caught up. From Champagne and white wine, I went through the card, and the cellar, that night. The barman, an honorary Scouser for the evening (and early morning), did not hold back in his largesse with measures. At one point, Al fancied a Canadian Club. Returning from the bar 20 minutes later, clutching his drink, Al looked slightly confused.

'I asked for a Canadian Club,' he said. 'They gave me a whole bottle.'

'That's to save you a few journeys,' I laughed.

Marina and I finally turned in around four in the morning, leaving Charlie to it. Marina was up at nine, nipping downstairs for the papers while I ordered breakfast from room service. When she returned, she looked stunned.

'I've just seen Graeme,' Marina said, almost disbelievingly.

'Where?'

'Heading back from breakfast.'

'No chance.'

'He was there, Kenny, I'm telling you. Graeme was up for his breakfast.'

Moments later there was a loud bang at the door. When Marina opened it, Charlie fell into the room. Smashed. Charlie did not have the look of a man who had joined the tables of sober-suited, sober-headed businessmen starting the day with a full English in a well-known London hotel dining room.

'Charlie, is that you up for breakfast? Marina saw you at breakfast.'

'No, Kenny, I'm just coming in!'

'Oh, very good. We've just ordered some breakfast. What do you want?'

'Usual stuff,' Graeme replied. So I called room service again.

'Some toast and orange juice please, and a pot of very strong coffee.' Graeme grabbed the phone.

'Is the orange juice fresh? Is it squeezed? Yes? Well give us two bottles of Champagne then.'

'Charlie, leave it. We'll not drink it.'

'We will,' said Charlie, putting down the phone. Amazingly, the hotel somehow found two bottles we hadn't consumed earlier and delivered them to our room. As the waiter placed the bottles on the table, Charlie looked at them but couldn't focus. His eyes were rolling.

'I need to go to my bed.'

'Charlie, you've left us with two bottles of Champagne.'

'Kenny, how can you even think about drinking at this time of the morning?' replied Charlie and, lurching out of the door, he stumbled back to his pit. Marina and I sat there with the Champagne.

They didn't go to waste. I found some plastic bottles, filled them up with bubbly, and passed them round the train. Charlie slept until 10.30 but made Euston in time. Just. After 90 minutes' kip, Charlie had regained his thirst. Marina and I were sitting quietly in one of those old-fashioned compartments, six seats facing each other, when Charlie piled in and the party began again. We must have had 20 people in the compartment at one point, sitting on laps, lying in luggage racks, swigging Champagne from plastic bottles, and so it went on, all the way to Lime Street.

The open-topped bus tour of the city fulfilled another of my boyhood dreams. Looking out from that bus, it seemed to me that the whole city had turned out to congratulate us. Hundreds of thousands lined the streets. They climbed up trees and on top of bus shelters, waving, smiling and singing. Seeing their happy faces meant so much to me. It was a wonderful feeling, being able to bring pleasure into people's lives. As I admired the crowds spilling off the pavements, I did feel a shiver of frustration that this could never have been achieved in my home-town. The perfect scenario would have been winning the European Cup with Celtic and then doing a ride through streets I knew and loved. Sadly, the tensions between Celtic and Rangers made that impossible. Divisions ran too deep in Glasgow. Liverpool was different. I appreciated that rivalry defined relations between Anfield and Goodison, but it was never poisonous, and in among the red scarves, I saw dashes of Evertonian blue.

'Look at that,' I said to Al. 'That's great. It's not their team but it is their city, so there must be pride.' I'm sure Liverpool fans felt the same when Everton won the European Cup-Winners' Cup in 1985. As I looked down the bus, I saw Joe, Ronnie and Roy deep in conversation with Bob. Liverpool's famous Boot Room were preparing for another season, another success.

6

AND COULD HE PLAY!

THE best compliment I ever received in my life came from the greatest manager of them all, Bob Paisley. It came after our victory over Bruges when the Press chased Bob's opinion of me. His response was wonderfully simple: 'He'll do for me.' Bob's approval meant the world to me. Although Jock Stein shaped me at Celtic, I grew even more under Bob and, even now, I treasure every kind word he uttered about me. I remember warmly Bob's appraisal that 'great players are normally like soloists in an orchestra. They perform alone and tend to look down on their team-mates with lesser ability but that was never Kenny. He brought others into play.' I was never a virtuoso, like Maradona or Pelé or 'Jinky' Jimmy Johnstone from my Scottish homeland. I couldn't dribble past seven players like wee Jinky could, leaving full-backs trailing with a burst of speed. I could create a chance for a team-mate, even a shot at goal for myself, but it was never out of nothing. Somebody would pass to me. I quickly understood that Liverpool's success was built on a formidable work ethic, a concept that chimed with the way I was raised by Jock. The team was more important than I was. If I went through one-on-one with the goalkeeper and somebody was well placed beside me, I'd take as much pleasure in drawing the goalie and tapping it to my team-mate to put in the back of the net as in scoring myself. I never gauged my value on the 172 goals I scored in 515 appearances for Liverpool. Just making a contribution to the cause was my aim. Trophies mattered to me, not individual plaudits.

Graeme Souness heaped praise on me, claiming, 'I can think of only two players ahead of Kenny – Pelé and possibly Cruyff. Kenny was better than Maradona, Rummenigge or Platini.' Leaving aside my gratitude to a friend for his kind words, I think Graeme might well have been pissed when he made that comparison, and how do you judge greatness? World Cups, European Cups, domestic titles? Individual contribution or number of team triumphs? It's very subjective. When Uefa and Fifa rank their top 20 footballers of all time, I'm often included, which is flattering, and it's nice to be fondly remembered, but who judges it? I never saw Billy Liddell play, although I know of his legend through Liverpool folklore. Big Hansen and Nealy have roomfuls of medals and I don't see them getting a mention in the all-time lists.

Newspapers applauded me for having an eye for a pass but I might as well have been blind if the Liverpool players hadn't moved as brilliantly as they did. Sharing a field with so many talented craftsmen helped me settle and prosper. Often, Liverpool were simply unstoppable. When Spurs visited Anfield on 2 September 1978, the experts on the television and on the terraces believed this would be a right close game. I saw Ossie Ardiles and Ricky Villa striding down the corridor, two of the stars of Argentina's World Cup triumph, and the scorching weather must have made them feel they were back in Buenos Aires, admittedly without the tickertape. The Kop were very respectful, clapping Ardiles and Villa on to the pitch, but that's where the warm welcome expired and the Argentinians must have wondered what hit them. Liverpool blitzed them. Spurs had Ardiles and Villa but we had possession. Having a World Cup-winner's medal in your back pocket means nothing if you don't have the ball.

The first six goals we rattled in were decent enough. David Johnson and I got two apiece, Ray Kennedy and Nealy, with a penalty, also scored but Liverpool left the best until last that amazing day. Easing up was never in our psychological make-up, and Bob wouldn't tolerate it. Keep going, keep passing, keep scoring – that was Bob's mantra. Pride played a part as well, a desire to obliterate Spurs pumping inside every red shirt. I was always conscious the Liverpool punters paid good money to watch us and deserved to be entertained. So we conjured up what the newspapers called 'the Magnificent Seventh', one of the finest goals ever witnessed at Anfield. Traditionally, I associate great goals with winning a cup. Whenever the pundits congregate on television to discuss 'the greatest goals ever', I often find myself shouting at the screen, 'The goal must carry significance. It must win something. It cannot simply be about the beauty of the goal. It must be decisive in some way, shape or form.'

I accept our final goal against Spurs that sultry afternoon was of no consequence since the points had long belonged to Liverpool, but it was still special. As a pure technical and team goal, it didn't get much better. It was not so much an attack as a journey, the voyage beginning at a Spurs corner. Standing at a post, assuming his usual corner position, Terry Mac took off the moment Clem caught the ball. Clem found Ray and possession moved quickly from me to David Johnson in the centre circle. This was typical Liverpool, one-touch passes sweeping the ball forward. All the time, Terry Mac hared up the pitch. Running on to Davie's pass, Stevie Heighway met the ball first time, whipping in a cross to the far post where Terry Mac rose to head past Barry Daines, Tottenham's keeper, who must have been absolutely startled. Where the hell had Terry Mac sprung from? One moment he was on Liverpool's line, a few seconds later he was 100 yards away scoring! In the last minute of the game! What made him bother running that far to finish off a move that Bob hailed as 'good a goal as scored at Anfield'? That was the Liverpool way – giving everything. That was what made Liverpool so formidable.

'That's some fitness regime you've got going at Headquarters!' I told Terry Mac afterwards.

Following games like that, my performance occasionally drew in-depth analysis in the newspapers, a reaction I found slightly awkward. Tommy Docherty declared that I saw goalscoring situations developing quicker than other players did, so compensating for my supposed lack of pace. This obsession with how fast I covered the ground annoyed me. I'd have liked to be a yard quicker, and an inch taller, but come on! Other footballers had greater handicaps. Maybe people were fed up talking about my strengths so they looked for weaknesses. If all the attackers at work in English football in the late Seventies and early Eighties had lined up for a 100-metre race, I promise you I would not have finished last. Anyway, speed is useless without control and vision. I knew where all my fellow strikers were before the ball came to me: Tosh, Davie Johnno, Rushie, Paul Walsh, John Aldridge and all the others. Bob kindly observed that what made me unique was my vision, that I could find a red shirt. Throughout my playing days at Liverpool, I had a picture in my mind of team-mates' positions. Playing with my back to goal meant I could shield the ball from my marker, who had to read whether my intentions were to keep the ball or lay it off.

Taking responsibility came easily to me on the field. My old Celtic coach, Sean Fallon, once portrayed me as 'greedy in the box' but that wasn't true. I never went for glory. I often laid the ball off. Sometimes the keeper expected me to lay it off so I shot. I couldn't bend it like Beckham, but I could curl a moving ball.

When newspapers debated my fitness levels at Liverpool, arguing whether my stamina was good enough, I just looked at the appearances total for 1977–78. Of the 62 games, I was ever present, a record matched only by Phil Neal. In keeping up with the pace of the English game, fitness was never an issue. I just needed to adapt to the different style of play, and that didn't take long. Celtic games were actually more intense because of the fans' demand to 'attack, attack, attack'. At Liverpool, we were more cautious, particularly away from Anfield, displaying a caginess that Celtic supporters would never tolerate. In possession, Liverpool moved the ball quicker than Scottish teams did. Scottish teams were more dependent on individuals, such as Jinky, who'd go past five people for fun. Such wingers were rare down south. When Celtic played Leeds, wee Jimmy roasted Terry Cooper.

My fitness record was helped because training at Melwood was on grass, a welcome respite from the shale in Glasgow, so my ankle problems eased. Eventually, I threw away the strapping that supported my ankle and had been part of my everyday uniform at Celtic. I was at my peak with Liverpool, both physically and in terms of expressing myself with a ball. During my early days at Anfield, the Doc described me rather too generously as 'a football genius whereas Kevin Keegan's qualities were man-made'. To say Kevin 'manufactured' himself, as some people did, was fine because he worked hard at his craft, but so did I. Nobody poured more time and sweat into improving themselves. God never said: 'Kenny Mathieson Dalglish, you are born with all these skills, now go out and shine.' That talent was nurtured through hard graft and good advice.

'Play with your head up, Kenny,' Dad instructed me when I was young. Dad was a decent player until he suffered an injury. He resumed playing in the Army but never made it professionally. He coached and encouraged me. 'Learn, learn, learn,' he'd say. I'd watch games on television, pick up ideas from Rangers stars – Ian McMillan for one – and try their skills again and again.

'Look at how McMillan shoots,' Dad urged me as we hurried into Ibrox one day. McMillan had this trick where he waited for a defender to drift across, blocking the keeper's line of sight, and then he bent the ball around the defender. Seeing the ball late, the keeper usually had no chance to prevent a goal.

'See what he did there?' Dad said.

'That'll do for me,' I replied. McMillan's ploy served me well down the years.

After studying a few of my displays at Anfield, Ian St John remarked that I was 'an old-fashioned Scottish inside-forward' like McMillan, a compliment that thrilled me and my dad. At Motherwell, the Saint worked with a clever, creative inside-forward, Willie Hunter. Although such a breed usually had No. 8 or No. 10 on their backs, I wore No. 7 but operated in a similar style.

Scottish players have traditionally been associated with footballing intelligence but also, back then, with dribbling irrepressibly down the wing. Jinky at Celtic and Eddie Gray at Leeds United, real tanna-ba' players as we called them, were brilliant at taking a ball deep into enemy territory.

For a nation not blessed with numbers, Scotland produced a lot of successful footballers. As a breed, we're tough, capable of enduring difficult times, and I have long believed that leading financial companies often employ Scots in their sales force because the aggressive accent makes them intimidating in negotiations. On the football field, the 1970s and 1980s were eras of brutality, when centre-halves had licence to batter into forwards from behind. I envy the way skilful players are protected now. Back then, referees either turned a blind eye to the punishment meted out by defenders or simply didn't have the laws to stop the slaughter. The tackle from behind had yet to be outlawed, so centre-halves felt they had a free hit. First minute – BANG! Every time. Defending is more of an art now, encouraging attackers and making the game more of a spectacle.

When I played, every match-day brought a different assassin. At Leeds United, Norman Hunter could play a bit but Christ could he kick, as I discovered when Liverpool played Bristol City, where he'd moved by the time I came to play in England. Similarly uncompromising opponents were encountered at Nottingham Forest – Kenny Burns and Larry Lloyd were as hard as hobnailed boots. Big Mickey Droy ploughed into me at Chelsea. Malcolm Shotton pounded my ankles at Oxford United. At times, I felt I'd strayed into a war zone in the role of target, so I dreamed up a clever means of protecting myself – stopping a yard short of where the defender expected. I knew he'd either slam on the brakes, and then I'd accelerate away, or his momentum would take him into me and I'd get a free-kick. Whichever way, it was too late for him to kick me.

Football was a game of survival and I treated the pitch as a jungle. One day, I overheard Bob saying that 'few defenders can kick Kenny out of the game', a judgement from the great man that filled me with pride. I knew I had to stand up for myself, otherwise defenders would walk all over me, so I fought hard and sometimes dirty. Just as I accepted that defenders would assault me, so they acknowledged the possibility of retribution for a particularly bad tackle. Sometimes I got my retaliation in first.

My most shameful act came at White Hart Lane. Chasing Ray Kennedy's ball down the left wing, I found myself closely attended by Steve Perryman next to the touchline and the full-back Don McAllister on my right. Their elbows were raised but not malevolently, just pumping forward and back like pistons as they raced me for the ball. I'd been here before, feeling an elbow suddenly crashing into my face from an unscrupulous opponent, so my survival instinct kicked in. Fearing an elbow, I took pre-emptive action. This was crazy, I accept now, because there was no signal from the Spurs players that they planned anything malicious. Perryman wasn't a dirty player and nor was McAllister. My violent response lacked logic as well as humanity. As we closed on the ball, I punched McAllister, who went out like a light, spark out on the grass. Perryman knocked the ball out for a throw-in. Yards away, the Spurs fans who'd seen my crime screamed blue murder. Luckily for me, there was none of the close television scrutiny that instantly detects any misdemeanour nowadays. If the cameras had caught me, I'd have been hung, but as the referee didn't notice, I escaped. As the Spurs fans seethed, I grabbed the ball and threw it to Terry Mac. In those days, teams didn't stop for an injury. Even if somebody was dead, we played on. Fortunately, McAllister got to his feet. Slightly sheepishly, I muttered a few contrite words when our paths crossed shortly afterwards.

'Listen, I was out of order. I know you're going to have a boot at me. Make it a good one. You've one free shot then that's us quits.' McAllister was never going to decline my offer and I was duly clattered. No problem. At the final whistle, McAllister and I shook hands. When we met at Anfield a few months later, I went down the right, pushing hard to catch the ball and went over on my ankle. When I limped back on, a cocky voice greeted me.

'By the way, that wasn't me!' It was Don McAllister and he was smiling broadly. Fair enough. Respect flowed more freely then. Sadly, grudges fester in modern football.

During an international against Belgium, I exacted a particularly vengeful price on Michel Renquin, the Standard Liege defender. For 45 minutes, Renquin kicked me, attempting to inflict as much damage as possible. Renquin was as merciless as the referee was hopeless. After the fourth bad kick, my patience was close to snapping.

'One more and I'll have him,' I promised myself. The fifth assault was not long in coming. Taking possession with my back to Renquin, I shaped to go inside and then flicked it outside. As I turned, my Belgian tormentor came in hard, burrowing into my Achilles. I rolled on the ground, guaranteeing his booking. Renquin deserved it and should have been cautioned far earlier. He didn't learn. As he pulled my shirt moments later, I swung my elbow back and caught him in the mouth. BANG. Take that. All my anger at his persistent fouling poured into that swing of the elbow. Renquin went down, squealing in pain and spurting blood. No remorse invaded my conscience. Renquin should have thought of the ugly consequences before trying to kick me out of the game.

In the dressing room at half-time, I said to the doctor, 'My arm's sore, Doc.'

'Take your shirt off,' the doctor instructed. It had long sleeves and I struggled to lift my arm to slip it off.

'Your arm's swollen, Kenny,' said the Doc when I finally removed the shirt. 'You've got two puncture holes just above the elbow.' I didn't want to admit that Renquin's teeth must have been the cause.

'Just strap the arm up, Doc, and get me back out.'

In the second half, I tried to inspect Renquin to see the damage I'd inflicted but he never came close. He'd learned his lesson and my ordeal was over. At the final whistle, Renquin did come across.

'Good game,' he said. As Renquin opened his mouth, I felt a certain satisfaction to note he had no front teeth. 'Shake hands?' Renquin asked.

'Get lost,' I told him.

Whatever my anger over his first-half violence, I was out of order. I went home to Liverpool with a few bruises but Renquin went back to Belgium without two front teeth.

However sore and aching my legs, I preferred to play against these rough types of defenders. They held no surprises. It was a physical test, never a mental one. Facing defenders of the class of Derby County's Colin Todd was far harder. Like Liverpool's Lawro and Big Al, Colin read the game so well, never needing to resort to hostile measures to deprive me of possession. Colin nipped in, nicking the ball. Anticipation was Colin's weapon of choice, not aggression, and I respected him deeply.

Against opposition who routinely fouled, Liverpool simply played more passes to feet inside the area. 'Make sure it's in the box,' stressed Bob, knowing a mistimed tackle would result in a penalty. Diving was not in my nature and I only went down in the box with good cause – either I was caught or I lost balance while trying to evade a challenge. Cynicism never accompanied my descent to the floor. If Norman Hunter or Mickey Droy kicked me, I didn't want to go down. My pride would never let me show the enemy I was hurt. I always tried to play on in the manner of a winger I greatly admired, George Best, who just rode tackles or leapt up and carried on. I hope that, like George, I never gave referees many problems, although bookings for dissent came my way – a surprise because I thought the officials wouldn't understand my Glaswegian accent. Referees engaged more with players then, conducting a bit of banter. If I was moaning, Neil Midgley said, 'Shut up, Kenny.' Neil, bless him, has passed away now but he was a good referee. Neil made mistakes but he'd chat.

'You're having a nightmare, Neil,' I'd tell him.

'You're not playing too well yourself, Kenny,' he'd shout back. Industrial language wasn't frowned upon – Neil and the other refs understood the factory-floor nature of match-days. Referees forgave a few swear words as we pursued trophies. That was all that mattered to me, collecting silverware, and I craved a second European Cup.

7

PARIS

I STILL recall the look of hurt in Paul's eyes. I still remember my son's plaintive words when he was just five and watching an old Granada TV highlights' show about Liverpool's loss to Nottingham Forest in the European Cup. 'What does it mean, Dad, "The Party's Over"?' Paul asked me. What do you say to a bairn? How can you explain that some Granada producer probably thought it was clever to use a Frank Sinatra track over footage of us traipsing off at Anfield on 27 September 1978, our grip on the European Cup broken? Television people saw only the professional footballer, never the relatives affected by their insensitivity. They never thought of the inconsolable children. Paul was so young but he already supported me and loved the club, so it broke his heart when Liverpool struggled. At the time, Granada's choice of music made me angry, but even more so when I saw the distressing effect on wee Paul. Granada were disrespectful to our past achievements and naïve to think Liverpool might not hit back.

I'd never dispute that Cloughie's side were deserved winners, but that European Cup draw was a joke. When the call came through, informing Bob of Liverpool's next opponents in Europe, the Boss was in his room at Melwood as usual. It wasn't grand enough to be called an office or tiny enough to be considered a cupboard. It was just a small room with an old table and a metal filing cabinet with a phone on top. Bob's control centre had two windows. He could watch the kids on the pitch that was sarcastically called Wembley from one, and the first team training from the other. Bob stood at the windows, inspecting his troops and warming himself in front of a radiator because his tracksuit bottoms had holes in the knees. Bob would shuffle to the phone and then emerge from his room for one of Melwood's great traditions. I knew if the Boss came across to the training pitch taking big steps, then it was a draw he relished. Small steps meant difficulties.

'Big steps,' began Bugsy before quickly changing his tune. 'Oh, no, wait a minute, small steps.' The defence of our trophy would begin against Forest, European champions versus English champions. England were the dominant nation, and the feeling within the Liverpool dressing room was that Uefa, the governing body, wanted to break that power.

'There's a one in thirty-one chance of us getting Forest – and we just have done,' I said. Everybody in the Liverpool dressing room respected Forest, who'd done brilliantly in winning the League. Cloughie had them very organised, very efficient, and we knew Forest were a really strong force collectively. Individually, John Robertson did the magic on the left, servicing Tony Woodcock and Garry Birtles. Ian Bowyer and John McGovern patrolled the middle, nicking the ball and getting it forward. If Forest had a genuine recognised star, it was Peter Shilton, a fantastic goalkeeper. Just like us at Liverpool, I knew Forest were unhappy with the draw. This was their first time in the competition and they risked going out of Europe without even getting out of England. The draw stank.

For all our frustration, Liverpool should still have gone through. We had the experience, the players and the confidence because of our long unbeaten record in Europe. Cloughie tried to butter us up with praise, saying that 'Liverpool are a great team' and attempting to foster a sense of complacency. Bob just laughed. The Boss knew what Cloughie was up to, the old mind games routine. We'd heard it all before.

'You know you are a great team,' Bob told us. 'Now just go out and prove it.' Cloughie could have used every trick in the psychology manual and it wouldn't have worked. Liverpool messed up against Forest because we made a silly error in the first leg at the City Ground, becoming obsessed with equalising after Birtles scored. We should have seen the game out, knowing that 1–0 in the away leg was fine in Europe, but because we were playing English opponents, we adopted a Football League mind-set and pushed on, a foolish reaction. Forest hit us on the break, Colin Barrett making it 2–0. As European champions, we should have been more mature, less gung-ho, but an unexpected bout of naivety cost us. At Anfield a fortnight later, Forest held out and we were out.

In victory, Forest were very dignified, which was no real surprise to me. I knew Cloughie would never allow his players to gloat. They shook hands with us and headed off into the second round. Forest were certainly more respectful than I felt Granada were. People respected Liverpool because of the gracious way we conducted ourselves during times of success. Gerald Sinstadt was Granada's reporter and he certainly copped some stick for 'The Party's Over'.

'Go and prove the party's not over, lads,' Bob said. We did, winning the League that season, so Sinstadt was a good judge, wasn't he? The Kop was quick to make its point, singing: 'Gerald Sinstadt, Gerald Sinstadt, how's your party doing now?' The moment we heard it, all the players joined in. Afterwards, poor old Sinstadt must have felt a wee bit sheepish coming in to interview the new champions.

A couple of years on, I was walking with Paul through reception at Anfield when we bumped into Sinstadt.

'Gerald, Paul's got something to say to you,' I said. Sinstadt looked at Paul. 'How's the party going, Gerald?' Paul asked. We didn't forget.

Fortunately for us, the party got going again quickly back then.

That League success swept us back into the European Cup, thank God, as we'd really missed the competition. Liverpool belong in the European Cup. Sadly, we didn't last long in the 79–80 season after being thrown in against Dinamo Tbilisi in the first round. Over the years, I feel a myth has grown unchecked that Dinamo had so little fear of Liverpool they cockily warmed up in front of the Kop. Newspapers were riddled with idle chatter that Liverpool supporters apparently marvelled at the Georgians' skills before the first leg on 19 September.

'If they were doing it to show they weren't afraid, that just proves to me they were afraid,' I said to Graeme. We won, but only 2–1, and a fortnight later set out on a journey into the unknown.

Liverpool's plane was an Aeroflot jet, which the Soviets insisted we hired, conveniently making them a bundle of roubles. For a bunch of communists, I felt they showed distinct capitalist tendencies. Our journey became increasingly complicated as the Iron Curtain still hung across the Continent, and any destination in the Soviet Union involved a stop in Moscow – another Soviet demand. So we dutifully filed out of the plane, heading through immigration as Red Army soldiers scrutinised us as if we were some band of dissidents. The stopover seemed pretty pointless, paranoid even, but we shrugged and got on with it. The Soviet solders and immigration officials didn't look the types who'd welcome any friendly banter. We then reboarded the plane to Tbilisi, landing in one of the grimmest parts of Europe, even by Communist standards.

Liverpool's hotel was pretty basic but we were assured it was Tbilisi's finest. Fortunately, Bob always made sure we came well-prepared, bringing our own chefs, Harry White and Alan Glynn, who worked in the hotel trade in Dublin. Harry and Alan ensured we had tea and toast for breakfast and that the hotel cook was onside, a vital move. I was always suspicious about what foreign cooks might slip into the food but Harry and Alan man-marked the cook closely, watching him in the hotel, keeping him sweet with a bottle of whisky or two. European football required intelligent tactics off the field as well as on.

'Anything we don't use, you can keep,' Harry and Alan told the cook, who was incredibly grateful, because provisions were modest in Georgia. Tbilisi was pretty primitive.

'Be careful in the lift,' I told the players after one perilous descent towards reception. 'There's water streaming down the side. Don't go near the electrics.'

'It's a hole,' seemed to be the overwhelming verdict of the players – a noisy hole as well. Under a Soviet regime that didn't seem big on laughs, the natives of Georgia were forbidden from staging demonstrations – until Liverpool arrived. My precious sleep was disturbed at 2 a.m. by chants of 'Dinamo, Dinamo'. Peering out of the window, I saw hundreds of people marching up and down outside our hotel. The noisy protest was so obviously organised it must have been sanctioned by the Soviet authorities. The Georgians would never have dared gather in numbers like that without permission from Moscow.

During my trips behind the Iron Curtain, I gained the strong impression these Soviets used the European Cup as a vehicle to generate great publicity for all the Soviet countries. Whenever a western club visited, the Communists wanted a show of strength, and that meant giving their sides every chance of winning. Liverpool were not just up against a team in Tbilisi. We were up against an ideology. The whole experience was eye-opening and anyone travelling behind the Iron Curtain with thoughts about communism being the future would have changed their mind sharpish. Power to the people? Many didn't even have electrical power. Accommodation was decrepit, food short and the whole place seemed blanketed in a cloud of smog and depression. Who'd want to live like that? I never blamed the Georgian people, who were just trapped in a brutal system. In the morning, some of the locals even queued around the hotel just to see what westerners looked like.

The Georgians' sad, controlled existence meant they really let rip on match-day. Dinamo Tbilisi fans were incredibly passionate, leaping out of the stands, running to the edge of the pitch as their team gave them plenty to cheer. Dinamo stormed to a 3–0 win, playing some wonderful football in the second half, which we simply couldn't live with, and again Liverpool crashed out of Europe at the first hurdle. Even the refreshment in the dressing room looked trouble.

'Don't touch the tea,' said Bob, 'you don't know what they've put in it.'

Sitting on the bench for both legs against Dinamo was Frank McGarvey, the Scottish striker whose spell at Liverpool has often been a matter of debate. Arriving in May 1979 from St Mirren with a good reputation, and a valuation of £270,000, McGarvey should have fitted in but he never settled. We Scots did everything to look after one of our own. Al, Charlie and I took Frank out for a drink, helped him look for houses and offered every welcoming gesture.

'How are you enjoying it, Frank?' I asked him.

'I'm not sure, Kenny.'

'What do you mean?'

'Everybody's really nice to me.'

'Well, that's good.'

'I'm not sure about that, Kenny. I'm uneasy.'

'You plank! They all want you to do well, Frank, that's why they're all nice to you.'

'The cleaning lady is really nice to me!'

'Frank, that's because she's a Liverpool fan. They're all Liverpool fans. You've just come down from Scotland and they're trying to make you welcome.'

Frank never overcame those doubts, which I always thought was a great pity for him, and for Liverpool. In truth, I must admit Frank's style of play was far too individual for Liverpool. We dubbed Frank 'the Incredible Turning Man' because he'd

En route to a Scottish Cup winner's medal for Celtic against Dundee in 1974.

Great men, brilliant managers – Jock Stein (*left*) and Bill Shankly at Celtic Park.

I won one of my 102 caps for Scotland against Holland at the 1978 World Cup, although our victory over the eventual runners-up proved to be in vain.

Arriving at Anfield with Bob Paisley in 1977 to begin a fresh chapter with Liverpool.

Chairman John Smith (*left*) and secretary Peter Robinson (*back, right*) join Bob Paisley to watch me sign.

Pursued at Melwood by Phil Neal, a fine Liverpool captain under Bob Paisley and Joe Fagan.

Running out at Middlesbrough for my Liverpool debut, which I marked with a goal.

I took over Kevin Keegan's No. 7 shirt for the 1977 Charity Shield game at Wembley.

Back at Wembley in 1978, Liverpool won the European Cup with this goal against Bruges.

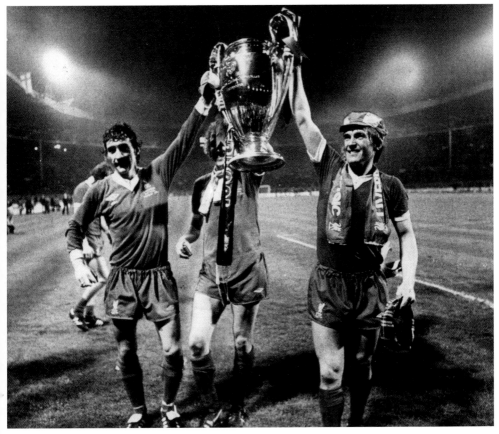

Terry McDermott joins me to parade the European Cup before our jubilant fans.
Bob Paisley raises the trophy on our triumphant homecoming tour of Liverpool.

Sammy Lee's tight marking stifled Bayern's Paul Breitner (*left*) to help us reach another European Cup final in 1981.

Alan Kennedy (*centre*) is mobbed by David Johnson (*left*) and Terry McDermott after his goal beat Real Madrid in Paris.

We often used to play cards to wile away the hours on long train journeys. Ray Clemence (*left*) and I are enjoying this game, while Terry McDermott seems to be assessing my hand!

Another Championship party in 1982 for the Boot Room (*left to right*): Ronnie Moran, Roy Evans, Bob Paisley, Tom Saunders, Joe Fagan and John Bennison.

Sign him up! Paul shows deft control and balance as a toddler at Melwood.

On the attack in the 1982 Charity Shield win over Tottenham at Wembley.

Sir Stanley Matthews presents me with the Footballer of the Year trophy in 1979.

twist and turn with the ball when some of the lads, particularly Terry Mac, wanted it laid off straight away, so keeping the momentum that made Liverpool such a force. Bob took a chance on Frank McGarvey and it didn't work out, but anybody arguing that his 10 months at Anfield were an expensive mistake has simply not done their sums. Celtic paid Bob what he'd paid St Mirren. Liverpool's association with Frank was disappointing but it could never be entered in the club ledger as bad business.

Sitting next to Frank on the bench in Tbilisi was Avi Cohen, a real character much loved in the Liverpool dressing room for his sense of humour. When Avi first walked through the door, I went out of my way to talk to him. After a few words, Avi asked me, 'Do you speak English?'

'Are you joking?' I replied, failing to mask my annoyance. Even now, I'm still not sure whether Avi was winding me up, although the lads found it marvellous entertainment. 'Do you speak English?' became a constant refrain of theirs.

The Boss came into the dressing room, chuntering on about something. Eventually, he said, 'The Press are saying Avi is an Orthodox Jew and that he can't play on a Saturday.' All the lads looked intrigued.

'So what did you say to the Press, Boss?' somebody asked.

'I told them Avi won't be out of place here. Several of you lot never play on Saturdays!'

Sadly, no laughter accompanied Liverpool's travails in Europe for those two seasons. Finally, early in September 1980, Bob came bounding across Melwood. 'Come on, who do you think you want?' he smiled. We'd never have guessed. At last, Uefa granted Liverpool an easier start to a European campaign, a visit to Oulu, a small market town in Finland where the locals were incredibly hospitable, to play Oulun Palloseura. For these Scandinavians to have Liverpool Football Club actually in their town was a major honour and the Raatti Stadium was rammed, crackling with atmosphere as Finns and Scousers mingled.

As usual, Liverpool fans travelled in numbers and their loyalty never ceased to astonish me. They got everywhere, behind the Iron Curtain and up near the Arctic Circle, using their ingenuity to cover vast distances, sometimes skipping the train fare by hiding in the toilet when the ticket inspector came round. Liverpool supporters were masters at keeping the cost down. Outside grounds, some fans mugged ticket touts. They'd only hurt them in the pocket. When the tout produced the tickets, the fans grabbed them and ran. Such behaviour never troubled me. Why should it? The touts tried to fleece them, exploiting their passion for Liverpool. Our supporters made so many sacrifices, following the team they loved. It cost them serious money and cost some their marriages. I found it a truly humbling experience to talk to fans on the road in Europe. They'd hang on every word, no matter what I said, but I was fascinated by their adventures. Some of the punters were familiar faces from the club plane, or friends of local players. Nowadays, apart from Carra and Stevie, no Liverpool players enjoy the contact with fans that we did back then. Kop and team had a truly special relationship. Abroad, we made sure we got the fans tickets, rewarding their loyalty. On most midweek trips, we saw school-aged kids.

'They must get a lot of holidays,' I mentioned to Graeme. 'Or their dads are taking them as a treat.'

Unfortunately, there were few treats for them in Oulu. The Finnish champions were playing their first game in Europe and the wait had made them impatient. Oulun had a right good go and we were fortunate to leave with a 1–1 scoreline. Unimpressed with our display, Bob sent out the same team again for the Anfield leg on 1 October.

'Do the job properly this time,' Bob told us. We didn't let the Boss down. Souey and Terry Mac got hat-tricks in a 10–1 thrashing as we coasted into the second round.

The moment we knew it was Aberdeen next on 22 October, the mood around the dressing room changed. Facing a Scottish side was huge for Al, Souey and me. We all knew what a lively reception was in store. Scarcely had the draw been made than all sorts of noises flooded out of Scotland about what Aberdeen would do to Liverpool, about us Anglos being sent homeward to think again.

'You have to understand,' I told the other players. 'We cannot lose this. Come on. It's a big game for us.' The English players took the piss.

'Even if we lose up there, we'll beat them at Anfield,' Terry Mac said.

'Don't start that,' I replied. 'Don't. We have to win up there. Our lives depend on it.'

Before we departed north, all the non-Scottish players were made fully aware of what this tie meant. Nothing less than victory over Aberdeen was acceptable. Catching the mood, the newspapers raised the stakes, giving it the full 'Battle of Britain' treatment. Fittingly, we landed at RAF Lossiemouth with our canny squadron leader, Bob, ready for the Scots. As he headed off for the press conference, Bob said, 'I'm just going to give Gordon Strachan a wee bit of toffee.' Bob brought out the toffee for special occasions only, for when he wanted to give an opposing player a compliment to soften him up. The Boss was a master at dishing out toffee. On the morning of the game, the newspapers were awash with Bob's praise for Strachan. They'd taken the bait. Bob talked about how Liverpool respected Aberdeen's winger, how it was a great stage for such a talent as Gordon to shine, and how the world watched him.

'We've seen the headlines, Boss,' I said as he came into break-fast. 'We've seen you've said how good Strachan is.'

'I just gave him a bit of toffee,' smiled Bob.

When we arrived at Pittodrie, the Aberdeen fans seemed in no mood to repay the compliment. The reception for Graeme, Al and me was horrendous, real vitriol spitting out from the terraces. If we'd been wearing a Scotland shirt, they'd have cheered us, but we represented an English team so they battered us. The one blessing was that Graeme's 'Champagne Charlie' image meant the Aberdeen fans slaughtered him even more. Charlie liked that, and so did Al and I, because it took the heat off us.

Our game plan was Liverpool's usual away tactic of keeping the ball, quietening the 24,000 fans and taking the sting out of a heated occasion, but we knew the scale of the mission. Alex Ferguson was doing such a magnificent job with Aberdeen we had to respect them. With so much money and playing talent at Celtic Park and Ibrox, I appreciated what an incredible achievement it was by Fergie to break the Old Firm stranglehold. He'd assembled a really good side at Pittodrie. For opposing forwards, like me, stepping into this cauldron, Aberdeen posed a particularly formidable challenge. Fergie had built a brilliant centre-back pairing. Alex McLeish attacked the ball while Willie Miller swept up, handling the one-on-ones. Bob told us that when we got in the final third, we must move the ball quickly to get past Alex and Willie. Within five minutes, we'd scored from a fast move, Terry Mac chipping Jim Leighton for the only goal of the first leg.

The Scottish newspapers claimed we were fortunate to leave with a 1–0 win. 'Lucky Liverpool' was the gist of the headlines, but I didn't care. I just felt relief, because losing to a Scottish side, and hearing the crowing of the Scottish journalists and public, would have been torture. Terry Mac did us a right good favour with that goal. The pressure was off.

The second leg kicked off on Bonfire Night and Aberdeen certainly lit a fuse, upsetting us by winning the toss and making us kick towards the Kop. Down the years, it has become one of the great traditions of European nights at Anfield that Liverpool attack the Kop in the second half. From St Etienne, before my time, to Olympiakos more recently, Liverpool have performed heroics running towards the Kop as the clock ticked down. Maybe it was the sight of all those expectant faces, all those Liverpool flags and scarves, or maybe it was the noise, pulling us towards the goal, but there was always something special about this second-half experience. Against Aberdeen, we were annoyed to be playing towards the Kop so early, and took our anger out on Fergie's defence. Miller conceded an own goal, Nealy swept in another and the tie was over before half-time. After the break, Al and I really rubbed it in. Battering Aberdeen 4–0 pleased a lot of people and it certainly delighted us. The verdict in the newspapers was that Liverpool comprehensively outplayed Aberdeen. Fergie had been completely outwitted by Bob, and wee Gordon was too busy chewing on toffee to hurt us. I'm convinced that this defeat was when Fergie first realised the importance of psychology. What Fergie now uses as mind games, Bob just called toffee. It certainly worked.

As bitter memories of the party being over faded, Liverpool strode closer towards the final in Paris. In the March quarter-final, CSKA Sofia were overwhelmed in a tie notable for Graeme's hat-trick at Anfield and David Johnson's strike in Bulgaria.

'Well done, Doc,' I shouted at Johnson, who was becoming more and more influential. David was known as the Doc because he always carried a small BOAC airline bag filled with all types of pills.

'My head's killing me,' I occasionally said to the Doc.

'I've got a tablet for that,' replied the Doc, fishing around in his magical medical chest of a bag. He had absolutely no medical knowledge, of course, but the Doc knew where the goal was. When I arrived, the Doc thought he would be bombed out by Bob but he stayed and played an important role.

Through to the semis, we knew our next opponents would be of the very highest order. 'Inter, Real Madrid or Bayern Munich,' I said to Terry Mac as we trained. 'I don't think Bob's going to have very big strides.' Moments later, our beloved manager walked out of the Melwood pavilion and we stopped training, transfixed by his movement.

'Smallish strides,' I correctly concluded after much scrutinising. Bob was quite happy with Bayern. He knew the Germans could field some of the best talent at work in the modern game, stars such as the European Footballer of the Year, Karl-Heinz Rummenigge, but Bob trusted us. Even when Liverpool were held 0–0 at Anfield on 8 April, the Boss remained relaxed.

'We'll score out there,' said Bob, his confidence strengthened by the knowledge that Graeme would be back from injury, stiffening the midfield. By the time we got to the Olympic Stadium on 22 April, Bob's team-talk had already been done for him. Living up to arrogant stereotype, the Germans gave us all the incentive we required by spouting information to their fans on the best travel plans for the Paris final. Even Bayern's experienced players, who should have known better, mouthed off about us. I was seething when I heard Paul Breitner calling us 'unimaginative and unintelligent', a comment as disrespectful as it was incorrect. Just before we went out, Bob said to Sammy Lee, 'Go and mark Breitner.'

Liverpool traditionally relied on tried and trusted tactics in Europe. I was occasionally withdrawn into midfield, but this was a new development. Bob rarely assigned individuals to man-making roles but he clearly identified Breitner as Bayern's chief threat. Being the mouthpiece for all Munich's dressing-room rubbish about Liverpool told Bob that Breitner was the ringleader. Only somebody assured of his team-mates' support, or immensely thick, would have ventured opinions as provocative as Breitner's denigrating remarks about Liverpool.

Sammy accepted his evening's mission willingly. Typical Sammy. A local boy, he loved Liverpool with a passion and would do anything for the team. Friendly and unquestioning, the only person Sammy ever criticised was himself, and he'd apologise for everything, even breathing. 'Sorry, sorry, sorry,' he kept muttering, like a Scouse Ronnie Corbett. His committed, genuine nature made him one of the most popular players in the Liverpool dressing room. When he marked his 1978 debut with a goal, against Leicester City, we were all made up. Sammy hit the ball from 20 yards, not the most venomous strike ever attempted in front of the Kop, but it somehow meandered into the net.

'I've scored. I've scored,' yelled Sammy, almost in disbelief. 'I've scored at the Kop,' he added, realising the extra significance. Scoring in front of all his family and friends meant the world to Sammy. His wholehearted nature endeared him to everybody at Anfield. Sammy ran himself into the ground shuttling between the boxes, making light of his lack of height. In confronting some of the bigger units patrolling central midfield, Sammy's size was against him, so I consider his achievements in the game should command even greater respect. His was a difficult position to play in for Liverpool, up and down non-stop, demanding great stamina. Continuing the rich tradition of Brian Hall and Jimmy Case, Sammy put in a good shift and he never let anyone down at Liverpool. I always felt the only ingredient holding Sammy Lee back from being a truly top player was self-belief. If Sammy had believed in himself more, and not got so wound up if he made a mistake, he'd have been up there with the very best. That was Sammy's nature. Bob certainly believed in him, seeing what Sammy could bring to the team, what an important cog he was in the midfield engine. So he set Sammy to work on Breitner.

'Smother him, don't let him move, don't let him breathe,' Bob said. Sammy's not a dirty player but he wouldn't let Breitner go. Wherever the German went, a short, freckly Scouser blocked his path. Whenever Breitner got the ball, Sammy was in his face, closing him down, pressing him to lose it. Whenever Breitner saw a window of opportunity, Sammy slammed it shut. Sammy followed him everywhere, almost into the Bayern dressing room at half-time.

I'd long gone by then. My night in Bavaria lasted just nine minutes, and my frustration at limping off was compounded by the manner of my incapacitation. Bayern's winger, Karl Del'Haye, topped me. Being put out of a game by an opponent of imposing physical stature was something I'd resent but could accept – not Del'Haye, though, not some skinny winger. He was so light-weight in frame and ability I never thought he posed a threat as I laid the ball inside. Del'Haye went straight into my foot and I strongly suspect the German's intent was to remove me from the fray deliberately. Replacing me was Howard Gayle, who ripped the backside out of Wolfgang Dremmler. Howie was flying, utterly unstoppable and the Germans were run ragged. Watching from the dug-out, I saw the game getting very tasty with tackles going in from every angle, from every player, demonstrating the desperation to reach the final. When Howie got booked, Bob had to make a call. The Germans had really wound up Howie and if he'd lost it again, Liverpool would be down to 10 men. In the seventieth minute, Bob took Howie off and sent Jimmy Case on, so that was our subs used up. Just as I began thinking that if any injuries occurred, we'd be struggling, the Doc signalled to Bob.

'My thigh's gone,' he shouted. Furious, Bob jumped off the bench. Looking at our irate manager, I knew there was no chance the Boss would hand Bayern any advantage on the threshold of Paris. The Boss turned to the security people guarding the dug-out, pointing at their pistols.

'Give me that gun,' Bob shouted at one of them. 'I'm going to shoot him.'

Fortunately, the security man didn't understand. The Doc got the message and immediately forgot his thigh problem. With seven minutes remaining of normal time, he ran down the touch-line, whipped in a cross and Ray Kennedy's wonderful volley did the rest. Bayern needed two. No chance. Rummenigge equalised but even that goal was lucky. Colin Irwin jumped to head the ball and it spun away to Rummenigge. Colin and Richard Money were brilliant that night. Our defence was much changed, only Nealy and Alan being regulars, but nobody let Liverpool down in Munich. At the final whistle, the boys all queued up to shake Breitner's hand. They were all smiling, wondering what was the German for 'unimaginative and unintelligent'! If Liverpool were that unintelligent, Breitner can't have played well as Liverpool were in the final. Breitner certainly never had the imagination to escape Sammy's clutches. Thanks for the ammunition. Sadly, I never had a chance to voice my reflections on Breitner's pre-match critique with the man himself. I'd hobbled down the stairs for treatment on my ankle after Del'Haye's attack.

Immobilised in plaster, it was touch and go whether I'd be fit to face Real Madrid in the final. Determined to make Paris, I fought my way through five weeks of rehab and nerves. When the plaster was removed, I guested for Bob's staff team against the ground-staff and apprentices at Melwood. As usual, Bob was in goal with a pair of mittens on and he never caught anything, just punched. Joe was in front of him with Ronnie and they made sure nobody got through, not always in the most legitimate manner.

'Play on,' Bob shouted regardless. Old Tom, only 60, was a jinky winger. At least Roy was fit. He was the only member of the coaching staff who'd run. The pitch was a decent size, 60 by 40 yards, and Bob made sure I covered every blade of grass. I ran and ran, and whenever I eased up, gasping for air, Bob shouted from his position in goal, 'Come on, Kenny. Start running.' My tongue was hanging out like a knackered dog, rolling from side to side. Still Bob screamed, 'Start running.'

'Bloody start!' I said to myself, and I thought I'd learned the trick of how to survive these games, rationing my runs forward because I knew nobody was tracking back. Bob was no fool. He knew this was a clever way of building up fitness. It was the length of the game that really killed me – it went on until Bob's side were winning.

With the apprentices showing common sense when tackling me, I gradually eased my way back from injury in time. Before we flew out to Paris, a few of us gathered in Sammy's wine bar to watch the England–Scotland Home International. Sammy was almost as passionate about England as he was about Liverpool, but even when us Scots invaded his wine bar, he was good as gold. Even when Big Hansen kept waving a large Scotland flag at the bar, Sammy just smiled. Even when England got stuffed, Sammy accepted all the banter with surprisingly good grace.

Heading into Paris, we swiftly discovered that Liverpool fans in their thousands had beaten us to the French capital. We heard them before we actually saw them. Their songs carried far and wide, tunes like:

> We'll visit the Folies Bergères,
> They like to see the Scousers there,
> The women are lovely with skin like a peach
> But no one can move it like Kenny Dalglish.

Very flattering! Once we'd settled into our hotel in Versailles, on 26 May 1981, Bob delivered a particularly significant team-talk on how we'd face Madrid.

'We are going to frustrate Madrid,' said the Boss. 'We're going to deny them possession. Keep the ball, keep the tempo slow.' In the morning, Bob took us on a stroll through the park in Versailles and spoke more about mighty Madrid, about their six trophies, and our chance for an upset. I'm no student of history, and certainly not French history, but I appreciated the image of aristocrats falling to a revolution.

For all the talk of Real's illustrious history, I didn't really care who our opponents were. The newspapers banged on about Real Madrid. Christ, everyone knew their tradition and I certainly didn't need reminding. As a wee boy growing up in Glasgow and passionately interested in those who played football like gods, I could hardly escape Madrid. They beat Eintracht Frankfurt, 7–3, in 1960 at Hampden Park and that team remains indelible in my memory: Dominguez, Marquitos, Santamaria, Pachin, Vidal,

Zarraga, Canario, Del Sol, Di Stefano, Puskas and Gento. But Liverpool were not playing Di Stefano, Puskas and Gento. The shirt was familiar but was the heart inside the same? Liverpool had a great incentive to overcome a famous name – victory was our only ticket back in to the European Cup. The League had been a disaster. We'd finished fifth, so this was it. Paris or bust.

Bob read out the team: Clem, Nealy, Alan Kennedy, Tommo, Ray, Big Hansen, me, Sammy, the Doc, Terry Mac and Charlie. One more instruction fell from Bob's lips –

'Sammy. Take Stielike.'

Sammy was collecting some distinguished German scalps. As with Breitner, Sammy forced Stielike deep. He didn't like it, getting booked, and lacking any influence on the game. Madrid attempted similar tactics, attaching Jose Camacho to Souey, and I knew what Graeme was going through. When Scotland hosted Spain at Hampden, Camacho marked me, but fortunately he was cautioned after 20 minutes so he was restricted. Graeme needed all his guile to escape Camacho. The game was tight, cagey, short on chances, even decent moves. Real's best outlet on the wing, Laurie Cunningham, was quiet, and any hope of fluency was tempered by the unpredictable pitch at Parc des Princes, a rugby pitch with rock-hard lines. One Real shot hit the six-yard line, reared up and caught Clem in the face. Not for the last time in my Liverpool career, Uefa chose an unsuitable stadium.

Our annoyance with the poor surface was forgotten nine minutes from the end. Liverpool advanced down the left-hand side as Madrid harried, forcing the ball out. From the third throw-in near the corner, Alan Kennedy burst into the Real box and into Liverpool legend. A popular figure, Alan enjoyed many nicknames. He was 'Belly' after Bel Mooney, the writer on the *Daily Mirror*, who mentioned him once. He was 'Billy', as in Billy Bungalow, because he had nothing upstairs. He was 'Barney' to the punters after Barney Rubble from *The Flintstones*. He certainly

made a name for himself in Paris. Barney took Ray Kennedy's
throw on his chest. An imposing goalie, Agustin Rodriguez
seemed to set himself right and I expected Alan to square the
ball to the Doc, who was screaming for it in the centre. Barney's
response was so unexpected it could have been included in the
old 'What Happened Next?' section on *A Question of Sport*. Barney
drilled the ball towards the near-post, beating Agustin. I don't
know who was more surprised, Real's goalkeeper or Liverpool's
players.

'What were you doing up there in the first place?' I asked
Barney afterwards. He wasn't sure.

'Did you think of crossing to the Doc?' I asked.

'I thought of it,' Barney replied. I'm glad he didn't.

The newspapers weren't particularly charitable to Agustin,
repeating the usual criticism that no keeper should be beaten at
the near-post, but I thought blaming Agustin was harsh. Barney
never picked his spot. He flashed his shot and it went in.

'Did you mean it?' Terry Mac asked. Barney smiled.

'Yes,' he replied. Barney's shooting prowess was a matter of
some conjecture inside the Liverpool dressing room. Bob always
had faith in him as a full-back.

'If Alan Kennedy doesn't play for England, I will jump off the
Pier Head,' Bob said just before signing him. We were in Vienna
at the time and Alan was invited to join a five-a-side game in
training. He was awful.

'Don't you want to come to Liverpool?' I asked Alan back at
the hotel.

'What?' spluttered Alan.

'That performance this morning was as if you didn't want to
come here.'

'No. No.'

'You were hopeless.'

Alan needed time to settle because he'd come from Newcastle
United, who played a more direct game, hoisting balls to Super

Mac and John Tudor. One of his first games was against QPR at Anfield and in the dressing room afterwards, Bob announced, 'They've shot the wrong Kennedy.' Barney took it well. He was a real character. One year, Lada gave three cars to Liverpool and when Alan mentioned it, there was a rush for the dressing-room door. A few stayed. The Doc took one Lada, Barney definitely got another and whoever got the third kept the news quieter than the car's exhaust. Barney struggled in his Lada. He couldn't do a three-point turn, more a 24-point turn. When he parked, Barney took the gear-stick out.

'It's so nobody will steal the car,' he explained.

'Barney, if you left the engine running with the door open, nobody would steal it,' I told him.

One year, he marched into the dressing room and declared, 'I'm going into the Christmas hamper business. Who wants one?'

'I'll order one,' I said to help Barney out.

'Thanks, Kenny. They're good. Perfect for the wife and mother-in-law. Wines, chocolates.' We all piled in, all the boys ordering some of Barney's hampers. Shortly before Christmas, Barney informed us, 'Listen, sorry, lads. I've got your hampers but I've had to make some changes. I never got the chocolates. So I got underwear.'

'Pants?' I said. 'I'm giving my mother-in-law pants?'

'Sorry, Kenny. They didn't have chocolates. But she'll get a mug as well.' By that time, the boys were falling about laughing.

'It's not just any mug,' Barney insisted. 'It's a Dunoon mug.'

The boys almost never recovered from that revelation. They were rolling around the floor by then. Poor Barney. His whole hamper business was carnage, but if we hadn't forgiven him by Paris, we certainly did when he scored.

Few teams celebrated as well as Liverpool. We moved out of Versailles and into the wives' hotel in the centre of Paris. Some of the boys got invited to the Moulin Rouge but I stayed in because Marina felt sick. We didn't know at the time but she was pregnant with Lynsey. It often happened that nine months after a European Cup final, the Liverpool dressing room reported an upsurge in babies, although Marina was already pregnant by Paris. So she sat up in bed, chatting with Richard Money and his wife.

'What have you got in your pocket?' I asked Richard.

'A medal,' he replied.

'No, you've not. You've got a *winner's* medal.' I kept saying it. Richard kept answering as if it was the first time he'd heard the question. Mind you, we were both lashed. We talked about the game, talked a little about Madrid, but I never thought: 'We've just beaten the club of Di Stefano, Puskas and Gento.' It never mattered to me whether the scoreline was 1–0 or 4–0 as long as we'd won. I just wanted the victory, the trophy, the glory.

Winning the European Cup gave us the right to face the champions of South America, the Brazilians of Flamengo, in Tokyo later in 1981 to decide the club champions of the world. The journey was madness. We flew to Anchorage and I swear the time when we arrived was earlier than when we left Heathrow. We went from Anchorage to Japan and it seemed as if we skipped two days. My body clock was all over the place. I kept waking up at 3 a.m. in Tokyo. To kill some time before the game, the usual idiots – Hansen, Terry Mac and me – went to a three-tier driving range next to the hotel, where the Japanese fixed us up with clubs and handed us an empty bucket each.

'Where are the balls?' inquired Alan, very slowly.

'There,' replied one of the golf boys, pointing to a drain-pipe.

I pressed a button and golf balls cascaded out of the pipe, running all over the driving range. We soon realised the trick was to put the bucket underneath before pressing the button! The place was amazing. I hit a ball into this vast piece of sloping grass and watched as it rolled back down yet another pipe, funnelling back to the clubhouse. With so many golf balls, it sounded like hailstones crashing down.

The golf was more enjoyable than the match against Flamengo.

The pitch was burnt to a cinder and we weren't much livelier. Liverpool wanted to win but it felt an obligation, not high on our list of priorities. Latin Americans, in this case Flamengo, and players such as Zico took it seriously, and they celebrated wildly when they won 3–0. If Liverpool had won, we wouldn't have been gloating about being champions of the world. Anyway, the Liverpool dressing room was the world champion home of banter, as a precociously talented young striker was about to discover.

8

RUSHIE

WHEN a quiet, rake-thin teenager from Wales shuffled self-consciously into the Anfield dressing room, I noted with quiet pleasure that the lads had just been presented with another target for our relentless banter sessions. I also detected Ian Rush was desperately shy, which was understandable really. Here was this young boy coming from Chester City into a room full of players who'd won European Cups and League Championships. Hailing from Flint, a small mining town, Rushie must have found Anfield a complete culture shock, and Liverpool didn't make allowances for sensitive types. Mockery came as easily as breathing to us but proved an ordeal for Rushie, who simply didn't understand that all the banter was to make him feel part of the Liverpool family. It pained me to discover eventually that all this high-speed teasing nearly destroyed Rushie, or 'Omar' as we first called him. Rushie tried to grow a moustache but it was a long way short of the bushy class of Omar Sharif.

'Is that eyebrow pencil?' I asked him one day.

'Where?' Rushie replied nervously.

'Under your nose, above your lip. It looks like eyebrow pencil.'

His moustache was a rich source of entertainment for the boys. Omar's fashion sense provided especially powerful ammunition for Al, Souey and me. Anything Rushie wore, he got pilloried for. As he stripped near me, I was afforded a close inspection of his latest outfit, and, one day, he wore corduroy trousers that seemed at half-mast.

'Is the tide out, Omar?' I asked.

Embarrassed, he spluttered some reply. He always seemed tongue-tied. When I hear Rushie on the television now, speaking so eloquently, I must confess to a certain surprise. To start with, Rushie's heading was weak, so we gave him the ironic nickname of 'Tosh' after John Toshack, a Liverpool legend famed for his strength in the air. Even now, I still call Rushie 'Tosh'. In today's politically correct times, some people might consider our behaviour was bullying, but it wasn't. It was character-building and this was how Liverpool forged a formidable collective spirit, holding us together in difficult times. This was why we won. We teased each other off the pitch and fought for each other on it. Just as it strengthened me, the banter toughened Tosh mentally, so he could handle the pressure of opponents. There was method in the mockery. And trophies.

As a defence mechanism, Rushie sought the company of a new Irish boy, Ronnie Whelan, or 'Vitch' as he became known. Ronnie was first called 'Dusty' because he mangled the word 'just', making it 'dust', but when Liverpool played some East European side whose surnames all ended in 'vitch', we tried it on ourselves. 'Dustyvitch' stuck for Ronnie and was soon shortened to Vitch. His phone number is still down in my mobile as Vitch. Tosh and Vitch knocked about together, roomed together and slowly became immersed in Liverpool ways by first winding each other up. They practised banter on each other before taking on the big boys. Together, they were the Chuckle Brothers.

In the dressing room, we held a competition for Plank of the Year. Most seasons, it was a two-horse race to claim this prestigious trophy for the most stupid player, and every August Tosh and Vitch were usually installed as joint favourites. Liverpool took every competition seriously and Plank of the Year inspired incredibly competitive behaviour. Ronnie told tales about Rushie, describing the latest daft thing he'd done, just so his rival picked up more votes. I considered Vitch's allegations very credible because Tosh did come out with stupid statements. He often mixed up words.

'I was driving along this road near Flint and had to go off on a detail,' Rushie said one morning. He meant detour. Whenever Rushie made a rick, we leapt on it. So did Ronnie, pointing it out and saying it was surely worth another vote in Plank of the Year honours.

As much as I loved all this banter, I must admit Liverpool were lucky not to lose Rushie. Finding the constant mockery too much, Rushie went in to see Bob, asking for a move. The Boss calmed him down and thank God he did. If this gifted striker had packed his bags, it would have been criminal. Rushie took time to realise the stick being dished out by the rest was a sign of dressing-room acceptance. Promoted from the reserves, Rushie slipped on the No. 7 shirt against Ipswich on 13 December 1980 when my ankle was playing up. Rushie failed to find the net in seven games but I could see he was a special talent. We were all left in no doubt against West Ham in the Milk Cup final replay on 1 April 1981. Bob picked Rushie, so I had a quiet word with him as we gathered in the tunnel at Villa Park.

'You move and we'll find you,' I reassured him. 'Don't worry, don't delay, do what you think to be right. And it will be all right.' It was. Rushie terrorised West Ham, doing everything apart from score, but he showed his class and enjoyed the celebration of our 2–1 victory. He just needed a goal. Two nights later, Vitch made his debut against Stoke and scored past Peter Fox. Ronnie was up and running but Rushie took longer to settle. I think he needed more self-belief before being able to express himself on the pitch. I forgot he was only 19. At that age, if somebody said hello to me I went bright red. As senior players, we should have realised Rushie was a kid, but because he was in our dressing room, we treated him as an equal, an adult, and therefore fair game for our jokes.

Maybe I should have taken a step back and seen the effect on him. If I'd known how distressed he'd become, I wouldn't have been that harsh. Fortunately for Rushie, Stevie Nicol arrived in the dressing room in 1981, and this daft soul offered more tempting material for ripping into than Rushie did. Nico saved Rushie's life. Even Rushie hammered him and it made me smile to see the poacher turn gamekeeper. Of course, we still carried on winding up Rushie but he changed, not us. He became more confident.

In later years, Rushie remarked that I took him under my wing but I never did. A big fixture against heavyweight opposition was no time or place for educating apprentices. It was sink or swim, deliver or be damned, and Rushie needed to grow up fast. Included by Bob for the League Cup tie against Exeter on 28 October 1981, Rushie scored in the 5–0 thrashing and never looked back. By the end of the season, he'd netted 17 times in 32 League games and a star was born. He was beginning to bite back in the banter, a sign of growing confidence. Towards the end of that 1981–82 season, we travelled to Middlesbrough for a game at Ayresome Park. The League title was already secured, so Souey suggested a small libation on the afternoon of the match.

'Up to your rooms now,' came the usual command from Bob, sending us off for our pre-match nap in the hotel. The moment we got upstairs, Souey said, 'Come on, there's a great pub round the corner. Everyone follow me.' With that, Charlie headed for the door. Standing reluctantly on the landing was John McGregor, a Glaswegian who'd come to sign that day.

'Come on, John, we're going for a walk,' I told him.

'I can't,' replied McGregor, fearful of Bob finding out. So we left him and walked to this smashing pub. We must have been in there a good hour. As the boys ordered beers, my view of the bar was suddenly blocked out by a large glass of wine placed in front of me by a smiling Souey.

'There you go, Dugs,' said Souey.

'Charlie, it's massive. Do I drink it or swim in it?' My head was certainly swimming by the time we returned to the hotel. Sleep was brief before the call came to board the coach to Ayresome Park. Graeme, blessed with a unique metabolism, typically showed no after-effects of the afternoon session. I was OK.

'Tosh,' I shouted midway through the first half.

'What?'

'Careful.'

'What do you mean, Kenny?'

'You're going to get a kick in a minute!' It was true. Rushie hardly had a touch.

'Oh, you're playing well, aren't you?' Rushie shouted back. Good. The introvert from Flint was answering back. His mettle had been forged in the fire of a demanding dressing room and I knew then that Liverpool had a real diamond.

For all our unorthodox build-up, I was impressed that we still managed to come away from Middlesbrough with a point. The trust between Liverpool's players and Bob was immense, and we betrayed it a wee bit on that occasion, although I must stress that we'd never, ever have done anything that unprofessional if anything had been riding on the game. Little adventures like that simply added to our unbreakable team spirit and I find it sad that such team outings wouldn't happen in the modern game. Some players aren't interested, most managers wouldn't tolerate it, and there's always some punter about with a camera-phone. Thank God there weren't camera-phones back then.

Trips to Middlesbrough were often eventful for Liverpool. On one occasion, Souey got the boys along to help open a sports shop owned by his mate, Willie Maddren. The lads were all standing there and, BANG, the floor caved in. It was probably the only time Rushie lost his balance.

Tosh seemed to derive particular pleasure in punishing Everton. Season after season, he inflicted pain on our neighbours' defence and I often wondered whether it was personal. I knew all the

Merseyside folklore about Rushie supporting Everton when growing up. As the club he loved as a child never signed him, maybe Rushie had something to prove. Not a man with a vindictive streak, he certainly had a scoring streak against Everton. Game after game, time after time, Rushie pummelled them.

In particular, 6 November 1982 should be a date scarred in Gwladys Street memory as the fireworks kept coming. Everton fans will want to forget what happened but it must surely still haunt them as this was the stuff of the darkest nightmares. I really admired Howard Kendall's Everton side, with a top keeper in Neville Southall, respected midfielders in Steve McMahon and Kevin Sheedy and attackers of the quality of Adrian Heath and Graeme Sharp. Sadly for Howard, an injury to Kevin Ratcliffe meant his defence was badly weakened. Howard gambled with a loan signing, Glenn Keeley, alongside Billy Wright in an inexperienced back line. Keeley must hold the record for making two appearances for Everton on one day – his first and last.

Rushie and I immediately set to work dismantling this makeshift defence. Rushie hit the bar and I was denied a totally legitimate header for some phantom offence early on. Nobody saw it. We'd all lined up on the halfway line for a re-start when the linesman began signalling. This injustice spurred Liverpool even more. Intercepting the ball in the middle of the pitch, Al roamed forward and slid the ball through for Rushie to score. Keeley pulled me back and was dismissed. God knows why he tugged my shirt – he'd have caught me anyway. Everton, now depleted, were there for the taking. Rushie beat Neville with a shot from the edge of the area and Lawro added the third. The game finished with a demonstration of Rushie's phenomenal ability to time his runs and elude a keeper. Twice he raced from halfway to beat Southall, finishing up with four. Afterwards, Rushie sat in the Goodison dressing room holding the match-ball.

'You deserve the town-hall clock!' I told him.

My respect for Rushie was now colossal. Our success was based on an understanding of each other's strengths – I got the ball, Rushie moved, I passed, he scored. Nothing complicated. Creating goals always gave me as much satisfaction as scoring them. I found it curious that newspapers occasionally described Rush as 'a creature of instinct', as if he'd wandered into football from some wildlife programme. Creature of instinct? What did that mean? That he never analysed his own game? Rubbish. Rushie certainly did that. If newspapers had called him a 'creature of intelligence', I'd have understood. At Melwood, he educated himself in the art and science of timing runs, learning how to play off and with people, and how to stay onside. He examined the strengths of the Liverpool players, so he knew what was coming. At the beginning, sometimes I'd play the ball in there when he wasn't expecting it. At 19, Rushie still required time and experience to tune in to Liverpool's wavelength, and vice versa. Slowly, he assimilated Liverpool's culture of pass and move. Anyone standing still was in trouble, so Rushie knew he had to move.

'Don't go running and standing in the space,' I told him. 'Just leave a space, Tosh. The ball will be there for you. Time it.'

Many strikers possess pace in abundance but only the special few, like Rushie, have brain in sync with flying feet. When I had possession slightly deep, Rushie knew the ball was coming and he needn't be anxious. He could see there were acres in front of him to work with, particularly if the opposition played as high a line as Everton. When Kevin Ratcliffe was around, the style suited Everton because he could shift, but only the quickest of defenders or slickest of offside traps could catch Rushie. He waited and waited, biding his time until the optimum moment came to strike. When I pushed the ball into space, Rushie would be off and running like a greyhound, darting through, using the timing and speed of his run to destroy defenders. He'd either sprint round the keeper and roll the ball into the net or lash it from the edge of the box. When one-on-one with the keeper, Rushie was utterly ruthless. Sometimes I felt as if the keeper needed putting out of his misery as I'd back Rush to score one-on-one with anybody. Even as good a keeper as Neville Southall got battered that day when Rushie scored four. Having trained with him regularly for Wales, Neville would have had a close understanding of Rushie's game yet still had no chance.

I was pleased that Rushie's homework was rewarded. Opposing centre-halves were scrutinised for failings he could prey on. He watched them like a hawk, picking up any flaw, such as a tendency to react slowly to passes down the channel. He would lurk on the shoulder of the last defender. Pass, control, goal. Rushie was so much more than a brilliant run-through striker. Not only could he see a pass, he could ping the ball with either foot. His touch was so good I even thought in later years that he would drop back and play as a second striker. The only reason he didn't was because he was still capable of such damage up front.

More than Rushie's lethal instinct was on parade at Goodison that extraordinary day in November 1982. Liverpool's requirement that forwards close down defenders found a wholehearted disciple in our new No. 9.

'When they have the ball, everybody becomes a defender,' Bob said. Blessed with such pace, Rushie suddenly swooped on a defender, hustling him into losing possession. Rushie and I often went on the pitch armed with the knowledge of which defender felt most uncomfortable with the ball. We'd close down the others so the weakest defender had the ball and then we'd pounce on him. Down the years, Liverpool forwards hunted in packs, a tactic started by Shanks, carried on by Bob and, in 1983, by a new manager.

9

ROME

I NEVER sensed Joe Fagan was at ease with management. When Bob stood down, Joe was the reluctant successor. Asked by the board to climb the stairs from the Boot Room to the manager's office, Joe took the steps wearily. 'It's lonely up there,' he once remarked. Joe felt isolated and missed the banter of the Boot Room, but as a conscientious employee of Liverpool Football Club, and a man with humility running through his veins, Joe thought it would be wrong to refuse the job. Liverpool meant that much to him. I completely understood the thinking of a board who valued continuity. The good principles laid down by Shanks were carried on by Bob, whose assistant was the obvious man to maintain a great tradition.

Joe stuck to the old routine, keeping things simple. At times, he pulled me a bit deeper, but otherwise Liverpool's tactics never really changed. Joe was observant and straightforward. Like Bob, he lived life simply and had the respect of everyone in the dressing room. We knew his heart was in the right place – in Anfield and in the pursuit of more silverware. Joe was slow to rile, so when he did become angry, raising his voice, we knew we'd transgressed.

'You've let the club down and the fans down,' Joe said. The look of disappointment in his eyes really hit us hard, making us regret any lapse, however minor, such as being late.

'I don't care what your excuse is,' Joe declared, 'if you're told a time, you get here for that time.'

If anybody messed about at Melwood, Joe chilled the blood with the tone of his rebuke. One day, Terry Mac volleyed the ball at Tommo and Joe immediately stopped everything.

'Don't ever take the mickey out of the session,' barked Joe.

Discipline mattered but he could be relaxed. When he was Bob's assistant, Joe knew about the 'walk' before the Middlesbrough game. The alcohol on some of the lads' breath must have been a wee bit too strong.

'Have you been out?' Joe asked. Our sheepish looks betrayed our guilt.

'OK, OK,' smiled Joe, who was no stranger to drink's charms. During testimonials, Joe and Ronnie Moran kept a half-bottle of whisky in the dug-out.

'We'll have a wee nip if we score,' Joe always said. If the game went on without a goal, Joe said, 'OK, we'll have a wee nip if we get a shot on goal.' When the game meandered on with Liverpool still not threatening, Bugsy said, 'Joe, why don't we just do it for a free-kick?' Still no joy. 'Let's just settle for a throw-in!'

Joe was a worldly-wise man who understood footballers and certainly knew how much my legs ached after matches. The thought of pushing my body through training early in the week was too much, so I put my concerns to Joe, who listened intently.

'Kenny, you don't need to train as often as everybody else because you're getting a bit older,' Joe said. 'I can give you until Wednesday off.'

'Come on, Boss,' I replied. 'I need longer.' Joe wouldn't budge, so I rested until Wednesday, and after we won the next game, I said, 'Same again next week, Boss, or do you want to make it Thursday?'

Liverpool's marathon involvement in cup competitions meant we had plenty of midweek games, so the opportunity to rest up presented itself infrequently. Still, I was grateful for Joe's appreciation of my need to take a break, spending time sleeping or

relaxing on the golf course. The only time I fell out with Joe
Fagan was when he dropped me for a Spurs game in 1984. He
had every right to pick whatever team he wanted, but Joe should
have informed me before telling the newspapers.

'Kenny's not been at his best and there's no room for senti-
ment,' Joe told the Press. I resented learning about my demotion
from the papers rather than from the manager. After training
that morning, Joe called me in.

'I'm not going to play you tomorrow,' he said.

'I know.'

'What do you want to do about it?'

'What can I do? You've picked your team. I've seen it in the
paper.' And I walked out. It wasn't a pleasant moment because
I usually had so much respect for Joe. And Liverpool lost.

Otherwise Joe's attention to detail served Liverpool well as we
fought our way along the road to Rome for the 1984 European
Cup final. The start could not have been smoother. Bob's big and
small strides were no longer a feature of Melwood life but our
first-round draw against Odense would have been worthy of a
giant's steps. Denmark's champions hardly sent fear coursing
through us. Odense was the home of Hans Christian Andersen
and having Liverpool as guests on 14 September 1983 was inevitably portrayed as a fairy tale for the natives. Many Danes follow
Liverpool. When I picked up the match programme, I immediately
noticed a picture of Nealy and Clem holding up the European Cup
in Paris. Liverpool were big news in Denmark, bigger than Odense,
and when I scored the only goal, the number of Liverpool fans,
some visiting, many local, became readily apparent.

The Anfield leg was always going to be a formality, so only
14,985 turned up. Joe again picked an attacking team, including
Rushie, Michael Robinson and me. The night proved of particular
significance for me, and I still reflect on it with pride because my
two goals took my European tally to 15, eclipsing Denis Law's
British European Cup record. Setting a new mark was prestigious

enough but overtaking such a legend as Denis sprinkled even more stardust on the achievement. For my generation, Denis was every Scottish boy's hero. Denis Law! Goalscorer! Style and panache! I became a 10-year-old again just thinking of the great Denis Law. As kids, we all admired Denis, adored his Jack the Lad swagger on the pitch. I loved that goal celebration, fingers holding the shirt-cuff. When he scored against England, young Scots like me felt like we'd ascended to heaven. In one game, Denis scored at the Mount Florida end of Hampden Park, which some people know as the Rangers end. From a corner, Denis whipped it in at the near post. He was a hero to everybody, not just for his goals but because there was a humility to Denis, a lack of pretence, and he's never changed. Among my proudest possessions at home is Denis's Manchester United shirt from Bobby Charlton's testimonial.

My record-breaking brace against Odense was matched by Michael Robinson. Robbo was a good alternative for Liverpool up front, a change for Rushie or a complement to him with me dropping deeper. It annoyed me that people felt Robbo was never really a Liverpool player. After one game, I was walking up the corridor to reception when I passed a group of journalists and overheard one talking dismissively about Robbo in comparison with me. I was furious. Robbo wasn't there to defend himself, so I did the honours.

'Michael Robinson has attributes that I don't have,' I said to this reporter. 'Don't you come down this corridor and shout your mouth off about a player not being able to do it. If you want to stay in this corridor, you keep your mouth shut and your opinions to yourself.' Robbo was just round the corner and heard everything.

'Thanks very much, Kenny,' he said.

'If he comes down here, he should bloody behave,' I replied. 'It's a privileged position. He shouldn't be mouthing off. And don't worry what he thinks anyway.'

I meant that. Michael was bigger, stronger, probably quicker than I was, and certainly better in the air. One night in 1984, Liverpool beat Newcastle 4–0 in the Cup and Michael was brilliant, selling his marker a dummy and cracking the ball in.

'The whole stand moved when you dummied, Robbo!' I told him.

Another reason I stood up for Robbo was that he was a good lad, who loved a natter about anything, and it never surprised me to learn he became a popular chat-show host in Spain. Robbo's always got something to say, particularly over a meal. Most Liverpool players had pretty basic tastes but not Robbo or Souey. They liked seafood and a glass of Champagne, and Robbo loved an oyster.

Robbo started again in the second round, an awkward tie against Athletic Bilbao. A first-leg stalemate at Anfield didn't perturb me because Liverpool were always capable of scoring an away goal, but I knew how careful we needed to be in Spain. They had tough players, such as Andoni Goicoechea, the defender known as the 'Butcher of Bilbao' for that horrendous tackle on Barcelona's Diego Maradona at Camp Nou just a few weeks before we arrived in the Basque country. Watching the footage of Goicoechea storming into Maradona, ripping his ankle ligaments, made me wince.

'Don't retaliate,' Joe warned us. I'd actually faced the Spanish defender before in the international arena and found him no problem. Nor did Goikoechea prove a physical threat at the San Mames Stadium on 2 November. For all the talk about hostility on and off the field, the moment Rushie headed in Alan Kennedy's cross, the Basque fans were really good to us. Bilbao were protecting a long unbeaten home record in Europe but the 47,500 crammed inside San Mames gave us a standing ovation for the quality of our performance.

Frustratingly, my prospects of facing our famous quarter-final opponents, Benfica, seemed badly compromised on 2 January

1984. The setting was Anfield, the time three minutes into the second half. Coming up in the inside-left position, I went up for a header with Manchester United's centre-half, Kevin Moran. My trade involved countless moments like this, manoeuvring a ball away from a determined defender, but not this time. The lights went out. I was on the floor, my vision blurred, my head filling with excruciating pain. I was always advised by medical people that the adrenalin accompanying competitive activity dulls any hurt. Not on this occasion. What the hell happened? I learned later that Moran's elbow hammered into my face, fracturing my cheekbone, a challenge that enraged Liverpool. Souey was furious and tried to get at Moran. I admired that in Graeme, that desire to take revenge for a team-mate's suffering.

As I lay in hospital, I reflected on whether Moran's attempt to disfigure my face had possibly been deliberate. Surely not? That would just be too reprehensible and I genuinely believed no professional would commit such an offence on another. No bad blood flowed between the two of us. Only Kevin Moran can possibly know whether he intended putting me into Accident and Emergency. A centre-half rarely far from the fray, Kevin had enough stitching in his head to make a knitting pattern, so perhaps he threw his arm up to protect himself and it caught me. I never asked him. Kevin certainly never apologised and I never expected him to. If he had shown some contrition that could be construed as an admission of guilt. In later years, Kevin was my captain at Blackburn Rovers and proved a particularly able leader who served me well. That's the nature of professional football. We all move on. Kevin's a good man, and nobody ever said sorry to him when his eyes were cut.

All the relief I took from an immediate prognosis of a full recovery disappeared on being informed how much of an important season I'd miss. 'Nine weeks,' predicted the medical staff for my convalescence period after surgeons completed the jigsaw that was my face. Fortunately, they were able to put all the pieces back in the right place. It was mid-season, my fitness levels were high, but it was still a considerable time to be on the sidelines. By all accounts, I was hardly a picture of athletic health when my Liverpool team-mates visited me in hospital. I knew my face was badly swollen, a point confirmed by the players' reaction.

'You look like the Elephant Man,' Graeme remarked charitably. I laughed. Why should I mind? I'd have been unhappy only if he'd made the comment before the accident. When the Southport boys popped by to see me, Lawro never lasted long. He took one look and slipped out. 'It was the hospital that made me queasy,' Lawro insisted later, 'not your face.' Apparently, Lawro was taken round the corner and given a cup of tea to restore him.

However short, I appreciated the boys' visits. Every morning, Joe came by with the newspapers but I noticed he always seemed to avert his eyes and never seemed prepared to stay.

'See you later, Kenny,' Joe said each morning.

'Oh, thanks, Boss,' I replied as my manager disappeared quickly out of the door. My face must have been a mess. Looking in a mirror has never been a regular pastime of mine but I became curious, and slightly alarmed, about my team-mates' concerns, so I sneaked a glance. Moran's elbow had made an almighty mess. My cheekbone was held together with a chunk of wire.

Fortunately, no permanent damage or scarring occurred and I began plotting my comeback. Thinking big, I targeted the Benfica tie at Anfield on 7 March. I knew I'd be rusty but I managed to get in a warm-up game, turning out in the Liverpool Senior Cup against Southport at Haig Avenue. Joe rightly decided I was not quite ready to start against the Portuguese champions, keeping me on the bench until half-time. Replacing Robbo, I received great support from the Kop, a gesture further strengthening my determination to make up for lost time. The pleasurable feeling of actually playing again was enhanced when Rushie headed in. Benfica left Anfield making noises about how 1–0 was still a good result and how they'd turn the tie around in Lisbon.

'We'll see,' I thought. I'd spent too long in a hospital bed to surrender lightly in Europe.

Before stepping out at the Stadium of Light on 21 March, Joe gave us an important instruction.

'It's a massive stadium and if the fans are on their side, it really helps Benfica,' the Boss said. 'If we can turn their fans, it'll be a real burden on them, so get on top of them early.'

More than 70,000 filled the Stadium of Light, all screaming their support for Benfica, but Joe's prediction came true. When Ronnie headed in after nine minutes, the heat went out of the crowd. Needing three goals, Benfica's supporters knew the game was up, particularly when Craig Johnston scored just after the half-hour. The whistle for half-time was drowned out by boos. As we walked off, Graeme, Al and I looked at each other. The sound of derision was music to our ears. Joe's plan for a high tempo was paying off. Liverpool ran amok, Craig darting in behind their defence time after time. Rushie and Ronnie added more goals as Benfica collapsed.

One challenge remained before Liverpool could reach the final in Rome and I suspected it would be a very physical challenge. I can honestly say I have never been in such a war zone as this confrontation with Dinamo Bucharest, masquerading as a European Cup tie. The Romanians came to Anfield on 11 April with malevolence on their minds. Sammy Lee's header gave us the edge but Dinamo gave us an absolute battering. I was clattered, Rushie got clobbered, and make no mistake there was murder going on. Foolishly, Dinamo tried to mix it with Souness. Their captain, Lica Movila, marked Graeme for the whole game, and every time Graeme ran forward he was checked by a wee tug on his shirt.

'No, no, one more and you're getting that,' said Graeme, showing Movila his hand. The warning was clear. If Movila stepped out of line again, he faced an appointment with Graeme's right fist. Stupidly, Movila carried on niggling. As the clock hit 70 minutes, Graeme hit Movila. The ball was going out for a throw-in, everyone was looking out wide, so Graeme just punched Movila. The Romanian never saw it coming and the referee and linesmen certainly never saw it. I understand that Movila has since said his team-mates initially thought he was lying on the ground play-acting. Somehow he managed to explain through a broken jaw the price Graeme exacted for his persistent fouling. Movila was carried off and the game finished with the Romanians promising all manner of revenge on Graeme back at their place.

'You. Souness. Bucharest,' one of Dinamo players shouted at Graeme, making a throat-cutting sign. The Romanians lived up to their promise on 25 April, shouting at our bus and making threatening signals as we drove to the ground.

Fortunately, the police escort did their job and we reached the 23 August Stadium with windows and bones intact. Ensconced in the dressing room, I picked up the programme and had to laugh. On the front was a message: 'Welcome FC Liverpool'. Some welcome! I knew what was coming and it certainly wouldn't be welcoming. In his brief team-talk, Joe didn't need to encourage us to keep calm. I was well aware that open warfare had been declared by Dinamo, and the 60,000 crammed into the 23 August Stadium screamed for Movila to be avenged. From the first whistle, Dinamo players took it in turns on Graeme. One Romanian tried to top him, another caught Charlie so hard that his dented shinpads were visible through ripped socks. Such intimidation would never faze Souey, who enjoyed the challenge.

'You're a bit of a masochist, aren't you,' I said to Souey afterwards. He smiled. Typical Graeme. Few midfielders can ever be mentioned in the same breath as Graeme Souness, because whatever the type of game, he had the qualities to deliver. If the other team wanted to take Liverpool on at football, Graeme could pass

them off the park. If the opposition wanted a battle, Graeme
wouldn't flinch, as Dinamo discovered. I've never met anybody
as competitive as Charlie, and I lost count of how many arguments the two of us had in the dressing room. After one game,
Graeme was fuming because I'd gone for goal rather than pass
to him.

'You should have squared, Dugs,' Graeme ranted. 'Why did
you shoot?'

'Because I fancied I'd score,' I replied. I had done, but my
terse reminder that the ball ended up in the net wasn't swaying
Graeme.

'You should have passed,' he insisted.

'But you'd have missed!' I hit back. The row went on. Neither
of us conceded an inch.

'You two are unbelievable,' said Big Al. 'Neither of you has
ever lost an argument even when you argue with each other.'

This refusal to surrender made Graeme Souness such a special
player. Nobody could break Graeme. Whatever stunts Dinamo
attempted that bruising evening in Bucharest, Souness carried
on. When Rushie scored early, the Romanians' venom intensified and it was a real battle out there. Dinamo knew the game
was probably over, even when they equalised, so they just went
about trying to settle scores. When Rushie added a second late
on, the fight finally went out of Dinamo. Afterwards, Joe was
delighted.

'Dinamo met us on a day when every player was on song,' the
Boss told the Press, and we were. Dinamo also met us with the
wrong tactics. These people didn't understand that Liverpool
players looked after each other. I got battered, so did Rushie, so
did Graeme, but we won the war and the right to travel to Rome
– via Tel Aviv!

Eight days before the European Cup final, Liverpool were
invited to play a prestigious friendly against Israel. The game was
serious, keeping the fitness ticking over, and it was also a relaxing

trip off the pitch, very relaxing for some. Some of the boys went out drinking and when one of them stumbled, it kicked off briefly. Bruce Grobbelaar thought somebody punched Rushie and there was bit of shoving. One of the reporters on the trip spotted this and alerted a Liverpool director, Sidney Moss.

'Mr Moss, they're fighting in the square.'

'Put all those supporters in jail,' came Mr Moss's reply.

'Mr Moss, it's not the supporters, it's the players.' Moss shrugged. He didn't seem that bothered. It was only a skirmish anyway.

Far more important issues occupied Liverpool minds. I have no brief against Rome, a magical city, but it was a disgrace that the 1984 European Cup final was staged there. The Olympic Stadium was the home of Roma, our opponents in the final. Uefa should have shifted the final because why should one team enjoy home advantage? This surely trampled on Uefa's principle of fair play. If the final had been scheduled for Anfield, Roma would have screamed to the high heavens, pressuring Uefa to move it. So people should have understood Liverpool's feeling of being cheated by Uefa. It was rubbish to suggest, as some did, that Wembley was effectively a home ground for us in 1978. Bruges was as close to London as Liverpool was.

Uefa should have put different venues on stand-by and then chosen the final setting from among those clubs knocked out in the quarters. Preparing a stadium doesn't take that long. Clubs arrange replays within 10 days, and even a World Cup has been reorganised at relatively short notice, Mexico standing in for Colombia two years after Rome. Stewards, police and stadium staff could all be made aware they were required on a certain date. The European Cup, the most important club prize on earth, was at stake, not some village fete. No club should be given an advantage as Roma were in 1984. Walking around the Olympic Stadium before kick-off on 30 May, we were left in no doubt that this was Roma's fortress and their fans would happily resort to violence and intimidation to protect their territory. I'll never forget the abuse, the swearing, chanting and slit-throat gestures, even the occasional missile.

Outside the ground it was worse and my anger with Uefa intensified as I saw and heard what Liverpool fans endured. In making the journey from the centre of Rome, crossing bridges and negotiating underpasses, Liverpool fans were ambushed. Bottles, bricks and stones rained down on them and some poor souls were even stabbed. Uefa never thought about this danger when persisting with the city of 'La Dolce Vita' as host venue. I bet it didn't feel like the sweet life to Liverpool supporters being attacked by local *tifosi*.

Before kick-off, Joe stressed again the need to keep calm, to draw the sting out of Roma's fire. Stepping from the dressing room into the tunnel, I looked around and Roma were nowhere to be seen. I suspected typical Italian mind games, keeping us waiting so the nerves built up. Suddenly, Sammy launched into a Chris Rea song, a particular favourite of ours.

I don't know what it is but I love it,
And I don't know what it is but I want it to stay,
And I love it.

Lawro, Al, Souey and I immediately joined in, and so did the rest, seizing on those familiar lyrics, words we'd sung a thousand times on the bus to matches, and on nights out in Sammy's or Lawro's wine bar. We can't have been singing for more than a minute but it is a moment that has gone down in football history. For many people, it represented a sign of Liverpool's complete calm before the heat of battle. Legend goes that Roma were stunned by the singing when they eventually deigned to join us in the tunnel. Their coach, Nils Liedholm, has since observed that he felt at that moment Liverpool had the psychological edge on Roma. I hate to dispel a popular belief but we were probably singing to quell the butterflies floating around our own stomachs. If it disconcerted Roma as well as relaxing us, then good.

As we emerged from the tunnel, Roma's fans threw everything at us. Our earlier stroll around the pitch had been unchallenging compared with this. This time, we got smoke-bombs, flares and the interminable screech of klaxons. A huge banner was dragged over the heads of Italian fans, with 'ULTRA ROMA' in large letters and a picture of the European Cup in the middle. Watching all this, I gained the distinct impression that the locals considered the final not so much a match as a coronation. With so many Italian fans holding up flares, the stands looked like a scene from an inferno. Amid the plumes of smoke, I spotted our 20,000 supporters. Liverpool fans love a witty banner and I noted they had not left their ingenuity at home. One banner read: 'Shanks Marmelized Milan. Paisley Munched the Gladbach. Now Fagan's Making Roman Ruins.' Placing Joe alongside Shanks and Bob was a splendid tribute by Liverpool's followers.

Just before Erik Fredriksson got the game under way, I looked around and noted the quality of the opposition. Roma had classy attacking midfielders Falcao and Cerezo, who were typically cultured Brazilians; Italian World Cup-winners Bruno Conti and Francesco Graziani also graced the white shirts; but for all the talent on display, the final became mired in caution. Nealy scored for us but Roberto Pruzzo replied. Amid the sterility of the second period, it dawned on me that we were heading for extra time and penalties. I realised Roma were too terrified to attack, preferring to man the barricades. When Fredriksson blew for the end of the additional half-hour, Joe set to work preparing Liverpool for penalties.

'Don't worry,' Joe said. 'You've done all you can. Now do your best again.'

Joe looked at the players. This was crunch time, when he needed the strongest to step forward.

'Who wants to take a penalty?' Joe asked.

Nealy, Souey and Rushie immediately volunteered. Having been substituted, my evening's work was done and I must confess to feeling little frustration at not being involved in the shoot-out. Although taking penalties was part of my job at Celtic, I never took them at Liverpool, barring one in pre-season. When Joe contemplated his potential penalty-takers, I would never have featured. Al certainly wouldn't have taken one. He was behind me in the list and I wasn't even eligible! During the preparations for the shoot-out, I heard Stevie Nicol talking to Joe.

'I'll take a penalty,' Nicol piped up. This worried me. While admiring Stevie's courage, I remembered with alarm his previous attempt from 12 yards, and that was messing about at Melwood.

I considered Roma to be favourites, because Brazilians and Italians were good at dead-balls. Standing between the posts, ready to defy Liverpool, was Franco Tancredi, a highly respected goalkeeper. Turning my attention to Roma's chosen five, I saw with quiet delight their body language hardly screamed confidence for this imminent test of nerve and technique.

'Falcao won't take a penalty,' I said to Craig.

'It can't be in his contract!' Craig replied. '£300,000 a year and they want you to take a penalty! The bloody cheek!' Joe was still busy with the players and I noticed him having a quiet word with Bruce.

'Try to put them off,' Joe told Bruce, who nodded, instinctively understanding what the Boss meant. How Bruce would interpret this permission for psychological warfare was his affair. Looking at Bruce, I felt hope surge through me. Bruce was a fantastic athlete, a reassuring sight as he walked to the goal-line. Sometimes Bruce was criticised in the newspapers but what I loved about him was his decisiveness – he came for crosses, missed a few, but everybody knew he was coming. Bruce was a good character, who often talked of his time in the bush.

'Shepherd's Bush, Bruce?' I asked.

'What?'

'In London,' I explained. Bruce would sigh, make some dismissive noise and then talk again of his time in Africa.

In games, Bruce never felt involved unless he was shouting. He'd even scream, 'Shoot,' at the opposition. By the time he'd got to Rome, Bruce had long negotiated a rough spell when he'd found it difficult to replace Clem. People had a question mark against him but, in the main, he was a fantastic servant to Liverpool. I'll never forget his superstition of bouncing the ball to knock the light switch off in the home dressing room. Sometimes one of us would have to go and switch it off just to get Bruce out of the place. One day we went to Plough Lane and beat Bobby Gould's Wimbledon.

'Christ, I thought I had you going,' Bobby said to me afterwards.

'What do you mean?'

'Didn't you notice the light switch?'

'No.'

'I read Bruce likes to volley the ball until he knocks the light off, so we put a cover over the switch just to upset him.'

'Bob, he only does it at home!' I laughed.

Back in Rome, I knew Bruce wouldn't let us down, but such was the tension I could hardly focus and the next few fluctuating minutes went by in a blur. Nealy should have taken Liverpool's first as our regular penalty man but Nicol grabbed the ball. He walked up, placed the ball on the spot and fulfilled my fears by missing. Di Bartolomei put me in an even darker mood by placing his shot past Bruce. Roma had the advantage and their fans began planning their victory party. It needed cool heads to destroy these celebrations on the terraces and, fortunately, Liverpool had a cool head in Nealy, who made it 1–1, bringing Conti under the harshest of spotlights in sport.

Conti had experienced the joy of becoming a champion of the world, overcoming great German players such as Karl-Heinz Rummenigge and Paul Breitner in the 1982 final in the Bernabeu, but the Italian had never before encountered anything like what awaited him 12 yards away. Bruce bounded around on his line, turning his legs into spaghetti, doing everything to psyche Conti out. Poor man. He was clearly stressed out and his kick flew over the bar, throwing a lifeline Liverpool's way.

So it went on. Souey rattled his kick in, Ubaldo Righetti made it 2–2. Rushie then made his way towards the spot, a choice by Joe that surprised me. Tosh was confident, however, and did his duty expertly, making it 3–2 to Liverpool and really cranking up the pressure on Roma. Graziani walked from the centre, his steps seeming to me to resemble the gait of a condemned prisoner heading towards the gallows. Bruce clowned about, leaping all over the place, pretending to be scared, trying to put Graziani off. As with Conti, Graziani was tipped over the edge by Bruce's carry-on. His penalty hit the bar and disappeared, probably into the Tiber. Bruce never even had to save a penalty, Graziani and Conti were that traumatised by the occasion and Bruce's antics. When Graziani missed, all the Liverpool players cheered, of course. The shoot-out was turned on its head. Then I realised who was taking Liverpool's fifth penalty.

'Oh no, it's Barney,' I said to Craig as Alan Kennedy walked towards the spot. At Melwood, Barney kept hitting the right-hand stanchion. Under immense pressure in Rome, would he do the same? He went exactly the same way but with a fraction greater accuracy, beating Tancredi, bringing Liverpool a fourth European Cup. Game over, party started. The boys were itching to get over to the celebration at the hotel but I was held behind for a drugs test. God knows why they wanted to check my urine. Uefa's dope-testers wouldn't have found anything stronger than adrenalin and pride flooding through my system. Mind you, if they'd tested me the next morning, they'd have detected an incredibly high level of Champagne.

'Hurry up, I've got to get to the celebration up the hill,' I kept telling them. The boys started without me but I soon caught up and it was another special evening, ending with a real singsong with punters who'd filled the foyer. Having scored the winning goal in a European Cup, Barney was the toast of the night. At one point during the wonderfully drunken evening, we were singing the Phil Collins version of 'You Can't Hurry Love'. Already totally gone, Barney was prone to mix up words anyway. He was singing at the top of his voice: 'You can't hurry up'. So we all joined in, shredding the lyrics even more. Towards dawn, when I was making even less sense than usual, Marina sensibly dragged me up to our room.

'I must tell something to Charlie,' I insisted to Marina on stumbling into the room.

'No, Kenny, don't. He's in with Danielle,' said Marina. 'Give them some peace.' I wouldn't be dissuaded. Picking up the phone, I dialled Charlie's room.

'Oh you can't hurry up,' I sang down the phone.

'Piss off, Kenny,' replied Graeme, slamming the phone down. Charming.

A few hours later, gathering for the flight back to Liverpool, I was in a complete state, as was Graeme, and we vowed to lay off the booze for a while. During the open-topped bus ride round Liverpool, I was still struggling.

'We'll have a kip on the trip to Africa,' I told Graeme.

'Good idea,' he responded.

Liverpool had agreed to play the Royal Swazi Sun Challenge against Spurs on 3 and 9 June 1984 at the Somholo Stadium. At least the long flight would give us a chance to sober up. Graeme and I settled down in our seats on the short hop to Heathrow.

'No way am I having a drink,' I told Graeme.

'Right, we're playing Sunday, no more to drink,' he replied. At that point, the captain's voice came over the Tannoy.

'Welcome on board everyone – and a very special welcome to Liverpool Football Club. Congratulations on winning the

European Cup. On behalf of the airline we'd like to offer a bottle
of Champagne for each and every one of you.' As he signed off,
the trolleys came down the aisle. As the trolley closed in on
Charlie and me, I almost had the theme tune from *Jaws* crashing
through my throbbing head.

'I'm not having any more,' I told Charlie. 'No.' Then POP.
I heard the unmistakable sound of a Champagne cork being
given its freedom. Graeme and I looked at each other.

'Rude not to,' I said.

'Exactly.'

So that was us sorted. At Heathrow, we boarded another
plane to Johannesburg and I just about remember the captain
coming over the speaker.

'We are proud to have Liverpool Football Club on board with
us today. As a show of our admiration for your magnificent
performance in Rome, we will be serving a special thank you
from the nation.' Or words to that effect. It was getting a bit
fuzzy. POP, POP, POP. Champagne corks flew past me like the
Red Arrows. We changed planes in Johannesburg for the final
hop to Swaziland, squeezing into one of those small, twin-prop
numbers. As we neared our destination, Graeme prodded me
awake.

'Look out there,' he said. 'There's Spurs training.'

'Where?' I asked, peering out. I saw them.

'Christ, they're doing doggies.' And they were, sprinting up
and back. Madness. It must have been 100°F out there. Winning
the Uefa Cup had not encouraged Spurs to ease up.

'Fly a bit lower,' Bruce shouted to the pilot. 'Let's give them
a scare. Buzz them.'

Spurs certainly got a shock when our bus pulled up outside
the hotel just as they were getting back from training. Graham
Roberts, Alan Brazil, Steve Archibald and the rest were soaked
in sweat. Moisture also trickled off my forehead but it was pure
alcohol. We staggered into reception all red-eyed, hardly looking

ready for a showpiece tournament. At dinner, Liverpool ate in one part of the restaurant while Spurs sat demurely, nibbling away in another corner. A guy was playing the piano so we all joined in the usual songs – Beatles, Chris Rea, Phil Collins.

'Ask him if he knows "You Can't Hurry Up"' I shouted to Barney.

After we finished dinner, the pianist decamped to the bar, so we followed and carried on singing. Brazil, a friend from Scotland trips, sneaked in to join us.

'I can't stay long. The gaffer wants us in bed for nine thirty,' Alan said. Hansen, Souey and I burst out laughing.

'Nine thirty in the morning?' I asked.

'No! Night-time.' Brazil was serious. Spurs were treating this competition very professionally, certainly more than Liverpool were. Their manager, Keith Burkinshaw, soon marched across.

'Time for bed, Brazil,' he barked. 'Big game tomorrow.' Charlie knew Burkinshaw from Spurs, so he thought he'd intervene.

'Behave yourself, you're not sending the boys to bed at half nine, are you? Let them have a drink, man. We're just having a wee singsong.'

'Bed,' insisted Burkinshaw.

'Come on, Keith, let them relax,' said Graeme. Brazil shifted uneasily on his barstool.

'Bed,' Burkinshaw declared.

'I'll need to go,' said Brazil sadly. He sloped away, casting a final, doleful look at the bottles of wine lined up on the bar ready for inspection. 'Have a good night.'

Alan can rest assured we didn't let him down. By the end of the night, we'd been through the wine list and the pianist almost had steam coming out of his fingers. In the morning, Joe Fagan sensibly organised wake-up calls for all the Liverpool players. The shrill sound of the hotel phone stirred all but one.

'Where's Graeme?' asked Joe as I stumbled down the stairs.

'He's not well,' I replied, only half-untruthfully.

'What's the matter?'

'He's not feeling too great. I'll take his kit up for him.' Grabbing Graeme's kit, I dashed back upstairs.

'Charlie, there's your kit, you've got to get up. We've got to go for lunch.'

'I can't get up,' replied Souey, pulling the sheet over his tousled head. He was a mess, in no fit state for watching football, let alone playing it. Realising the impossibility of my mission, I returned to reception.

'Where is he?' asked Joe.

'He's not hungry. He thought it best to stay in bed.'

Joe knew it would be embarrassing if Liverpool Football Club turned up without one of their best-known players for this prestigious occasion, a tournament organised by the King of Swaziland, whose country was paying the winners of the European Cup handsomely, so I made a final attempt.

'Come on, Charlie, we need to go.'

'Dugs, I can't make it. I'm not well.' When I explained this to Joe, he shook his head.

'It was that food last night. I bet Graeme had the prawns.' Trying not to laugh, I made my way to the coach. Prawns? More like Pinot bloody Grigio!

'Gaffer, remember my calf, it's a bit tight, so I'll happily go on the bench.'

'Kenny, just play midfield, give us the first half, fill in for Graeme.'

Spurs had the full hit out – Garth Crooks, all the big guns. I knew they'd been training hard but I also knew Liverpool had been drinking hard. At half-time, I was panting.

'Gaffer!' I beseeched Joe.

'Just give us a few minutes.'

Joe took me off with a minute to go. Amazingly, we won 5–2. Back in the room, Graeme had perked up. He also had some news for me. Graeme and I were always honest with each other.

'Dugs, I think I'm off. Sampdoria.'

'I'm not surprised, Charlie.'

A man who loved a challenge on and off the pitch, Graeme's personality was suited to moving abroad. I sensed the European Cup final simply endorsed Sampdoria's view of Graeme, prompting them to get the chequebook out quickly. His last few days with Liverpool were certainly eventful. There was no way I would let Graeme know but I'd miss him. Charlie was always good fun to be around, particularly when we went about our regular wind-up work on Stevie 'Bumper' Nicol, our right-back as gullible off the field as gifted on it. One day, Graeme and I were hanging about after lunch at Anfield when Nico walked in.

'Have you seen Derek?' he asked. Derek Ibbotson was the man from Puma who sorted Stevie's boots.

'No, Bumper, sorry,' I replied. Nico wandered off, leaving Graeme and I to concoct a plan. Liverpool's switchboard lady, Nina, was often a willing accomplice in some of our practical jokes, so Graeme and I nipped down to reception to see her.

'Nina, do us a favour,' I asked. 'Write this wee message out for Nico. "Meet Derek Ibbotson at Burtonwood Services at 1 p.m. on Sunday and don't be late."' When Nina finished scribbling the note, I continued, 'I'll go to the players' lounge. Phone and I'll pick up. Ask for Nico.' Nina was as good as gold and within a minute of Graeme and I returning to the players' lounge, the phone went.

'Bumper, phone-call, Nina.' Sticking brilliantly to the script, Nina told Stevie she had a message from Derek. When Nico returned, he never mentioned anything.

'Christ, we thought you were getting boots off Puma,' I asked. 'Where are they?' Nico stayed silent, although he had a quiet gleam in his eyes. Nico felt he was going to meet up with Derek, collect a pile of boots and we'd all be envious.

The following Monday, as we boarded the bus for training, Al parked Nico in the corner of the back row, so he couldn't get out. Al wasn't in on the wind-up. He always did this so Nico couldn't escape if he wanted some fun at Nico's expense.

'Heh, heh, Al!' Nico laughed. 'You didn't think you'd catch me with that one, did you?'

'What are you on about?' Al replied.

'You know!'

'No.' Nico looked at Hansen, thinking maybe Al didn't know that he had made a wasted journey to Burtonwood. Hansen didn't. Graeme and I were falling about laughing. The next day, Nico went up to Alan.

'Big Al, you know what I was saying yesterday?'

'Aye, what were you on about?'

'You told me to meet Derek Ibbotson at Burtonwood on Sunday.'

'I never told you.' Nico looked confused.

'Well, I did fall for it. I waited two hours for him. I even took my wife.'

'Nothing to do with me,' said Al. He looked around the bus. 'Come on. Who set Bumper up? Kenny, was it you?'

'It was Charlie,' I said. 'We were going to tell Bumper it was a wind-up before he went to Burtonwood but forgot. Hope his wife enjoyed the trip.'

If Bumper felt safer after Charlie went to Sampdoria, I felt sadder. My room-mate and close friend was gone and, far more significantly, a great player for Liverpool was gone, a really popular one. When Charlie headed a goal at Maine Road once, everybody started laughing. We were not laughing at City but at Graeme scoring with his head. He was running round, slapping his head, celebrating a special occasion. I genuinely believe that Liverpool were their strongest ever when Charlie roamed midfield. Exuding an air of authority, Charlie just looked unbeatable. When Bob or Joe wrote Souness's name on the team-sheet, it immediately gave us a psychological edge. When that team-sheet was delivered into the opposition's dressing room, I always suspected a shiver of fear ran through anybody reading it. Opponents knew if that red No. 11 shirt was worn by Souness, they were in for a battle. Replacing Graeme Souness as midfielder, leader and character was going to be a hell of a job. Having discussed it, the players all reached the same conclusion that there would never be another Graeme Souness. However much a relief for the persecuted Bumper, it was deeply disappointing for the rest of us. Our leader was leaving.

'Do you ever fancy moving abroad, Dugs?' Graeme asked as he packed his bags.

'No, Charlie,' I replied. 'I'd really miss the banter in the dressing room. If I joined a foreign team and didn't speak the language, I'd always worry what they were saying about me. If we'd gone away from home, and I'd missed a sitter, I'd be convinced the other players on the bus back were having a go at me. I'm really happy at Liverpool.'

'The money's good in Italy,' Graeme pointed out. I knew Graeme wasn't leaving solely for financial reasons, but it was tempting.

'I'm well paid, Charlie. I'd rather have less money and more happiness. I love the football, we're winning trophies and the kids are settled. Marina and the kids would probably adapt better than I would to living abroad. And there's another thing. Marina's dad hates flying. I can never see him coming out to visit. He was in the toilet once on a plane and locked himself in. He was battering it, sweating. Terrified. They pushed the doors to let him out.'

So I stayed. Apart from Graeme and Kevin Keegan, few players have left Liverpool and gone on to better themselves. Liverpool adapted, survived and carried on.

'Forget Souness,' said Joe Fagan, standing in the centre of the room at Melwood with Ronnie and Roy in late July 1984, as Liverpool prepared for the new season. 'We've forgotten Souness,'

Joe added. 'He's gone. History. We move on.' As Joe uttered these words, I couldn't help thinking that his command to 'forget Souness' was a huge compliment to Graeme. To me, the very fact that Joe even mentioned Graeme hinted at a private concern the manager had of the potential impact of his departure. Ronnie then stepped into the middle, holding out a cardboard box to the players.

'Here are the Championship medals. If you qualified for one, take one.' As we leant forward and took our medals, Joe took up the talking again.

'The three trophies we won last season, the European Cup, League Championship and League Cup, are gone. It's in the past. New season now. We start again. We're European champions. We have to defend our title. No mistakes.'

10

HEYSEL

How many mistakes were made by the authorities in a season that ended stained with so much blood? Even before Liverpool arrived in Brussels for the European Cup final of 29 May 1985, our officials pleaded with Uefa to avoid making such a calamitous decision as using the Heysel Stadium. I was aware that Peter Robinson sent endless telexes to Uefa, the FA, the Belgian FA and Belgian police. As we stepped from the bus, even the players could see Heysel's unsuitability as a venue. Heysel was a disaster that should never have been allowed to happen.

The details of our road to Brussels now seem deeply insignificant, and reflections on the journey are necessarily brief. We began at Lech Poznan on 19 September with the build-up dominated by a declaration from the Poles' coach, Wojciech Lazarek, that he'd resign if Poznan didn't defeat Liverpool. During my time trekking around the Continent, I've heard some cocky predictions but this boast reeked of folly. Poznan were one of the smaller Polish clubs who had just ended up as champions in 1984. Liverpool were European champions, hugely experienced in bringing good first-leg scorelines back to Anfield. We all felt quietly determined to teach Lazarek a little respect. Stadion Lecha was hardly intimidating and Poznan's fans certainly weren't the fiercest on the European circuit. When we walked out of the tunnel, they threw toilet rolls at us, not the type of missiles to instil instant fear. Making a mockery of Lazarek's prediction, we took the lead through John Wark before you could say the words 'hostage to fortune'.

Wark had arrived from Ipswich Town in March, and was only now eligible to play in European competition for Liverpool. He was making up for lost time. Being Scottish, Warky immediately joined our clan, and Hansen and I took him under our tender wing. A non-stop giggler, he spoke more with his hands than with his mouth, gesticulating frantically like a tic-tac man. He had long impressed me as a footballer. At Ipswich, Bobby Robson paired Warky and Eric Gates in central midfield and it proved a very successful unit. When I'd played against them, I was struck that Gates was not exactly helpful defensively yet Warky still got a bundle of goals, ending as Europe's top scorer from midfield in 1981. Warky was a great finisher, hitting a hat-trick against the Poles in the second leg at Anfield. We won the round 5–0 on aggregate. On hearing later in the year that Lazarek had left Lech Poznan, I couldn't confess to being shocked or sympathetic.

Liverpool's drive towards Heysel pitted us next against Benfica, a second-round tie effectively decided in the rain at Anfield on 24 October when Rushie was irresistible. Just back from cartilage injury, Tosh had not lost his instinct for humiliating a goalkeeper, even one as good as Manuel Bento. Three times he scored on an evening also notable for Gary Gillespie earning a rare start. A genuinely nice guy, Gary was one of those steady centre-backs, very comfortable on the ball and a natural leader – he captained Falkirk at eighteen – yet, inevitably, he found it hard to dislodge 'Lawro' or Al at Liverpool. The only time Gary got the better of them was on the golf course. He played off two and still found Hansen a challenge. That year, Gary probably played more golf than football.

A fortnight later, Gary was back on the bench in the Stadium of Light, a torrid night not helped by Michel Vautrot, a referee even more atrocious than the weather. I was in our half with my back to Benfica's right-back, Minervino Pietra, and dummied to take the ball left, but then turned right. Pietra came straight through me. No mercy. No attempt to play the ball. Down I went, my ankle hurting bad. Jumping back up, I turned to confront Pietra, to remonstrate with him. I was furious. Never, though, did I consider retaliation. As I stared at him, Pietra looked like he was about to headbutt me. Instinctively, I threw my hands up to protect my face. All I did was try to defend myself, fending off what I thought was coming my way. My legitimate action of raising my hands drew a ludicrous and expensive response from Vautrot – a red card, my first and only dismissal. Four years later, I was amazed to flick on the television to discover Vautrot refereeing the final of Euro '88.

My anger at the automatic three-match suspension was partly softened by the first game being the European Super Cup, a bauble of little consequence to serious footballers. Liverpool's schedule was so busy that we'd agreed with Juventus to play the Super Cup over one leg only. So the lads went to Turin on 16 January, suffered a 2–0 defeat at Stadio Communale and nobody grieved. All that mattered was the European Cup and the boys made light work of Austria Vienna in the third round in March. I wasn't missed. Returning from exile against Panathinaikos in the semi-finals, I was keen to make up for my spell in the stands. We tore the Greeks apart at Anfield on 10 April, Rushie and me setting up Warky. Rushie popped in a couple and, such was Liverpool's control, the boys generously allowed me a free-kick, usually the domain of Alan Kennedy or Ronnie Whelan. In the past, I tried a couple of free-kicks but most ended up as throw-ins or in the Kop. An air-raid siren almost went off as I approached the still ball. This time, Sammy ran over the ball and I whipped it into the box for Jim Beglin to score. Following this 4–0 win, the match in Athens on 24 April was never going to present a problem. The lads were so relaxed Joe even permitted us a spot of sightseeing.

'Go and have a look at the Acropolis,' urged the Boss.

'But it's just an old ruin,' replied one of the players. We still went.

'It's falling to bits this place, look,' said another player. He was right and we never stayed long.

The tourist trail never interested us on European trips. The only souvenir we wanted was victory and Lawro ensured we collected that in Athens. Lawro scored quite a few goals on the quiet, occasionally ghosting forward, exchanging passes and carrying on. He had tremendous pace and if he did make a mistake, he'd invariably be back after it, clearing up quickly. Few defenders read the game as well as Lawro, or were as versatile. He was at home at full-back and in midfield as well as central defence. After his goal in Athens, Brussels awaited.

Even before seeing the appalling state of Heysel, we knew the assignment on the field would test us to the very limit on 29 May. Individuals of profound technical talent could be found throughout the black-and-white-striped ranks of Juventus. The most renowned of their marquee names was Michel Platini. The leader of France's vintage Euro '84 winners, Platini was right at the very pinnacle of his game. My admiration for Platini was immense – he could score with shots from range, and from free-kicks, and he could also drive through the middle, creating chances for others with his delicate touch and wonderful vision. Helping Platini sharpen Juventus's cutting edge was Polish striker Zbigniew Boniek, who was well known from his goalscoring exploits at the 1982 World Cup, and Paolo Rossi presented another class act in attack. Other famous names, including Bonini, Scirea, Cabrini and Tardelli, rolled effortlessly off the tongue when reading out the Juventus teamsheet. As a football match, the 1985 European Cup final was always going to be difficult. Liverpool were up against it. As an event, it was always going to be trouble. More of an athletics than a footballing arena, Heysel was too old and too badly configured for fans to be accommodated safely.

'It's not suitable,' Peter Robinson told me. I know how tirelessly Peter worked behind the scenes, trying to convince Uefa it was the wrong choice for such an emotionally charged event as a European Cup final. Peter worried in particular about the neutral zone Z behind one goal, as Liverpool fans were in pens X and Y to one side.

'They're letting anyone in there,' Peter said. 'Liverpool fans, Juventus fans, Belgians. It's supposed to be just for Belgians but everyone's getting in. It's dangerous. Liverpool and Juventus should be allocated tickets.'

Fans arriving at the ground without tickets were always going to buy them off Belgians for this neutral zone. A lot of Italians began filing into this section alongside the Liverpool area. Even two hours before kick-off, PBR implored Uefa to tackle the problem in the neutral section before it got out of hand. Uefa didn't listen and nor did the Belgian authorities.

As we strolled around the ground before kick-off, the atmosphere seemed fine. I noticed a lot of people in the neutral part of the terracing but the mood appeared good. One of the Liverpool fans threw a ball over the fence, the boys were keeping it up and then knocking it back to the supporters. Liverpool's punters loved that, so we had this wee game going, volleying the ball back and forth with banter being swapped as fast as the ball. As I returned to the dressing room, I can honestly say I saw nothing untoward going on. But, tragically, Peter's nightmare started to come true, and as we got stripped, a catastrophe unfolded outside. Struggling with a cold, I was laid out on the treatment table, dosing up on some legal medicine, dozing intermittently, but I listened for anybody coming through the door with any updates on events on the terraces.

'We need you and the captain to make an announcement,' I

heard somebody from Uefa telling Joe. 'We need an appeal for calm.' So Joe headed off, followed by Nealy. By all accounts, their appeal to Liverpool fans to 'behave' helped.

'Don't go outside,' ordered Joe on their return. The Boss was clearly distressed by what he'd seen, and the abuse he'd been subjected to by Juventus fans. For Nealy, wearing a Liverpool tracksuit guaranteed instant derision and a stream of Italian spit.

'What's going on out there?' I asked. I just didn't know. Joe wouldn't tell us. Nealy certainly didn't. High up on the dressing-room wall facing the pitch was a skylight with frosted glass so people couldn't see in. Some of the boys managed to force it open but still couldn't work out what was happening. Confusion reigned. Uefa were all over the shop.

'The game's off,' came the word. 'The game's on,' came the update. Reliable information was at a premium. After a 90-minute delay, the green light came from Uefa. Oblivious to the extent of the carnage in zone Z, we headed along the tunnel. I knew there had been an incident, clearly a serious one, but the magnitude? Damage to man or property? Nealy claimed in his book that Liverpool's players knew there had been fatalities. I didn't. Nealy had been outside, talking to the authorities when he appealed for restraint by Liverpool fans, so maybe he knew, but the rest of us were in the dark. What had gone on? Sensing the fraught mood, I guessed the final would be over in 90 minutes. No extra time or shoot-out would be allowed to extend the hostility. To my knowledge, nobody at Uefa had a word with the referee, Andre Daina, about the importance of finishing this as quickly as possible, but then they didn't need to. Everybody understood that everything had to be done to avoid the tension rising higher. Juventus fans seemed to be threatening a riot. Police horses dashed about. Glancing around, I noticed huge spaces on the terraces. Thousands of people had left Heysel. I had no idea that 39 spectators had perished. Even without knowing the facts, my intuition that this final was a farce, and as an event utterly bankrupt of any sporting integrity, was confirmed when Juventus were awarded a penalty 14 minutes after half-time. What a joke that was. Gillespie's trip on Boniek was certainly outside the box but it looked like Daina couldn't wait to give the penalty to Juventus.

'There's no way that was a penalty,' I remarked to a Uefa official a few years later.

'Some of us know that,' he replied.

Uefa must have known it wasn't a penalty. They must have seen it occurred outside the box. No doubt they also understood keenly they had to get the game over. Making the most of Daina's generosity, Platini tucked away the kick. Conceding goals, particularly unjust ones, normally stirred me to anger, and determination. I'd dash through the gears as quickly as possible, looking for a goal back, for revenge, for justice. Not this time. Even when we were denied a blatant penalty when Bonini brought down Ronnie Whelan a yard inside Juventus's area, my mind and body were stuck in neutral, unwilling to become engaged. The 1985 final of the European Cup passed me by. Despite the mood of barbarism between the fans, no such tension existed between the players. Juventus players must have felt bad. It didn't matter whose fans lost their lives because both teams were hit by Heysel. Liverpool were affected because of the horrible atmosphere and nightmarish situation in which the club found themselves. Trauma engulfed everybody inside Heysel. When Daina signalled full-time, I was so numb and detached I never went up for my medal. That was me straight off, down the tunnel, no looking back, racing to reach the hushed dressing room. Each player was lost in his own thoughts. As I stared around, my heart went out to old Joe. This was his last game in charge, and it bequeathed him countless sleepless nights. Joe looked haunted, his body suffering waves of stress.

Showering and dressing quickly, I rushed off to find Marina. She was fine, thank God, clearly distressed but not as bad as those wives who'd been threatened by Juventus supporters. One Italian tried to drag Paul Walsh's girlfriend to see the bodies. Only when the girls began explaining to us what had happened did we realise the enormity of the occasion. The wives had attempted to leave the stadium by a back entrance but ran into ambulances and a row of dead bodies. When Marina relayed this detail to me, I was even more furious. If Uefa were going to carry on with the game, they should have protected innocent people such as our wives.

As we boarded the bus, it gradually became more apparent what had occurred. The main facts are now well established: 39 people died when a wall collapsed as they sprinted away from Liverpool fans who were charging at them. Unfortunately, they had nowhere to go, just retreating into that crush and losing their lives. Desperate. Even now, the authorities still don't comprehend that what happened at Heysel was a legacy of Rome a year earlier. Still fresh in the minds of Liverpool fans was how brutally they had been treated by Italian supporters outside the Olympic Stadium in 1984. Kopites remembered the stones, the flying bottles, the attacks around the ground. The ambushes that befell Liverpool fans in Rome angered all supporters, who determined they would not fall victim to Italian venom again. At Heysel, Liverpool fans were hemmed in, so when rocks and chunks of concrete began coming through the air, some of them inevitably felt 'this is Roma re-visited'.

'We copped this the last time,' a Liverpool fan told me. 'It's different people but same principle. Are we going to stand there and let somebody throw stones at us?' Not many people would. Why should they again be used for target practice by Italians? Nothing forgives the violent reaction of a few Liverpool fans, but the whole controversy needs placing in context. After 21 years of playing in Europe, Liverpool fans enjoyed an unsullied reputation. Before Heysel, Liverpool had not been associated with trouble. I'm offering reasons, not excuses. If somebody comes

into my house, I'll defend my house. If somebody throws bricks
at me, I'll defend myself. Why are those who retaliated instantly
denigrated as the bad guys? If Roma fans hadn't attacked Liverpool
in 1984, our fans wouldn't have been so quick to retaliate in
1985. If Juventus fans hadn't lobbed bricks, there would have
been no charge by the Liverpool fans. No spark, no fire. No
stones, no reaction. Juventus fans shouldn't have been in zone
Z, a neutral area. During the inquest into Heysel, people seemed
to forget that Juventus fans were aggressive. Watching the footage,
I noted a masked Italian running out from the stand, pointing
a gun. Nobody knew at the time it was only a starting pistol, so
why wasn't he arrested?

Uefa has always sought to dodge the finger of blame. They've
never answered questions legitimately directed at them. Why did
they choose the wrong stadium? Why did they compound their
mistake by authorising a neutral section? If this end was supposed
to be neutral, then why did the list of dead show 32 Italians,
four Belgians, two French and a man from Northern Ireland, so
more than three-quarters of those who died were Juventus fans?
Uefa's 'neutral' area was anything but. In Rome, Liverpool fans
had one end and it wasn't full because the Olympic Stadium was
so vast. Why didn't Uefa have the same arrangements in 1985?
Juventus could have had their share of Heysel and Liverpool their
share. No neutral section was required. How on earth could Uefa
think they could separate the passionate followers of Liverpool
and Juventus with a thin piece of chicken wire? Chicken wire!
Why did Uefa fail to organise a line of stewards between
supporters? Why did they fail to control the situation once the
trouble began? Uefa had plenty of failings to answer for but never
did. Instead, and to my eternal anger, the hurricane of questions
and criticism blew towards Liverpool.

The only major decision Uefa got right on the night, a call some
people still disagree with, was to play the game. Uefa's fear, and
one I shared, was that a dreadful situation could have worsened.

If everybody had been turfed out of the stadium, more trouble might have erupted in Brussels. Uefa couldn't hold the European Cup final over, but they should never have held the presentation, not if they knew people had died. That was so undignified.

The following morning, some grieving Juventus fans made their way to Liverpool's base in Brussels. To leave the hotel was to run the gauntlet. Climbing on board the bus, we were left in no doubt about the depth of Italian fury. Juventus fans were sobbing, hitting the bus with their bare hands, their emotions so raw. One man pushed his face right up against the window. He was inches away from me and I saw and understood his anger. This man might have lost a brother, a son, a friend among the 39. Football's a central force in millions of lives but it can never be more important than family. For all my veneration of Shanks, I've never agreed with his famous quote that 'football is not a matter of life and death. I can assure you it is much, much more important than that.' That's wrong. I can't have that. Football can never be more important, but staring through the window at that poor Juventus man, I couldn't help thinking that the Italians should have vented some of their rage at Uefa and the Belgian organisers.

Liverpool's retreat from Brussels was one of the darkest journeys I'd ever made. Not only had we left the European Cup behind, we'd also left much of our good reputation behind. My heart went out to Joe, who broke down on the tarmac at Speke Airport, overwhelmed by emotion, requiring Roy's support. Joe's last game as Liverpool manager ended in tragedy and a decent, honourable man deserved to be retiring in a more dignified manner.

Unfairly vilified from many quarters, Liverpool Football Club showed its remorse for what happened at Heysel. On the Friday, all the players and staff attended a requiem mass at Liverpool Metropolitan Cathedral. Joe was still in pieces, needing his wife's help to enter the church. I joined the offertory procession while Bruce and Big Al carried a wreath bedecked in the red-and-white ribbons of Liverpool and the black and white of Juventus. Bob Paisley read from the Book of Isaiah. His distinctive voice flowed like a soft breeze down the church, his words stirring more emotions. 'The Lord will destroy death forever,' read Bob. 'He will wipe away the tears from every cheek and take away the people's shame.' Shame? That word hit me hard. Why should Liverpool feel shame? Regret, yes. But shame? I felt no shame, just sadness for those who died, and anger at Uefa for not listening.

As I sat there, seething with frustration, Joe bravely took to the pulpit to lead the prayers. His words carried such beauty and soul, making a fitting tribute to the 39. 'We pray for their families and friends who have suffered through bereavement,' read Joe. 'We pray that the sporting spirit, so treasured on Merseyside, may never be lost to violence or to bitterness.' Amen to that. In a moving and eloquent way, Joe articulated Liverpool's deep sympathy towards the people who lost their lives, our respect for them and their families. In tragedies like this, people feel helpless. What do I do? What can I do? Liverpool responded correctly, solemnly. Juventus had an outpouring of grief. Liverpool had an outpouring of sympathy. Gathered in that cathedral, we wanted to send a message of support to the Italians and I passionately hoped we achieved that aim.

Nobody cared to think Liverpool were suffering. 'It's a horror story one has to live with,' said Peter Robinson, whose warnings went so scandalously unheeded. PBR was right. Heysel was a horror story that Liverpool as well as the Juventus families had to live with it. The bereaved were the worst affected, of course, but it was not pleasant for anybody. Nobody can be proud – aggrieved, aggressor, footballer, official or politician. On 31 May, Margaret Thatcher, whose knowledge of football was notoriously limited, called for English clubs, particularly Liverpool, to be banned from European competition. The Prime Minister even

labelled Liverpool fans hooligans. I felt it the height of irres-
ponsibility for Thatcher to come out so quickly with such rash
statements when she didn't know the facts. She just saw it as a
political master-stroke for her – great publicity, Iron Lady, all that
baggage. It wasn't her job to ban us. Thatcher just made it easier
for Uefa to send us into exile. 'Look,' they must have thought,
'even the British Prime Minister has criticised Liverpool, so let's
ban them.' Within 48 hours of Thatcher's ill-advised comments,
Uefa banned English clubs – and I thought that football authorities, including Uefa, despised political interference. Thatcher
probably got all the English clubs banned. If she'd kept her
mouth shut, the rest of them might not have suffered.

I accept that Liverpool deserved some sanction, but why were
Everton affected? Howard Kendall's team won the League in
1985 and never got to compete in the European Cup. Heysel
was nothing to do with Everton. Why were Roma not punished
the year before? Why was that swept under the carpet and not
publicised? Roma fans bricked our boys, people had blood pouring
out of their heads, but they got no justice. Uefa certainly never
covered themselves in glory because they never accepted their
negligence. Juventus escaped criticism for their fans throwing
rocks and starting the trouble. The only people held responsible
were the Liverpool fans in that pen.

Of course, it was only right that the full force of the British
justice system should pursue those Liverpool fans who'd been
the most aggressive. I can't hide from the fact that a degree of
malevolence motivated some of those leading that charge. When
27 people were arrested by the police on suspicion of man-
slaughter, it was clear some were no angels. A few had previous
convictions for violent behaviour, but an analysis of any crowd
would probably reveal criminal records. Did any of the 39 who
so tragically died have convictions for violence? When it also
became apparent that a lot of the fans arrested didn't have
Liverpool addresses, the thought crossed my mind that maybe

they were supporters of other English clubs, simply using a crowded European Cup final as an opportunity for hooliganism. This was the mid-Eighties when the English disease, as the continentals called it, was at its ugly peak.

While the police went about their work, the Belgian parliament launched an investigation into events at Heysel. On 6 July, a Belgian judge laid the blame at the feet of politicians, police and football administrators. His verdict totally vindicated Peter's judgement and reputation as one of the best administrators in football. PBR offered good advice but the people of Uefa arrogantly refused to listen. The judge condemned Uefa, saying they were also culpable. Based near Geneva, in Switzerland, Uefa clearly felt themselves above Belgian law.

'How can that be right?' I said to PBR. 'How can Uefa be outside the jurisdiction of a country where they've held an event?'

Uefa should have been called to account. If Uefa had any shred of compassion, they must have felt guilty. The same as the Liverpool fans who charged across zone Z must have felt guilty at the consequences of their actions, although they never had any intention of killing anybody.

Amidt all the carnage and recrimination, some good came of Heysel. Policing standards improved, a dangerous stadium was rebuilt and fans taught themselves a bit of restraint. Liverpool supporters had six years to go away and think about their part in the tragedy, and learn from the awful events in zone Z. Liverpool and Juventus worked hard to rebuild their shattered relationship. Central to that was the strong rapport between Peter and the Juventus president, the tall, grey-haired Giampiero Boniperti.

Almost 20 years on, Liverpool and Juventus were drawn together in the Champions League. The Kop welcomed the Italians with a mosaic spelling out 'Amicia', showing that friendship had developed out of hatred. PBR and Boniperti were instrumental in that. Good links were made and both clubs have to be admired for the way they went about the reconciliation. Liverpool had the greatest ground to recover as they were banned from Europe. This was the situation I walked into as, even before Heysel, I knew I was succeeding Joe.

11

STEPPING UP

For the life of me, I don't know why Liverpool appointed me manager. PBR and the board could see my intense love for the club, and were aware I thought deeply about the game, but they also understood how committed I was to continue playing. That Liverpool No. 7 shirt was a second skin to me, and one I dreaded shedding. Looking back, I believe they carefully sounded me out about the possibility of management without my even realising it. A year before Heysel, PBR called me into his office at Anfield. Peter was his usual self, relaxed but always on top of everything. Calmly, as if opening a conversation about the weather, Peter said, 'Kenny, how do you see the future going?'

'Just concentrate on playing, I hope, Peter.'

'We want to give you a four-year contract.'

'Four years? Peter, I'm thirty-three. I'm not young!'

'We just want to reward you for what you've done for Liverpool Football Club.'

'Reward me? Shouldn't I be rewarding you for what you've done for me?' I meant it. Liverpool gave me the platform to reach for the sky. 'Look what I've done here. Look what I've won. I've only got those medals because you brought me here. Look, Peter, if you want to reward me with a new contact, I'm honoured. Just give me the contract and I'll sign it now.'

'There are no figures in it yet.'

'I'm no bothered. If I can't trust you, what chance have we got!'

'I'll have it ready for you tomorrow, Kenny. Come up then.'

So the following morning, before training, I reported back.

'Sorry, Kenny, it's not finished.'

'Peter, I trust you. I'll sign the blank contract, you fill in the details and I know I have a four-year contract.'

As I turned to leave, Peter remarked casually: 'Kenny, what do you see yourself doing in the future?'

'Play for as long as I can, then get into coaching or management. Football's all I know.'

I thought nothing of the glint entering Peter's eyes. PBR must have realised then that management was a road I wanted to travel down one day. Maybe he thought why not make that journey with Liverpool? That would fit in with the board's policy of promoting from within – Shankly, Paisley, Fagan, Dalglish? OK, my natural habitat was dressing room rather than Boot Room, but what was a few yards down the corridor among friends? Similar principles shaped both places. One day at Melwood, I missed a pass and Ronnie shouted at me, 'Play it simple.'

'It was simple. I just made it difficult.'

'Oh shut up, Kenny, you're not the manager yet,' Ronnie shouted back. Bugsy can't have known – I didn't know. That was my state of mind, though. I'd always enjoyed organising teams. Big Al reckons my managerial tendencies first came to the fore with Scotland during the 1982 World Cup. On the eve of a group game with Brazil, Jock Stein staged a practice match, his starting XI against me and the rest of the squad.

'Kenny, organise them like Brazil,' Jock shouted. 'Play five across the middle and one up. Brazil will have Serginho up. Eder, Socrates, Falcao and Zico will come up from deeper positions.' Fair enough. We had our orders. With that Jock blew the whistle.

'Leave them with the ball,' I told my team. 'Just leave them.'

Jock's chosen ones passed the ball across the back and we let them, just stayed holding our positions. Jock stopped the game.

'Hey, Kenny, you're smart, aren't you?'

'What?'

'I asked you to do something, and you're trying to mess it up.'

'I'm not messing it up. Do you think Brazil are going to run way up that high to get the ball? They'll sit here. You asked us to imitate Brazil's formation. That's what we were doing.'

'You're a smart arse. Always got an answer.' I also had a win – the reserves beat Jock's team 2–0, both goals scored by keepers! But however much I enjoyed pitting my wits against Jock, I wasn't thinking about becoming a manager.

My voyage towards the dug-out accelerated before Heysel. I was at home in Southport, pottering about, when the phone went.

'Kenny, it's Peter. The chairman and I would like to come across and see you.'

'Yes, no problem.' After agreeing a suitable time, I was about to put the phone down when PBR added, 'Kenny, are you not curious what we want to speak about?'

'OK. What?'

'We'd like to offer you the manager's job.'

'No problem, Peter, you can still come to the house!' Making a joke was my natural defence mechanism, winning myself time to absorb the immense significance of what was happening. Liverpool Football Club wanted me to become manager, assuming the office of men I revered – Shanks, Bob and Joe. Just writing their names causes me to catch my breath in awe. Now I was being told Liverpool believed I could follow in their famous footsteps. I couldn't really take it in.

When Peter and John Smith arrived, Marina hurried about, getting tea and sandwiches. Then she left us alone and they made their momentous offer, leaving me overwhelmed, honoured, shocked and moved. As we talked, I could hardly take in the details of what was being said apart from one extraordinary fact. After PBR and John Smith left, Marina rushed into the room.

'The club want me to be player-manager,' I told Marina.

Bob Paisley collects the League Cup after our Wembley defeat of Manchester United in 1983, the penultimate trophy in his haul of 19 for Liverpool.

Providing a tartan touch to our celebrations after beating United, Graeme Souness (*left*), Alan Hansen (*right*) and I show the trophy to the fans and photographers.

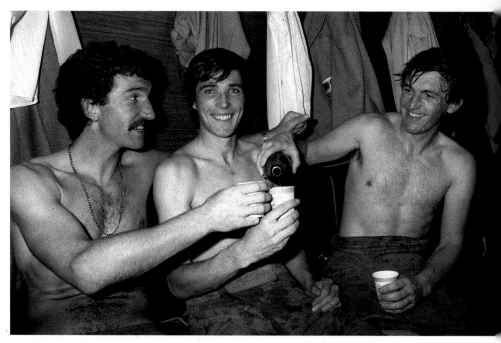

Another trophy to toast – in plastic cups – with Messrs Souness and Hansen as we close the
Paisley era by winning the 1982–83 League title.

Riding a tackle from Everton's Derek Mountfield during the 1984 Milk Cup final replay at
MaineRoad. Liverpool won after a goalless Wembley derby.

Smoke from the Roma fans' flares created a menacing backdrop to the 1984 European Cup
final in the Italian capital, but we emerged victorious.

Graeme Souness embraces Joe Fagan after we beat Roma on penalties to bring the giant
trophy back to Liverpool in Joe's first year as manager.

Joe Fagan pleads with hemmed-in Liverpool fans at Heysel. The roots of the tragedy lay in events in Rome a year earlier, and it was a terrible choice of venue.

Mounted police take to the pitch after the carnage that cost 39 lives at Heysel. This was the prelude to the final, which was won by Juventus but left me numb.

The face of Joe Fagan, like those of Jim Beglin and Craig Johnston, betrays the enormity of the situation that unfolded in Brussels.

Attending a memorial service with (*left to right*) Mark Lawrenson, Alan Hansen, Bruce Grobbelaar and (*far right*) Everton manager Howard Kendall.

A Juventus flag among the massed Liverpool supporters at Wembley for the 1986 FA Cup final was a pleasing conciliatory gesture.

The Boot Room generations at the '86 final – Bob Paisley, Ronnie Moran and Roy Evans, watched by future No. 2 Sammy Lee (*background left*).

Ian Rush has scored to pave the way to Wembley victory over Everton.

Craig Johnston strikes and the double beckons for one new manager.

Ian Molby, part of my inheritance from Joe Fagan, evades Paul Bracewell's lunge as we home in on the FA Cup in the first all-Merseyside final.

The best goal I ever scored? A sweet volley following a slick move sealed one half of the double in 1986 – the League, at Chelsea.

Silly hats were clearly *de rigueur* in 1986. We came from behind to overcome Everton at Wembley, finishing the second half of the job.

'You're kidding me on!'

'No, honestly. They said they want me to be player-manager with Bob working above me.'

'What are you going to do?'

'First phone my dad. Then phone your dad.'

Dad's advice was unequivocal. 'If Liverpool Football Club think you're good enough to be manager, have a go.' After Marina's father endorsed this view, I contacted PBR.

'OK. I'll have a go. I'll keep my player's contract and try it for a year. If I'm rubbish, I'll go back to my playing contract. I'll try my very best, but if it doesn't work, there's nothing lost.'

'Fine,' replied PBR, who sounded remarkably composed about a job offer that represented an almighty gamble. How could Liverpool's board possibly know whether their No. 7 could mature into a good manager? Peter and the chairman were putting a major sporting institution into the hands of an apprentice.

'I've not spent the last eight years sitting with Peter having great conversations about football,' I said to Marina. 'I talk to Tom during the week but not about management. It's very flattering they've come up with my name. I know Peter was taken by surprise when Bob went. Joe was a wee bit reluctant to take the job but three trophies in his first season was magnificent. The board knew this would be Joe's last season, so they've had time to think about things.'

Just because I understood the culture of Liverpool Football Club didn't automatically mean I was the right person. Others in the club fitted that bill. Why bypass Ronnie and Roy and go for a player? Why me and not Nealy? So many question marks hung in the air but the major two were answered. Liverpool wanted me and I wanted the job.

'I'll have a go for five years and then we can get a break,' I promised Marina.

So I rang PBR to accept with the understanding that news mustn't leak out.

'Agreed,' said Peter.

On the morning of Heysel, the newspapers were full of talk about Joe's future. 'JOE SET TO GO' screamed the *Mirror*. My name was mentioned as a possible successor but then so were those of Nealy, Bugsy and Chris Lawler. It made for lively reading when the squad gathered for breakfast in our Brussels hotel.

'Have you seen the papers?' asked one of the players. 'Joe's going after the game.' I walked away sharpish, keen to avoid engaging in any conversation where I had privileged information. Before such a big match, such stories were a distraction and the newspapers cannot have known for sure. At that time, the Merseyside reporters were very close to PBR. If Liverpool played rubbish, the journalists would reflect that in their articles and the players accepted and respected that. It was on the rare occasions when they strayed into speculation that resentment seeped from under the dressing-room door. Peter wouldn't have briefed the reporters on this story. The supreme professional, and a man with great respect for Joe, PBR would never have done anything to disrupt the team's focus before the climax of the season. Only one player in that Heysel dressing room knew the identity of Joe's successor. Well, two actually, because I couldn't resist telling Al. Before Heysel, Marina and I went for dinner with Al and his wife Janet in Southport. At the end of the evening, I mentioned I'd be manager.

'Right, Janet, get your coat,' said Al. 'We're off. The friendship's over!' I laughed. I knew one thing for sure and that was our friendship will never be over.

As we got on the plane to leave Brussels, the chairman called me over.

'Kenny, we're having to make the announcement today. I know we said tomorrow but what happened back there has changed all that. We'll do it when we get back to Anfield at four.'

'Chairman, I've no suit,' I replied, standing there in my tracksuit, Liverpool's usual travelling wear. 'I need a collar and tie for the Press conference.'

'You'll be all right,' insisted the chairman, clearly not in a mood for a fashion debate at a time when his club was being battered. 'Just go in your tracksuit.'

Sitting in front of Marina and me on the plane was Ronnie Whelan.

'Kenny, you'll know. Who's replacing Joe?' asked Vitch.

'I'm not sure.'

'Go on, you must know. Tell me.'

'OK, it's me.'

'Piss off.'

'It is!'

'Seriously, Kenny, who is it?'

'It is me! Honest.'

'Yes! Brilliant! Can I be captain!'

That was a rare moment of laughter on that cheerless flight to Speke Airport. Most of the players were lost in thought about the previous night. I looked forward, contemplating my new venture. I thought about other players who'd stepped into management. The job never really worked out for Billy Bremner at Doncaster Rovers or Bobby Moore at Southend United, but they never had the quality of coaching or playing staff gathered around them that I did. I was blessed. Not many people enjoy their first shot at management with a group of players who had been in two successive European Cup finals. I was more concerned about damaging Liverpool's reputation than my own. I thought about Joe, who was in tears, talking to the players, explaining this was it, goodbye, game over.

'I love this club and I love football,' Joe said, 'but I feel if I carry on any longer, people might not love me any more.'

As Joe spoke, the succession plans were being enacted. Roy and Ronnie were called over by John Smith and informed about me. The chairman stood up and said a few words over the mike, thanking Joe for all he'd done during his time as manager. So did Nealy. On landing at Speke, the world's media lay in wait, getting their cables in a twist in the frantic rush to interrogate poor Joe about Heysel while I headed off to Anfield. For somebody as extremely private as I am, facing the Press was an ordeal at the best of times. Even when flanked by Bob and the chairman, I still felt exposed. The chairman began proceedings by announcing my appointment.

'Kenny is entering the managerial side for the first time and we have every reason to believe he will have a successful period in office,' I heard him say. This was it. No turning back. The secret was out. 'We feel we have a man of great ability on the field who has an old head on young shoulders,' added John.

I stared out at the assembled press corps and familiar faces looked back, reporters I trusted, such as John Keith of the *Daily Express*, but to be honest the whole process was torture. My last experience of attending a press conference was eight years earlier, when I signed from Celtic. Even without the dark cloud of Heysel hanging over any Liverpool employee, this was an intimidating event, and I felt so far out of my comfort zone. My character means I'm more nervous playing golf in front of six people than playing football in front of 60,000.

I placed on record my feeling of great honour at being asked to become Liverpool manager. My ability to handle the Press was never a noted strength of my managerial career, and my unease riddled a first exchange with Ian Hargreaves, the respected football reporter from the *Liverpool Echo*. 'You know nothing about football and I know nothing about journalism, so we should get on well,' I told Ian. Looking back, I regret my attitude and I should have had a better relationship with the *Echo*. Ian and later Ric George were really important as the channel for me to impart information to Liverpool supporters. I should have been more cooperative. I showed a lack of understanding of what the local Press boys needed. Fortunately, PBR was close to the papers.

Having survived the Press inquisition, I escaped downstairs to find Ronnie and Roy, who were sorting things out in the Boot

Room. They looked at me with questions in their eyes. I was the new man, the Gaffer, not just a player any more. They couldn't shout at me. Sensing their concerns, I said to Bugsy, 'You're going to stay aren't you?' Turning to Roy, I added, 'You're not going away?' Both shook their heads. Anfield was their world.

'Good that's sorted then. I need you to stay.'

'We just want a job,' said Ronnie. Roy nodded.

'You'll always have a job, the two of you, while I'm manager,' I said.

Over the years, many hurtful claims have circulated that I abandoned the Boot Room. On the contrary, embracing the inhabitants and philosophy of the Boot Room was at the heart of my approach to managing Liverpool. Far from being a threat, the Boot Room was an ally. Settled in their successful routine, Ronnie and Roy needed a centre for their planning and discussions about training, and for their wee drinks after matches. As a player, I rarely went in. As a manager, I never went in after games, because I wasn't clever enough. Blessed with the sharpest minds, Ronnie and Roy set their traps to extract information from members of the opposing coaching staff. It would have been the height of stupidity for me to burst into the room and mess up this great Liverpool fact-finding tradition. After saying a few words to the Press, preferably as few as possible, I'd invite the other manager back to my office. Ronnie and Roy would be along the corridor, entertaining and working over visiting coaches and, sometimes, the opposition manager would pop in there en route to my office, giving the boys another opportunity to acquire knowledge.

Even though I made all the decisions, the Boot Room was a source of much sound advice and no manager could have had better support. I trusted Ronnie and Roy implicitly. They were totally honest, loyal men who'd never be stool-pigeons in the dressing room. When Liverpool stayed in hotels before matches, Ronnie, Roy and Old Tom gathered in my room after dinner. Those three would enjoy a tipple and I'd have a glass of sparkling water, just in case I was playing. We'd chat about the team, the opposition, tactics and potential signings. Friday night conversations were my Boot Room. For me, the Boot Room was as much about the people as the four walls within Anfield. The room itself went during redevelopment in Graeme Souness's time as manager, and even Roy never complained, believing there were 'too many ghosts'.

Tradition never intimidated me, anyway. Some managers – Cloughie at Leeds United springs to mind – marched into a new place and ordered the removal of photographs that saluted past triumphs. Cloughie's attitude was different from mine. Why be embarrassed about history? Why take down pictures? Don Revie helped make Leeds a great name, one Cloughie considered managing, so why run from that? History inspires. The challenge bequeathed by Shanks, Bob and Joe, and all their support staff in the Boot Room, was one I relished. I was still alive to the fact that some players shrank when walking down a corridor covered with pictures of famous successes. When assessing the merits of any transfer target, I tried to ensure they were made of the right stuff. Beginning with Steve McMahon in my first season as manager, every incoming player possessed the strength of personality to handle Liverpool's illustrious heritage, and Macca certainly did.

Just as Ronnie and Roy were part of the fabric of Liverpool Football Club, so was Bob Paisley. Having spoken to the boys in the Boot Room on that first day, the following week I went to the manager's office for the first time and found Bob sitting there quietly.

'Sit down, Kenny,' said Bob. I sat behind the manager's desk. This was it. I was now manager. I looked across the vast expanse of the desk. There was nothing there, no paperwork, nothing to read or sign. I heard the clock on the wall ticking. I stared at the phone.

'Bob, what am I doing in here?'

'What do you mean?'

'There's nobody in. There's nothing to do. Why do I need to be here?'

'The phone might ring.'

'Well I've got a phone in the house.'

'Oh, you've got to be here just in case anybody calls or anybody comes.'

Eventually, something happened. The manager's secretary, Sheila Walsh, came in.

'You can have new furniture, Kenny,' said Sheila. 'We have an allowance for changing the office furniture this year. New desk, new chairs, anything you want.'

'But this was Bob's desk, so I'll keep that. This was Shanks's chair, so why should I change? I'll tell you what, Sheila. Use the allowance to put a bar right along that wall so I can do some entertaining after matches. And put a desk in there for Old Tom.' Tom was always by my side. When I began spending less time in the office at Anfield, people wondered how much I consulted Bob. Those critics who surmised Bob was employed simply to give the new regime some old-school authority were just plain wrong. Bob was no token figure. It would have been remiss of me never to draw on all those years of wisdom, all that rich experience of outfoxing opponents, and Bob was really helpful. He came down from his office to talk to me, throw in wee ideas. If Liverpool were interested in a player, Bob might have a quiet word about the target with someone. Having Bob around was wonderful but it was my show and some decisions were required. Some proved very quick to sort out.

'Rushie needs a new contract sorting. What do you think?' PBR asked.

'Keep him,' I replied. End of discussion.

Another day, Peter asked,'Craig needs a new contract sorting. What do you think?'

'Keep him.'

Such decisions were no-brainers. Beyond expressing a desire

to retain a player, I never became involved in the finances. Why should I? In PBR, Liverpool had one of the best administrators the football world has ever known. As a manager starting my first job, I could not have had a better person negotiating transfers or wages. PBR never short-changed new signings, who always emerged from his office ready to run through brick walls for Liverpool. PBR had a clever trick during negotiations. After the initial dance with the player of 'the club can offer this' and 'I want that', Peter left the room and had a quiet word with me.

'Kenny, this is our top offer. Go and offer it to him. It will be good for your relationship.' So I'd sit down with the player and give him Liverpool's offer.

'That's your maximum, so it's a yes or no on that figure.'

'YES,' the player invariably replied, being indebted to me for seemingly getting him the best deal, which strengthened our relationship immediately.

PBR was actually very canny with money. Before the end of the tax year, he occasionally called me in.

'Kenny, we've got about £250,000 spare if you want to spend it.' Peter had done this with previous managers, so May signings were not uncommon. Frank McGarvey came in 1979 and Rushie arrived a year later.

PBR and John Smith made a fantastic partnership at board level, and I trusted them implicitly. Shortly after they appointed me, I chatted to PBR about reports in the papers that another manager was threatening to quit.

'Why would he be saying that in the papers?

'He'd be looking for a rise,' replied PBR without a pause.

'Peter, if I'm ever looking for a rise, I'll come and tell you.' I couldn't understand how managers could behave like that. I've never used a newspaper to air a grievance.

Always ahead of the game, PBR appointed Tom Saunders as Youth Development Officer in 1970 and later authorised Tom to be Liverpool's European scout, flying off to watch opponents and check on hotels. Back then, travel was a logistical nightmare but PBR sorted it for Tom, who'd spend a week getting to and from some distant Eastern European town, coming back and diligently typing up his report. Under PBR, Liverpool became the first British club to have shirt advertising, yet Peter's major love wasn't football. Cricket was his big passion. At Anfield, Peter watched some of the game but then slipped back to his office, catching up on correspondence. When PBR stood down, Liverpool really missed his astuteness, particularly in dealings with Everton. When Peter and Jim Greenwood worked in tandem across Stanley Park, relations were always good. For midweek matches, both clubs preferred to play on Tuesday, so Peter and Jim tossed a coin at the start of the season to see who went first and then alternated. Complete trust existed between Peter and Jim.

Despite my new status, I was determined to stay as unostentatious as possible.

'What car do you want?' Peter asked. 'A Mercedes?'

'Oh, Peter, I canna take a Merc.'

'Why not?'

'It doesn't seem right. I don't want to custard-pie the punters.' As a city, Liverpool was hit by economic strife in the Eighties, bringing hardship to many local people. 'The fans won't mind if I have some toys, but not to flaunt it. I'll have an Audi. People will feel comfortable with me in an Audi. It's less flash.'

As I drove into the ground on the first day of pre-season, I knew I had to address the players and set the right tone for the season. I stressed we were in this together, that Liverpool's principles would continue to guide the team.

'The rules stay the same, in at ten, collar and tie for games,' I told them. 'If you want a game of golf, not after a Wednesday. Don't go out Thursdays or Fridays.' After the specifics, I told the squad what I expected this season. 'There will be difficulties throughout the year but I want you to give a hundred per cent for Liverpool. I'll treat you as I liked to be treated. If you're not in the team, you'll know first.' To keep all the players on their toes, I never announced Liverpool's line-up until a couple of hours before kick-off. That meant if somebody got injured on the Friday, a fully motivated player stepped up without knowing he was destined for the bench. The players responded by running a sweep on my team selection.

One myth about my relations with the players needs destroying. The claim that Liverpool players couldn't understand me because of my Scottish accent was rubbish. My pronunciation could be clearer, more refined, but I am what I am – a Glaswegian who refuses to surrender his birthright. The TV commentator Alan Parry once asked me, 'Don't you think you'll have trouble communicating with players because your accent is so difficult to understand?'

'Pardon?' I replied, unable to resist the open goal.

The players certainly understood me. When Lawro was late back for pre-season training, I rang his home. His wife Vanessa explained Lawro was over in Dublin, doing some coaching. He was injured and couldn't have joined in training at Melwood but that wasn't the point. When Lawro finally called in, I made it totally clear he'd stepped out of line.

Although I was the Boss, I still socialised with players, including Lawro, who was part of the Southport set. We'd go out for a meal after the Saturday game, sharing a bottle of wine if we'd won. When Lawro and Hansen then went into the dressing room, they got dog's abuse off the others. 'Teacher's pet,' was the usual comment, although such an accusation was never made seriously. All the players knew I'd never talk about them with their colleagues.

The print boys seemed fascinated about how I would fare as Liverpool's manager, so they asked around. Graeme Souness surprised me with his comment. 'People are a bit frightened of Kenny,' said Charlie. 'He growls at them, makes them jump.

These are essential qualities for a manager.' I never understood what players had to fear in me. If they messed up in training or a game, I bit their heads off, of course. Bollockings helped them improve. Throwing tea-cups was never my style, but my aggressive streak would be on show if somebody fouled up badly.

I certainly wasn't scared of making decisions. Continuity was important but the Liverpool machine still needed tweaking. The hardest decision I made involved the armband. I knew the conversation with Phil Neal would be short and tense. At 34, he'd played more than 600 games, scored almost 60 goals, won four European Cups and captained Liverpool to famous triumphs. He was Bob's captain, Joe's captain, but not mine. After he sat down, I wasted no time explaining my plans.

'I'm going to change the captaincy,' I announced. 'I want a new kid on the block.' Nealy must have been livid. I wouldn't have expected such a proud man and hardened competitor not to feel angry. To have ownership of the Liverpool captain's armband is one of the great honours in sport, but that armband is only on loan. Nobody has a right to it, even a player as decorated as Phil Neal. The armband belongs to Liverpool Football Club. When Ron Yeats had the armband, he wore it proudly, but he knew he was simply the keeper of the flame before the torch was passed on. The same with Tommy Smith, Phil Thompson and Graeme Souness. These were great warriors in the red of Liverpool, supremely worthy captains, and so was Nealy. As manager, I felt the captaincy should go to Alan Hansen, somebody I knew well and trusted completely. Tempers have since cooled, and Phil and I get on fine now, but I understood he was enraged, and I understood why. But a charge of negligence could easily have been levelled against me if I'd not gone through with the decision. Liverpool's future lay with Alan, not Phil. We had two captains in effect.

Phil also harboured managerial ambitions, and must have been disappointed not to be offered the Liverpool job. Whether the board led him to believe he was a contender was neither clear to me nor mattered. Some people whispered that Nealy felt resentment towards me, but why? I didn't go looking for the job. I didn't elbow Nealy out of the way in a rush to throw myself in front of John Smith and PBR. Liverpool came to me. Nealy should have reserved any resentment for the board.

'The next time you talk to me – if you want to talk to me – make sure you call me Gaffer,' I told him.

'OK,' said Nealy. Sometimes the players forgot, saying 'Kenny . . . I mean Gaffer.' Who knows if Nealy's was an accident or not, but it was essential that I reminded him, as the situation could have festered.

Nealy's disappointment never showed on the pitch but after his testimonial, against Everton on 12 August, Nealy went to see the chairman, emerging from Anfield to tell the press he felt he had 'no future' at Liverpool. I never understood that because I felt he did have a future. I'd never let anything personal affect my match-day judgement. If Nealy had been made manager, I'd have carried on playing happily under him. But I was the boss, I wanted a new captain and Alan was the best option.

Even though we were close, Alan was never a spy. Smuggling stories out of the dressing room wasn't his style, and I never asked him to sneak on the players, anyway. Al deserved to be captain. He held the respect of the dressing room, and everybody wanted to be friends with him. He was incredibly popular. I never envied him . . . well, maybe his pace. His many admirers marvelled at his calm as a footballer but I knew Al's stomach would be churning. This great central defender for Liverpool and Scotland was not immune to nerves.

Al certainly had a nervous start to his Liverpool career. Signing in May 1977, Alan decided to take his summer holidays locally. Blackpool! He can't even swim, stupid idiot, so the sea was off-limits. Messing around on the beach one evening, Al managed to get done for streaking! He reported for pre-season training as if nothing had happened but he was met by John Smith, and must have thought he was for the high-jump. Liverpool's chairman looked at Al and said, 'As long as you can play, son.' He could certainly play. Bob hailed Al as 'quite simply the most skilful centre-half I've ever seen in the game' and I never considered such praise excessive. Al was elegance on long legs, and bright with it. He was a walking, talking record book, spouting stats and facts, so I nicknamed him 'Norris' after Norris McWhirter, the facts and stats man.

'Norris, you've got an answer for everything,' I said. Al could remember the minutes when we scored or gave away goals, and was always setting quizzes.

'In the year Liverpool lost only sixteen goals,' he asked one day, 'who finished as top opposition goalscorer?' The answer was 'own goal', three of them. As the seasons wore on, Al became cockier and his quizzes more fraudulent. Shamelessly, he'd make up facts, and if we caught him out, Al would always hit back with a question. Early on, Al and Terry Mac would have arguments, ending up with Terry asking, 'How many games have you played?'

'How many minutes have you played?' Al would reply. Not games. Minutes. Just to put us on the back-foot. The players just laughed. This was classic Al, brilliant on the defensive.

Big Al presented many credentials for captaincy. It was not just the looks, the grace as a central defender or the ready humour. What set Al apart was that Lady Luck had a serious crush on Liverpool's No. 6. Never in my life have I encountered some-body so frequently blessed with good fortune as Alan Hansen. If two people were sitting on 17 at blackjack, I'd put substantial sums on Al getting a four more often than the other person. No science explains why the sun always smiled on Al. No logic. It just happened. If he walked down the street, Al would spot a fiver on the pavement. At golf, Lady Luck caddied for him, a source of constant frustration to me. If we both hit balls into the rough, I won't find mine but Al will find his. His ball will be sitting up, winking at him, shouting, 'I'm over here.' It became a running joke between the pair of us.

'Kenny, I can lose a ball,' Al insisted. 'I have lost balls.'

'Al, if you lose a ball, you really have to lose it. You'll have hit it in the water, or on the railway line.' With such a guardian angel looking over him, Al proved a magnificent Double-winning captain for Liverpool, one of the club's greatest ever. Unfairly, Al never received the credit he deserved because the praise was too often directed my way.

After Phil's visit to the chairman and announcement to the Press, everybody knew his days at Liverpool were numbered. During the season, I received a call from Bolton Wanderers, whose request was simple.

'Can we have Phil as player-manager?' asked Bolton.

'Of course,' I replied. Relaying their request to Phil, I told him, 'It's in your best interests to go. Bolton's a great opportunity.' Liverpool were good to Bolton and helped out when they could. Bolton were short of kit, so Liverpool gave Phil some training gear to take across to Burnden Park. Leaving a great club like Liverpool was a wrench for Phil, but as he shook my hand, I couldn't detect any animosity.

'All the best,' I wished him. Phil nodded and was gone, disappearing from Anfield after 11 magnificent years' service.

At the same time, I took a call from Willie McFaul, Newcastle United's manager, enquiring about our other full-back, Alan Kennedy. Jim Beglin was pushing Barney, so this seemed a perfect opportunity to make a permanent change.

'No problem, Willie,' I replied. 'You can talk to him.' Soon Alan was on his way to St James' Park, or so I thought until Willie phoned, very agitated.

'Where is he?'

'He's come up to speak to you.'

'I've not seen him.'

'Honest to God, Willie, he set off to see you. I'll track the boy down.' Eventually, after much searching and message-leaving, I got Barney on the phone.

'Where are you? You should know the bloody way to Newcastle. You played for them.'

'Gaffer, I'm going to Sunderland.'

'What?'

I've spoken to them.'

'Listen, Barney, you're out of order. You need to phone Willie McFaul. He's really disappointed you never came to speak to him.' Alan had his way, though, and went to Roker Park, although it hardly worked out for him and he was off after a season.

Barney and Nealy were two fantastic servants who both made huge contributions to the success of Liverpool Football Club. It was sad to watch those famous full-backs go, but Liverpool needed new blood and a manager who craves popularity swiftly discovers a P45 in his pigeonhole. Any regard Liverpool players had for me as a team-mate was forgotten. I had to earn their respect as a manager and sometimes that meant being ruthless. Addressing the players in team meetings, I wondered how they felt about me now. Did they resent my promotion? How did they regard me as a player? A friend? A boss? I confessed my misgivings to Big Al one day.

'I miss the banter, Al. I know when I come in the room, and you lot are messing about, that it'll go quiet. I know I've got to go back out, leaving you to your little games.' Belying my public image of being surly and dour, I loved being in the thick of the banter, and I must admit some of the fun went out of football when I became manager.

My captain and I also discussed ways of bonding the team ever more strongly.

'What about the lunches?' asked Al, reminding me of the cost-cutting exercise that ended the meals back at Anfield.

'I'll get them going again,' I promised. 'If we all chip in, the ladies will put soup and something simple on for us.' The next morning, I called Anfield's three cleaning ladies, May, Theresa and Ada, into the office.

'We want to start the lunches up again. If we pay for them, will you cook?'

'We'll need to get permission,' said May.

'I'll get you permission, May, don't you worry about that.' Next stop PBR's office.

'It's important for the boys to have a laugh and a chuckle after training, Peter.' He agreed and the lunches were reinstated. May, Theresa and Ada stopped work at 11.30, cooked the meals and then went back to cleaning. For away trips, the girls heated pies and we'd eat them on the bus. The boys loved the three ladies even more now. The players' lounge became a lively place, particularly after games. It was really just a tea-room with a small area serving as a bar, a very well-stocked bar because a pal of mine worked at Whitbread.

'We'll give you three lounge passes and three tickets for the match,' I offered him.

'And you can have a keg of beer for the boys and boxes of wine for the wives,' he replied.

'Sounds like a fair swap,' I agreed. I loved this feeling of togetherness after the game, all the players and wives sitting about, enjoying a drink. Even if we'd had a tear-up, the opposition players were always invited in. A few punches and late tackles didn't matter when the players could make peace over a few beers.

As well as with Whitbread, I got the players a good deal going with Candy, the club sponsors, who made household appliances. A mate of mine from Glasgow, Jim McSorley, ran an incentive business. The idea was that people earned points and got rewards. With my backing, Jim took the concept to Candy, offering players for points in what was to be one of the most unusual and productive arrangements in Liverpool's commercial history.

As part of their contract with Liverpool, Candy got a lounge at Anfield. Jim negotiated a system with Colin Darwin and Ken Rutland from Candy whereby they'd vote for Man of the Match, the winner went into the Candy lounge and automatically received 200 points. As well as Man of the Match, we rotated players to visit the lounge. If a player popped in for 10 minutes, chatted, signed some autographs, it was worth 100 points, redeemable against Candy products.

'What do points make?' Lawro or Al shouted.

'Points make prizes!' everybody replied. The players soon expanded the points system. On one Liverpool flight, Al found himself sitting next to Colin from Candy.

'I'm not sitting here without 200 points,' insisted Al, only half tongue in cheek. 'You'll have to move otherwise.' A washing machine was worth 400 points, so a return flight next to Colin earned the family a new machine. The agreement worked an absolute treat. As one of the players said, it was like taking candy from, well, Candy. If any of my relatives needed a washing machine or tumble dryer, Colin or Ken sent it over from their Wirral factory when I'd racked up sufficient points. One day, I'd accumulated enough points for a real gem.

'It's the Candy washing machine deluxe,' I explained to Marina.

'What's the deluxe part?' she inquired sceptically.

'It comes complete with a plank of wood.'

'What?'

'You have to jam the wood between the washing-machine door and the wall, otherwise the water comes gushing out!'

When the machine was delivered to our house in Southport, I inspected it closely.

'This is not the deluxe,' I told Colin. 'You forgot the wood. I need the wood to keep the door shut!' Colin and Ken loved all that banter.

The Candy people were good as gold and slightly mad with it. On our golf days, after food and drink when it was getting dark, they'd park their cars right on the first hole and point the headlights up the fairway. After belittling each other's golfing prowess, a dozen of us would play up the first hole, all scores to count.

The boys from Candy liked a wind-up as much as a sporting challenge, and a particular target was the guy from Manweb electricity, Peter Hopkins, who worked with them. I got to know him really well when I moved to Blackburn. 'Hoppy', as he was inevitably called, wore a straw boater hat, which the Candy lads took great pleasure in setting alight at every possible opportunity. Hoppy would be standing there at the game, talking about the quality of electricity in the North-west region with smoke rising from his boater. Hoppy's great love was Leeds United, and on their visits there'd always be some bets flying around.

'A bottle of Champagne says we'll win,' Jim McSorley wagered. If we won, which we usually did, Hoppy would come in the office to settle up.

'I'll have a pint,' Hoppy would say. As Jim distracted Hoppy with an intricate question about Leeds' midfield, he lifted his tie and dipped it in his pint.

'Look your pint's ruined. Come on, have a glass of Champagne.'

'Oh, all right,' Hoppy replied. So Jim would hand him a glass that they'd drilled a hole in.

'Hold that,' Jim said, making sure the hole pointed towards Hoppy. Then Jim would pour the Champagne, which quickly fizzed out of the hole all over Hoppy's shirt. He never seemed to mind. Hoppy was used to the crazy ways of the Candy boys. When they hired a limo to get to and from the game, Jim insisted all passengers took off their shoes, and for some reason I never comprehended, Hoppy fell for this ruse. Every time Hoppy removed his shoes, Jim quickly rolled down the window and chucked one of them out. Hoppy would live up to his nickname by hopping into the pub, or wherever they were going, with one shoe on and the other in a field some-where.

If the Candy boys were my light relief, Old Tom Saunders provided constant, valued support. When I became manager, Tom was indispensable and we travelled all over, watching games together. In January 1989, we watched four in one day. First up were Bristol City, then we drove up to Wolves, stopped off at the Post House Hotel in Stoke, caught a game there on the telly, and then nipped to Crewe v. Carlisle – Liverpool were soon playing Carlisle in the Cup. Then we went home. Old Tom was never boring company. He'd experienced life, been in the Army, worked outside football and had stories to tell. A former teacher, he had been the youngest headmaster at Liverpool West Derby Comprehensive, and he understood how to bring the best out of people. If I was about to make a rash decision, Tom quietly voiced a constructive opinion, saving me from my mistake. 'It's my opinion but your decision,' he always told me. I valued the people who, like Tom, knew Liverpool Football Club and saw issues from a different perspective but always backed me. I was never afraid of people who questioned me.

Old Tom was always smartly dressed, suited and shoes polished, as if he was heading to church. He hailed from that generation who felt almost naked without a tie. His education was put to good use, helping me with *The Times* concise crossword. I had no chance with the main one – I always felt Poirot couldn't have solved those clues – but as I drove us between Anfield and Melwood, Tom read out the concise clues, asking me for the answers, even when he knew. Tom loved testing me.

His erratic map-reading certainly tested my patience. In the Eighties, retail parks were springing up outside towns, and we often ended up there because Tom thought the bright lights and pylons were floodlights. We really struggled in daylight.

'Is that it?' I'd ask, trying to read the signposts.

'I'll change my glasses. No, we've missed it. Turn round. Sorry.' Tom must have said that a hundred times.

'Kenny, you might not believe this but when I did National Service, I was put in charge of map-reading,' Tom announced one day. When I'd finished laughing, Tom continued, 'You'll probably believe this. One day, I led a convoy of a hundred Army trucks up a lane. Three miles we went. I was sure it was the right route but then we hit a dead end. All the trucks had to reverse out.'

'You've never got any better!'

I tried to be as well dressed as Tom. Many players who go into management prefer to wear a suit in the dug-out because it signals their new role. Being frustrated I wasn't playing any more, I just wore a coat. By the end of my first season as manager, any new suit would have to be double-breasted.

12

THE DOUBLE

IN THE wake of Heysel, the backlash against Liverpool guaranteed a closing of ranks at Anfield, bringing a real mood of defiance on the opening day of the 1985–86 season. Walking out against Arsenal on 17 August, I was strongly aware of the number of people on my side, wanting me to do well. The Kop were brilliant, and the staff were equally staunch. From the stands to the boardroom, I was reassured that everyone at Liverpool would give me time to make my mark as a manager, because of my status as a player and because of the painful situation Liverpool found themselves in. After Heysel, everybody craved peace and stability, and to focus only on events on the pitch.

For me, the build-up to this League fixture was a period of unremitting tension. Everybody seemed to have an opinion on Kenny Dalglish the manager. Good appointment? Bad appointment? One night, Marina and I discussed this national fascination with me.

'I keep hearing people are watching to see how I do, but why?' I asked. 'There's nobody takes greater pride in their job than I do. I want to be successful more than anybody else. Why wouldn't I be doing everything in my power?'

I had to succeed. I understood how much I must build on the work of Shanks, Bob and Joe. Ever thoughtful, Joe dropped me a kind letter. I wrote back, inviting him to the Arsenal game, and before kick-off, Joe sought me out, shaking my hand. 'All the best, Kenny,' he said. What class. Still haunted by Heysel, Joe didn't want to come to the game but he wanted to wish me well.

'Thanks, Joe, good to see you,' I replied. 'You know you're always welcome here.' But I scarcely saw Joe again. He left his love for football in a mortuary in Brussels. Joe also didn't want to be seen to interfere. An innately modest man, Joe hated feeling he was in anybody's way, particularly his successor, so he stayed out the road. That saddened me, because Anfield should always feel like home for those who brought Liverpool success and made such a huge contribution to the club.

With so many eyes on me, even kindly ones like Joe's, beating Arsenal was crucial. The team I picked was experienced but with a couple of surprises. Grobbelaar was in goal, Nealy and Kennedy flanked Hansen and Lawro. In midfield, Nicol, Whelan, Molby and Beglin lined up, with me behind Rushie. Everybody focused on my decision to start Jan Molby, who'd never really settled since joining from Ajax a year earlier. My reasoning was shaped by the memory of watching Jan for the first time, trialling for Liverpool at Tolka Park on 20 August 1984. Standing on the edge of the Home Farm box, Jan took a cross on his chest, kneed the ball up over the defender's head and volleyed it into the net.

'You've got to sign him now!' I laughed with Joe, whom I was sitting next to on the bench. 'If this Molby can do that, fine, sign him, do it at half-time.' No additional urging was required, yet Joe was never able to coax consistent performances out of the young Dane. Jan was only 21.

'Jan, we signed you because you're a good player,' Joe told him. 'Just go and play.' At Ajax maybe more tactical commands were given out. I couldn't believe such a creative player was languishing in Liverpool reserves and I couldn't wait to use him. One of the pleasures of my management career was getting Jan running big matches. Jan had unbelievable feet and I defied anybody to state categorically which was the stronger, because either foot could propel the ball at unbelievable speed towards goal. Jan scored against Manchester United in the League Cup with the hardest shot I've ever seen. Collecting the ball in our half, Jan strode forward and, as United backed off, Jan straightened and hit it with his left foot from 20 yards. Gary Bailey dived when the ball was coming out from the back of his net. Jan was a talented, versatile player. At Sheffield Wednesday one day, playing centre-back, he made three goals. Latterly, he suffered weight problems and was afflicted with ankle injuries.

With Molby in central midfield, I believed we would boss Arsenal. Putting Beglin on the left raised a few eyebrows but I felt he gave the midfield natural balance. Jim even crossed for Ronnie Whelan to head our first before I set up Stevie Nicol for the second. So there – I could manage and play. Liverpool were up and running. The relief I felt afterwards simply reflected the nerves in the build-up.

I knew the pressure would crank up again and it quickly did. In the opening months of my managerial tenure, Liverpool endured awkward times. Manchester United were flying, racing through their first 10 games unblemished, a fabulous achievement, and then Everton went eight points clear as Liverpool languished in the shadows. After we lost at Newcastle, QPR, Arsenal and Manchester City, one newspaper described us as 'the worst Liverpool side in 20 years'. Even accepting that some criticism was due, I felt such a comment was unfair, disrespectful and ignorant, but I knew the rules of engagement before stepping into the dug-out. A thick skin was required, a point the Saint made in his *Echo* column. 'Nobody likes criticism but Kenny will have to get used to it as a manager,' the Saint wrote. 'As a player he never received any criticism but as a manager he will be subjected to intense scrutiny, especially as manager of Liverpool. If things go wrong, he will get the blame.'

The Saint was only stating the obvious. I knew that if Liverpool slipped up, I'd be slated, and the barbs duly came my way. When we started improving, people talked about it being 'Joe's team', ignoring the fact that I'd made seven changes. Some players, such as Jan, were already there, just waiting a chance to express themselves. Craig Johnston was another. Having changed next to this charismatic Aussie in the dressing room, I was very aware of his frustration under Joe. 'He doesn't trust me, Kenny,' Craig said. Joe's caution was slightly understandable, because Craig was his own man, but I liked his energy. Brimming with enthusiasm, Craig had a gift for excelling at anything he turned his hand to. For a while, satellite dishes obsessed him. In the mid-Eighties, satellite dishes were still the province of MI6, but Craig got me one so I could watch Italian, Spanish and Portuguese football.

Another passion of Craig's was photography. Many of us mess around with cameras but not Craig, who really threw himself into it and had an eye for a brilliant picture. One evening, after Anfield emptied, all the players' kids were running around in the penalty area. Craig snapped a wonderful picture of my son, Paul, aged about seven, shooting into the Kop goal, and he made a life-sized print of it, which now hangs in a downstairs corridor of my home in Southport. Craig's love of photography faded for a while and he fell into music. He put a studio in his house and started playing the guitar. I've not encountered many individuals with such a diverse range of talents as Craig, who helped design the Predator boot, created a game show and developed mini-bar technology that registered your selection with reception. Craig was unbelievable.

Typical of his Aussie breed, Craig had a huge hunger for seeing the world. One year, Liverpool flew to Khartoum to raise money for underprivileged kids. With help from English donors, the Sudanese managed to build a beautiful hospital, but other parts of Khartoum were pretty bleak. Craig, naturally, went sightseeing, finding the bridge where the Blue Nile and the Red Nile meet. 'When the two of them join, it's the White Nile,' Craig insisted on telling us. Craig was so clever and well travelled that we believed him.

The big problem came when Craig wound up Bruce, whom he called 'Pally Blue'. Craig posed fictitious questions, so Bruce, who refused to admit to not knowing the answer, just made up a response.

'Why is the price of corned beef so high?' Craig asked. Nobody had a clue. How could anybody know? Bruce had a go.

'It's because of the tin mines in South Africa,' said Bruce. 'There's poor production so it costs more to make the tins to put the corned beef in.'

When Bruce and Craig engaged in their mind games, the rest of us backed off, laughing. For all his humour and many interests, Craig's main passion was football, particularly after Joe left. Training hard, Craig was one of the first players I knew who made it his business to look into healthy eating.

'Gaffer, you've got to get the boys into this diet,' Craig told me, showing me a list of lentils, rice and bananas.

'Get lost,' I replied, knowing Jan, Al and the boys would never surrender their pie on the way to games, and fish and chips on the way home. Yet Craig was ahead of his time. He realised the importance of rehydration and taking in the correct amount of carbs at the right time.

'What's macro-biotic?' Al whispered to me.

'Not a clue. A dance move?' We mocked Craig but his diet really helped him, giving him the sharpness he needed.

Sadly, Craig was his own worst enemy. He just didn't believe in his footballing abilities, and I could see that, when his form deserted him, Craig became depressed and the dark cycle continued. Several times during the season, I had to beat away this black dog of depression chasing Craig.

'Remember QPR away,' I told him during one rough period. 'It wasn't so much what you did on the ball but what you did off it. You give so much to the team, Craig. The players know it. The fans know it. I know it.' At least Liverpool had one magnificent season out of Craig Johnston.

If I possessed one particular gift for management, it was

empathising with players. I always felt a warm glow when I heard players praise my man-management, because to my mind that's the greatest quality of all. I learned from the masters, from Jock Stein at Celtic and with Scotland, and Bob Paisley at Liverpool. Tommy Docherty, and eventually Alex Ferguson, with Scotland enhanced my education. Without me realising it, all these shrewd football men instilled beliefs and ideals, particularly in the art of man-management. Although Liverpool's professionals found me demanding, they appreciated that I treated them as human beings, showing an interest in their families. That was little surprise to those who know me well, since an obsession with the family has always shaped me. A strong work ethic characterised my parents, and their industrious approach to life defined my DNA. Marina's family hold similarly strong virtues. Coming from a good family background was no guarantee of success, but it instinctively made me want a powerful family ethos in the dressing room. I've never seen a successful team that's not got a good dressing room. My job was made easier by the players sharing the right attitude – all for one, one for all.

Liverpool's form in my debut season as manager was greatly assisted by the arrival of Steve McMahon from Aston Villa for £350,000 in September, but he almost didn't join. This combative midfielder wanted to return to the North-west, moving closer to his Merseyside roots. When he eventually turned up at Melwood, 'Macca' explained how he nearly got rerouted by Villa's manager, Graham Turner.

'I told Graham I wanted to move back up to the north-west,' said Macca. 'When he finally agreed, Villa did a swap deal with a player at Manchester United. I told Graham I wasn't going to Man U and he said, "I thought you wanted to go back to the North-west." I meant a bit farther west!'

When Macca signed, the newspapers immediately declared Liverpool had finally concluded their hunt to find the successor to Graeme Souness, but I considered such a verdict unfair on

Macca. Like Graeme, Macca could create, score, put the foot in and get about the pitch, but comparisons were invidious. Graeme was unique. Besides, others came into the Liverpool side and ably performed parts of Graeme's old role. Liverpool's midfield had enough tough characters to give us a physical edge. Kevin MacDonald didn't make a bad contribution on the field, which was just as well because he was always complaining off it. First nicknamed 'Stroppy', Kevin was then dubbed 'Albert' after Albert Tatlock, the *Coronation Street* grouch. Albert grumbled about everything from the pitch to the weather and the food. He even moaned about other people moaning! Al and I listened to Albert chuntering away over something utterly insignificant and killed ourselves laughing, but Albert could play as well as whinge, and he was hugely important to Liverpool that season.

So was Ronnie Whelan, a quiet assassin who could put his foot in. No malice followed Vitch's boot into the challenge, just a wee reminder that Liverpool could show force as well as flair. Nobody really associated this likeable, skilful Irishman with hard tackles, but he often left opponents on the floor. When it came to stopping the other team, I knew Ronnie was the deadliest weapon in Liverpool's armoury, and he was also one of the most creative, developing an incredible habit of scoring important goals, particularly in finals, as distressed followers of Manchester United and Spurs will acknowledge through their tears.

With the midfield stiffened, we set about chasing the Double, but lost to Everton on 22 February. Bruce let one from Kevin Ratcliffe trundle under his body, presenting our neighbours with a victory even their most ardent supporters must have agreed was fortuitous.

'The next time we play Everton we'll beat them,' I promised Marina afterwards. As Howard Kendall's team led the League, it was a doubly damaging loss, not to mention the surrender of local bragging rights. Those three points to Everton became a turning point for Liverpool. I decided to push Jan just off Rushie as a shadow striker, using his accuracy to play in Rushie. Moving up the pitch, Jan stepped up a gear. He rattled in one goal at a frosty White Hart Lane, Rushie got the other, and that 2–1 win in March set us off on an amazing run. Until the end of the season, Liverpool dropped just one point, away to Sheffield Wednesday. That slip-up aside, our only other disappointment came in the semi-final of the Milk Cup when QPR got the better of us.

Craig brought energy and Paul Walsh scored a bundle of goals. When we got the ball in to his feet, Walshy danced around defenders. I was well aware that many centre-halves, particularly the old-school tall ones, found it tricky dealing with small strikers such as Walshy. He buzzed around as they swatted away at him ineffectually. They also discovered to their surprise, and cost, that Walshy could climb into the air, hang there and head the ball.

Initially, I struggled with the player-manager balance, being tougher on myself as a player than I should have been.

'Play yourself, Kenny,' urged Tom.

'But Walshy's doing brilliantly,' I replied, and he was, scoring 18 that season.

'It's difficult being a sub,' I told Tom. 'When I'm on the bench, watching, I get so tense and feel my legs tightening up. Then when I go out and warm up, I can't really focus on my exercises. I keep watching the game. It's better I stop coming on.' That decision made, I called in Ronnie and Roy for a meeting.

'Putting myself on is too difficult. If I'm going to be involved, it's best I start. Then if I'm crap, I can come off.' Ronnie and Roy agreed. When Walshy broke his wrist, I returned, playing the last nine games of the season as we accelerated towards the finishing line. The final hurdle was Chelsea at the Bridge on 3 May, a considerable challenge that was eased after 23 minutes when I managed to score what people consider one of my greatest goals. When Chelsea's keeper, Tony Godden, saved from Gary Gillespie, Rushie and Craig organised a short-corner routine. Chelsea managed to clear but Ronnie knocked the ball back in and Jim Beglin flicked it to me. Taking the ball on my chest, I let it drop and then caught it full on the volley. It could easily have gone in the enclosure but fortunately it flew past Godden. Those columnists who accused me of being awkward and unemotional might have rethought their views after my wild celebration.

'How did you score that?' asked some TV reporter.

'I closed my eyes and hit it.'

'You closed your eyes and hit it?'

'Is there an echo in here?' I laughed and walked off.

The title secured, we had other work to attend to – the FA Cup final against Everton at Wembley. On the eve of the game, another TV reporter asked my prediction for Cup final day.

'It'll be hot and sunny,' I replied. Some critics slammed me for what they perceived as flippancy, but it was my way of not giving anything away. Why should I reveal my thoughts on the Cup final, handing ammunition to Everton? I discussed the problem with PBR.

'Some TV people really wind me up, Peter. Some of them strap me up, landing me in trouble. I just think sod it, I might as well be sarcastic.' Anyway, that Cup final day *was* hot and sunny. Before the game, yet another TV reporter cornered me.

'Mr Dalglish, people call you monosyllabic.'

'What?' I replied, and walked off again.

By that tense stage of a marathon season, I was just hitting back with dismissive remarks. I knew it wasn't very informative, or even clever, but I tired of the attention. Putting on a show for the Press was not my style. Even those managers perceived as naturally flamboyant act up for the cameras. When the microphones came out, Cloughie was incredibly opinionated, but he may have gone home and been as quiet as a dormouse in front of his wife. People bang on about Jose Mourinho, calling him outrageous, controversial and colourful in public. In private, I hear, Jose's very sensitive. The Press perception of Fergie is not the real him, nor Rafa. Press conferences are deceptive. Having been stereotyped as dour and uncommunicative, I just couldn't be bothered to challenge that myth. I was too busy trying to win trophies.

The road to Wembley was not the most arduous. We beat Norwich in the snow, and overcame Chelsea, Watford and York before Rushie struck twice against Southampton to take us to Anfield South. Being part of the first Merseyside FA Cup final was a special experience. Driving on the bus to Wembley, I saw all the fans walking together, a merry mix of red and blue. I saw a father standing with his two sons, one holding a red scarf and the other lad clutching a blue one. Wonderful. This was the Mersey family on the move and I loved it. I also saw on TV, Scousers climbing through windows, dropping down ropes and pulling each other up, bunking in to the most famous stadium in the world for the oldest football trophy in the world. Nobody on Merseyside wanted to miss this occasion. When Wembley announced the official attendance as 98,000 I just laughed as there must have been at least 110,000 crammed in beneath the Twin Towers. The atmosphere was as magical between the fans as the rivalry between the players was intense. Swelling a lingering resentment over the European ban, Everton were now smarting at missing out on the League to us by two points.

For Liverpool, it didn't feel like a classic case of after the Lord Mayor's Show. After our exertions at the Bridge, we still had a full week to recover and prepare, but I could see that, mentally, my players were slightly drained. On the Thursday, Gary Gillespie went down ill so that meant Lawro and Al were the centre-backs. A troublesome knee caused me spasms of discomfort, and eventually kept me out of the World Cup, but I knew I had to start at Wembley.

'You need to be out of the dressing room ten minutes before kick-off just to reach the top in time,' I said to Hansen as we gathered at the bottom of the tunnel. Anfield South was a familiar home from home but our legs just couldn't get going. With every step up that long tunnel, the nerves grew. My hunch that this would be a gruelling afternoon was soon proved correct, and not until the second half did we find our stride. Until then, all Liverpool movement seemed laboured. Everton started far more strongly. Gary Lineker lurked on Al's shoulder, threatening to run through, and when Al switched off for a second, a rare lapse from one of the greatest central defenders ever, Lineker was away, released by Peter Reid's pass. Bruce saved the first shot but was unlucky the Everton centre-forward was there to tap in the loose ball. People pointed the finger of blame at Al but really the culpability lay with me. I'd lost possession and Reidy caught Al out with the speed of his pass to Lineker.

Undoubtedly a brilliant striker, Gary was not in the same league as Ian Rush, Liverpool's poacher supreme. As a predator, Lineker was more one-dimensional in my eyes. He hung around inside the box, waiting for the ball. Rushie offered more variety, more influence in the build-up. Liverpool's No. 9 was a force outside the box as well as inside. He closed down defenders and tracked back, contributing more for the team than Lineker did. I am such an admirer of thoroughbred attacking talent I could never dispute Lineker's area of expertise, or his success, but I just felt Rushie gave more and I'd pick him ahead of Lineker every day of the week. Gwladys Street might not appreciate the irony but, without Lineker, Everton won the Cup-Winners' Cup and the League. With Lineker scoring 38 goals, Everton won nothing.

At half-time, Howard's team still looked on course for the trophy. I glanced at Al, who'd long felt Liverpool were jinxed in the Cup, not having won it since 1974. Trophy after trophy had fallen into our clutches but not the FA Cup, and I began to think maybe there really was a curse on Liverpool. I looked across at Craig, knowing he needed picking up.

'There's forty-five minutes left,' I said to Craig. 'Don't blow it now, son. You've worked too hard to let it slip away in just one game. Let's not come off with anything left in the tank. Anything we've got, let's spend it out there.'

By the time we reached the distant dressing room it was almost time to come back out. The players were quiet. Needing to raise their spirits, I remembered something Old Bob had told me: 'In times of trouble, the best way to get players' attention is to speak softly because they have to concentrate on what you're saying.' At certain key points during this testing season, I'd raised my voice, shouting when required, but the managers I admired most in this tough profession were those who can go through the gears emotionally. If a player deserved some credit, protection or sympathy, I'd soothe them with praise, which made any angry outbursts more effective.

'If a manager shouts all the time, it washes over players,' Bob had said. 'Pick your moments.' Half-time in a Cup final with a group of shattered players slumped on chairs in front of me was not the moment for verbal fireworks. Quietly but firmly, echoing Bob's style, I told my team how close they were to turning a good season into a great one. Liverpool's tradition was to reach out that bit further, stretching for another trophy when other teams would give up the chase.

'Look,' I said. 'We've come a long way this season. We've won the League Championship. The Cup is there for us if we want it bad enough. When we come back in here, I don't want any regrets. The FA Cup final is not a rehearsal. This is it. Let's have a right go. Come on.' With that, we headed out into the fray again, a more confident step in our stride. Marching back up the tunnel, I thought I'd hit the right note with those words. My faith in the players was immense and if you can't believe in the team who've just won the League Championship, who can you believe in? I knew Liverpool were capable of taking away the FA Cup. We just had to get the ball down and play the Liverpool way.

I subsequently learned that Kevin Sheedy thought Everton had

Liverpool on the run, a miscalculation of the situation. Barring Lineker's goal, our defence was never on a state of high alert. Only 12 minutes was required for Liverpool's improved mood to make Sheedy reconsider his blinkered appraisal of the game's destiny. When Ronnie intercepted a pass from Gary Stevens, Everton's high line was always going to be vulnerable to a quick delivery behind it. Molby was beginning to make full use of Wembley's vast acreage and played the ball through, creating the opening Rushie loved best. One-on-one with Bobby Mimms, there could be only one winner. Rushie. 1–1. Who was on the run now?

Determined to regain the initiative, Howard gestured Everton forward. Alan cleared a cross and was desperately unfortunate the ball fell to Graeme Sharp, whose header brought a spectacular tip-over save from Bruce at his agile best. In television interviews afterwards, Bruce described it as a 'kangaroo save' because of the bouncing motion he made in leaping to push Sharp's header over. The Press feasted on this 'kangaroo' morsel from Bruce but it was a wind-up. It was not the first time Bruce flicked the ball over the bar rather than catch it and risk falling over the line. Kangaroo! I always felt Bruce's imagination knew no bounds.

Midfield now belonged to Jan. For someone lacking in natural athletic grace, Jan didn't half get up quickly to support Rushie. Just after the hour mark, Jan knocked the ball down the line for Rushie to chase with Derek Mountfield. The Everton centre-back was one of the best defenders in the game at that time, a player rarely beaten for speed or movement, but Rushie was a class apart. Controlling the ball, he looked square for a player and who was there? Jan. What a game Molby was having. He was everywhere. Taking the ball, Jan hammered it across. I missed but, fortunately, Craig had made another lung-breaking run and he rammed the ball past Mimms. 2–1.

Everton were on the run now. Sympathy for our neighbours and ancient rivals never entered my thinking. Ruthlessness has always been a feature of Liverpool's mind-set and, with six minutes remaining, Jan and Ronnie combined to send Rushie through on another murderous raid. 3–1. A still camera with a motor-drive captured the moment when Rushie's shot hit the back of the net, dislodging a camera. In the background was my secretary, Sheila, and Kelly and Paul jumping for joy as Liverpool won the Cup.

As we began to climb the 39 steps to collect the trophy, Al paused. 'Just getting my breath back, Gaffer,' he panted. So I stopped and Al accelerated past me. He just wanted to beat me up to get the Cup. The cheek! He deserved it, though. Al had contributed another superb season for grateful employers. While Al lifted the Cup, headlines were being prepared in salute of Rushie and Jan. In the dressing room, we all rushed to congratulate Kevin MacDonald, Liverpool's unsung hero that hot, momentous afternoon in north-west London. He got in among Everton's midfield, taking the fight to Reidy, reclaiming the ball time after time. Never one of the club's most celebrated footballers, Kevin Mac will always be remembered fondly for turning the blue tide back at Wembley in May 1986.

Liverpool were champions at celebrating and the party to mark the Double began in the Wembley bath, a big square tank about five feet deep.

'They must start running this on the Friday,' Al laughed. At that moment, Jimmy Taylor, a Liverpool fan and friend of the players leapt in with us. He was fully dressed – shirt, jeans, trainers, the works. Somehow he'd sneaked into the dressing room and just wanted to join us. As he surfaced from under the water, he said, 'If my time is up, I can go happily now. It can't get any better than this. We've done the double. We've beaten Everton at Wembley. That'll do me.' With that, Jimmy climbed out of the bath and walked away, a smile on his face and soap-suds in his hair. Laughter followed him out of the door.

When we emerged, it was less easy to celebrate. Liverpool had too much respect for Everton to gloat. The relationship between Howard and myself was fantastic. I knew he'd never have a pop at Liverpool and I certainly wouldn't at Everton. Howard was a superb manager for Everton, always close to his players, always wanting them to speak their minds so they'd do everything for him. Everton players had a strong bond with Howard and with each other, and with Liverpool in a strange way. We still see Andy Gray, Peter Reid, Derek Mountfield, Graeme Sharp and Kevin Ratcliffe for a chat and a drink. Back then, the hurt filling their hearts must have been so great. Everton lost the League to Liverpool after being favourites, and lost the FA Cup final after taking the lead, so this was a double whammy in every sense. That's why we kept the noise down in Everton's earshot.

Anybody who joined Liverpool was immediately taught the importance of being a good winner, of being sensitive to the anguish of vanquished opponents. I always believed this dignity in victory ensured that a lot of people outside Anfield didn't mind us winning. That tradition had begun during Shankly's distinguished era and been passed down the generations, so there was something wonderfully uplifting and appropriate to hear Liverpool fans chanting 'Shankly' at the final whistle. He started it all. Each Liverpool manager has carried the torch lit by Shanks. I never stopped to consider what winning the Double meant. Some of the papers compared Liverpool's feat to Spurs in 1961 and Arsenal in 1971. At no stage did I consider comparing myself with Bill Nicholson or Bertie Mee, and certainly not with a long night now in prospect. There was a Double to toast.

Liverpool stayed at the Mountbatten, a quietly elegant hotel on Seven Dials in Covent Garden. Heading down to the bar for some preparatory work before the night on the town, Craig and I got trapped in the lift.

'It doesn't get any better than this,' I remarked to Craig, putting my arm around his shoulder.

'What, Gaffer. Stuck in a lift with you?'

'No! Two trophies. Make the most of it, son.'

We did that evening. After laying the groundwork in the Mountbatten bar, I grabbed the FA Cup and announced, 'Come on, let's go down to Trafalgar Square. All the punters will be there.'

'No you're not, Kenny,' came a familiarly stern voice.

'Why not? The punters will all be there.'

'Exactly. Somebody might nick it. You spent all season trying to win the Cup. I'm not having you losing it now.' With that, Marina took the Cup off me. A shot of disappointment mingled with the alcohol in my bloodstream as my great dream of being in with the fans, savouring a trophy from their passionate perspective, faded. Professionals loved the occasion but supporters seemed to have more fun for longer. Punters could enjoy the build-up, the anticipation, the game itself and the party afterwards.

'Well, what about Stringfellows then?' I asked Marina, hoping for a compromise. Marina nodded, so the players, wives and girlfriends sauntered down the road to this celebrated nightclub, passing the Cup between us and waving to the punters. I looked proudly at my players, thinking what a band of brothers they were, strong men who watched each other's backs off the pitch and on. No cliques damaged dressing-room unity. For geographic reasons only, Liverpool's players split up when going for a drink back home. Southport boys, such as Lawro, Al, Vic, Macca and Albert, went out as a team. Over the Wirral, Rushie and Jan formed a good axis. But nothing could divide us as a team.

Arriving at Stringfellows, the players swiftly learned that the wives had been in the night before. The women were unbelievable. They all got on, all loved a night out, all seemed to share the belief that the game itself was an unnecessary interruption to the weekend's socialising. The wives attended the final but we were left in no doubt that it was a heavy burden for our nearest and dearest. They demanded we got to the final, of course. Every

August, Marina warned me, 'If you don't go to Wembley, you're in trouble.' Professional pride at reaching a final with Liverpool was complemented by the personal relief that the dog-house remained boarded up for a welcome few months.

Having half-recovered from a night at Stringfellows, we turned up at the airport with throbbing heads. Howard and his squad were seated in the front, so we had a slightly awkward walk to our seats at the back, particularly as Hansen was holding the Cup. Stuart Hall interviewed us, and as the television presenter asked me questions, Marina kidded around, pouring Champagne over me. Stuart turned his microphone to her.

'If Kenny does go to the World Cup, what will you do this summer?' Stuart asked.

'Easy,' replied Marina. 'I'll be looking for a toy-boy.'

Having shared a plane with Everton, we then shared a tour of the city. Liverpool couldn't really enjoy that because of our respect for the Everton boys, but I guess it was only fitting Everton did the bus ride. It gave the punters an opportunity to show their appreciation for the colossal effort put in by Howard's players. Hundreds of thousands lined the streets, filled with pride that the city had the two strongest sides in England. When the Liverpool bus finally came to a halt, I said to Marina, 'What do we do now?'

'Let's go home,' she said. On the way, we stopped at the chippie. Gary Lineker was outside in the car, waiting for Paul Bracewell.

'You're the last person I want to see,' said Brace.

'Everybody's got to eat, Brace.' The thought of ordering double chips briefly crossed my mind before restraint prevailed.

The next morning, when my head had cleared, I went in to Anfield to see the chairman and PBR. I don't have a cocky bone in my body but there was a definite spring in my step. A Double was not bad for starters. I was in for a shock. John Smith was in no mood for niceties. After gesturing for me to take a seat, the chairman barked, 'Why was Bruce Grobbelaar wearing that sweat-band around his neck after the game?'

'What?'

'We're adidas and he was wearing Umbro.'

'I never even noticed.'

'He shouldn't have done it.' The chairman then shook my hand and said, 'Oh and by the way, Kenny, well done.'

'No problem. I don't think it went too badly, so I'll carry on.' That was it. That was the Liverpool way. No basking in the glory, just a brief celebration, quick congratulation and move on.

Injuries prevented me from joining Scotland at the World Cup and Al was also omitted from the squad so we decided to treat ourselves to a break in Puerto Banus with Janet and Marina. The night before we left, captain, manager and wives went for dinner at a Chinese restaurant, which proved a surreal start. The owner had a bottle of '1986 FA Cup final Liverpool v Everton' Champagne behind the counter.

'Please take it,' said the owner. 'And well done.' As we headed off into the night, Al and I admired the bottle but drank its contents.

'Let's have a challenge. The couple who get the most free drinks on holiday wins a bottle of champagne.'

'You're on,' said Al. Janet and Marina were definitely up for the challenge. Heading down to the port, we went into Silks, a restaurant where many an hour can be agreeably passed. We paid for our first drinks then settled back, waiting for the great Dalglish–Hansen challenge to commence. Within 20 minutes, somebody sent over a bottle of Champagne, accompanied by a shout of 'Congratulations'. The Dalglishs and Hansens began fighting over the bottle.

'It's ours,' insisted Marina. 'We're claiming it. We smiled at them first.'

'No way,' countered Janet. This happened twice so the score was Dalglishs 1 Hansens 1. As we sat chatting, Marina noticed Freddie Starr entering the restaurant.

'Go and talk to him, Kenny,' said Marina, challenging me. She knew how shy I was. On this occasion, my reticence was obliterated by the alcohol, so I stumbled across.

'Hi Freddie, how are you?' He looked at me and smiled, shook my hand. I didn't know what else to say.

'See you Freddie,' I muttered eventually, returning to our table.

There's still an argument to this day as to who won.

At least the bill didn't leave me speechless, unlike Al the next evening. We were in a pizzeria and it was Al's turn to pay.

'Jesus Christ!' said Al on examining the bill.

'Alan, what is it?' asked Janet.

'It's bloody expensive.'

'Alan, don't make a show, just pay it,' said Janet. 'PAY IT.' Hearing the raised voices at our table, the owner came over, a man we knew well.

'Kenny, what's the problem?'

'I don't have a problem! Big Al does!' Al handed the bill over for the owner to scrutinise.

'That can't be right,' he said. 'They've put you down for twenty soups instead of two!'

'That's you out of jail, Al!'

The break was good, allowing me to re-wind and reflect on the season. Some critics dismissed my influence, claiming it was Joe's team, which was utter garbage. We'd changed the captain and the two full-backs, brought Macca in, and used Walshy, Jan and Craig more. We'd worked hard during the year, viewing endless videos, and made tactical variations at certain points, going to three at the back against more physical, aerial sides, such as Millwall and Wimbledon. At times, we played with Jan as a sweeper. The *Echo* lauded us as the 'Crown Kings of Soccer' but some columnists continued to criticise, and still do when judging my time as Liverpool manager. Just because we'd won the Double didn't end the argument in some people's minds. What mattered to me, though, was that Liverpool continued to employ me as manager. John Smith, PBR and the board made a very brave decision and winning the Double hadn't vindicated that. I hadn't earned my spurs, yet – far from it. The Double just whetted my appetite for more trophies.

13

CULTURE CLUB

A T THE start of each season, Ronnie Moran gathered the players at Melwood for a ritual announcement. 'Our ambition this year is to get into the Charity Shield,' said Bugsy. Achieving that aim meant we'd won either the League Championship or the FA Cup. Sadly, the warm glow of the Double didn't last for long and there can be no glossing over the painful truth that Liverpool's 1986–87 season was abject. The year was simply a succession of setbacks as we failed to meet Ronnie's minimum demand, although steps were slowly taken towards a brighter future.

After the 1986 FA Cup final, I went in to see PBR.

'Peter, I want to bring in Phil Thompson to run the reserves.' My reasoning was that Tommo would be more assertive than Chris Lawler, who was reserve-team coach. During a career as one of Liverpool's finest full-backs, Chris was nicknamed 'the Silent Knight' by Shanks. I felt Chris's personality was part of the problem – a nice guy, he was too quiet. Chris won the Central League twice in three years, but so Liverpool should be in contention. Roy Evans won it 11 years in a row. A change of voice might be helpful, I thought, a change of style. Tommo was louder than Chris, more vociferous. Shortly after I'd mentioned my plans to PBR, Chris went up to ask Peter about his annual bonus – bonuses were awarded at the board's discretion – and to discuss plans for the following season. Before

Chris could sit down, Peter said, 'Chris, haven't you spoken to Kenny?' Looking puzzled, Chris immediately came down to my office.

'I've just been to see PBR and he said I had to speak to you.' Chris must have known something was up.

'Chris, the first thing I need to do is apologise. I never knew you were going upstairs. I should have been the one to tell you. I'm bringing Tommo in.' Lawler looked bemused, and argued his corner, but my mind was made up. 'Look, Chris, why don't you stay for three months. You've got a better chance of getting employment if you're in employment. It's much easier for us to give you a glowing reference.'

'I don't know, Kenny.'

'Tommo's coming in. Think about the offer of staying three months.' Lawler came in the next day.

'No, Kenny, I want to go.'

'Well, OK. You need to go and see PBR. Get your finances sorted out.' Afterwards, I heard Lawler wanted to punch me, a reaction I understood. He was angry, but if I'd never made that decision, I'd have punched myself.

The disappointments began against Luton Town in the third round of the FA Cup with a 0–0 draw at Kenilworth Road. For a start, Luton refused to admit away fans, so the atmosphere was slanted unfairly in their favour. Luton's installation of an artificial surface further enhanced their advantage. For daring to suggest 'the pitch should be ripped up', as I did in the Press, I was widely castigated as arrogant. A joke did the rounds, mocking my concerns. Question: 'What's the difference between Kenny Dalglish and a jumbo jet?' Answer: 'A jumbo jet stops whining over Luton.' Very funny. Anyone with a footballing bone in his body knew that Kenilworth Road's pitch was a disgrace. If some of Luton's old players now find their mobility restricted by damaged joints, I'm saddened but not surprised, because artificial pitches took a painful toll. The main problem with Kenilworth

Road was the poor base, a contrast to the marvellous fourth-generation pitches nowadays. Laid on concrete, Luton's carpet lacked shock-absorbing qualities, so the impact of landing reverberated up the legs, battering the joints along the way. Ray Harford, Luton's assistant manager at the time, with whom I became closely acquainted during my time at Blackburn, confided that when he stood and watched training at Kenilworth Road, his back locked.

We just hoped that when we got Luton back to the green, green grass of Anfield, we'd teach them the error of their artificial ways but, and I still struggle to believe this now, they didn't turn up. Snow had fallen, and the journey north on the M1 was expected to be difficult, so Luton chartered two planes. Friends in the air business informed me that Luton booked two flight slots but never made them. Privately, I was told one of the Luton players hated flying, so they missed their slots and missed the game. On hearing that Luton would not be fulfilling the fixture, my first reaction was stunned shock. Some poor Luton fans had made it up by road. My second response was anger. How dare they? The third feeling was that Luton must be kicked out of the FA Cup. Sadly for all of us who wanted fair play in football, the FA bottled it. Luton's chairman, David Evans, was quite a powerful figure within football, as well as being close to Margaret Thatcher. When I learned that Luton had been reprieved by the FA, I felt that what should have been a straightforward football situation had acquired a political dimension. I still don't know why the FA didn't want to bring Evans to task.

At least Luton's absenteeism provided me with an opportunity for a wind-up. One of the players on the fringe of the Liverpool squad was a tall Scottish striker, Alan Irvine, a good guy who'd been on the bench at Kenilworth Road. We were in the Holiday Inn, and Alan didn't know the game had been called off. He came down in his suit and got on the bus not noticing the rest of the boys were in tracksuits.

'He thinks the game's on,' Hansen said.

'Let's have a wee bit of fun here,' I said and shouted down the bus for Alan Irvine to come up for a word. 'Look, we've got a problem,' I told Alan. 'We've got some injuries. How would you feel about playing centre-back?'

'I don't know about that.'

'Look, Alan. It's just like playing up front but you do the opposite.'

'I'm not sure, Gaffer.'

'Would you be more comfortable in midfield?'

'OK.'

'Just don't tell anybody you're playing,' I said. Alan was chuffed. He'd never started a game for Liverpool and he began preparing himself mentally. In the meantime Alan Hansen had told everyone about the wind-up. At Anfield we went as normal into the dressing room. The players sat down waiting for me to announce the team and have a chat about the game, but as Alan had no tickets I told them to go and sort their tickets out, leaving Alan alone. Alan was wandering around the dressing room in his collar and tie, waiting for them to come back.

'Game's off, Alan,' I finally said.

'I know,' he said.

Eventually, Luton made it north. I couldn't believe it when sod's law prevailed and another stalemate ensued, requiring another replay. Liverpool managed to make it south on schedule, but Luton had decent players, such as Brian Stein, Mick Harford and Mike Newell, and, unfortunately, we lost 3–0.

During that three-match exercise in exasperation, Liverpool endured another grievous blow with the loss of Jim Beglin at Goodison Park on 21 January. The challenge that broke Jim's leg came from Everton's right-back, Gary Stevens, and I felt it was a hard one. Only one person knew whether it was an accident and that was Stevens. Jim's injury was so horrific I almost retched when I saw the mangled state of his leg. Jim never played for

Liverpool again. He somehow managed a few games for Leeds United but really that was him over and done. That really saddened me because Jim was a very good player for Liverpool as well as an incredibly popular, gentle guy. Football's capacity for cruelty never ceased to disturb me.

A fortnight later, Liverpool was at Southampton, chasing a first-leg advantage in the semi-finals of the Littlewoods Cup, as the League Cup was now known. The 0–0 draw was notable for some disgraceful behaviour by Kevin Bond, and the intemperate reaction of his father, John. When Kevin spat at Walshy, our striker responded with a right hook and was promptly sent off.

Talking to the Press, I commented, 'I don't condone what Paul did but I can understand it. If somebody spits at you, it's hard not to retaliate.' Having referred to me as 'the moaningest Minnie I have ever known,' John Bond reacted by informing the papers that 'if Dalglish brought his kids up as well as I brought my kids up, he would be a happy man'. Well brought up? What was John Bond on about? His son showered a fellow professional in phlegm. Verbal abuse was one thing but spitting was a worse crime and the photographic evidence was graphic. With Walshy suspended, I took particular pleasure in scoring at Anfield as Liverpool reached Wembley.

We needed to beat Arsenal to prevent the season from being totally humiliating. Bad form dogged us in the League and Wembley offered our only salvation. When Rushie turned in Macca's pass midway through the first half, Liverpool's passionate support must have expected more incoming silverware. For seven years, Liverpool had never lost a game in which Rushie scored, so we seemed to be sitting pretty. Unbelievably, Charlie Nicholas rearranged the record book and the scoreline, although the identity of Liverpool's nemesis came as no particularly great surprise to me, since I'd observed his qualities on international trips. Charlie was arguably the most naturally talented footballer ever to emerge from Scotland. Jimmy Johnstone was a magical winger but moving past his prime when joining Sheffield United aged 31. Charlie looked the real deal, young enough at 21 to blossom further. In 1983, having learned of Arsenal's interest in the Celtic youngster, Graeme Souness and I sat either side of Charlie on a Scotland flight.

'Have you thought of Liverpool?' I asked.

'I wouldn't get a game,' replied Charlie, concerned that Rushie and I would bar his way to first-team action.

'Listen, I'm going to get pushed back a bit into midfield,' I told him. 'There's plenty of people at Liverpool. The pressure would not be so great on you to contribute. If you go to Arsenal, you'll be the "big saviour" with more pressure. You'd be better off with us.'

Charlie went to London. His return of 54 goals in 184 appearances at Arsenal wasn't shabby, but a forward of Charlie's calibre could have done more. He still got the better of Liverpool that frustrating day in April.

Our season was crumbling fast. Six days later, we lost at Norwich City, and I really lost my temper. As our ambitions drained away like water from the bath, Bugsy and I raged at the players for an hour. Eventually, my spleen vented, I left the dressing room and bumped into Dennis Signy, a reporter I knew.

'Kenny, I'd like you to meet Delia Smith. She's doing a column for us in the *Sunday Express*,' said Dennis, introducing me to the famous cook.

'Pleased to meet you, Delia. By the way, you've not got a recipe to turn a 2–1 defeat into three points, have you?'

'No,' replied Delia. Nor would she. Delia's love for Norwich ran deep. Still does.

With Liverpool looking vulnerable, the critics attacked me from every quarter. Typical was an abusive piece in the *Mirror*, claiming I was staring at 'the grim spectre of failure', adding that 'Liverpool will finish empty-handed for only the third time in fifteen seasons. It is not a prospect which will go down well on the terraces or in the boardroom where the chairman John

Smith has often been quoted as saying "winning is not the most important thing, it is the only thing".' The board were rock solid behind me, so I wasn't sweating on the mood of the chairman, who knew we were rebuilding in the background. But the most polite way I can describe the 1986–87 season is transitional, and the restructuring behind the scenes caused some controversy.

Geoff Twentyman, the chief scout who discovered Rushie and Al in the grass roots of the professional game, left midway through the season. Nobody could deny that Geoff did a fantastic job for Liverpool. Spotting players was a knack Geoff had an instinct for. Now, however, he kept talking about his arthritis playing him up, and night matches never appealed to him. He always took some-body with him. So I called in Ron Yeats, like Tommo, a person who commanded huge respect within Anfield as a former captain. Geoff was quickly employed by Graeme Souness at Rangers in a part-time role, far different from the full-time position assumed by Ron.

Before leaving, Geoff was credited with recommending John Barnes and Peter Beardsley to Liverpool, although Stevie Wonder could have seen those two were top players, but his greatest find was soon to leave. The season began with Rushie sitting in my office, expressing his desire to join Juventus because of the hand-some financial package on offer from a club rolling in Fiat money. Rushie was convinced Liverpool wanted to sell as the financial implications of the Heysel ban began to bite into club coffers, but I knew this wasn't true.

'Look, I want to keep you,' I told Rushie. 'I'll try to find a solution. I don't know what the position is, but I'll go around a few companies and try to get some commercial contracts if that would help. Do you want to stay?'

'The offer is so good, Gaffer.'

How could I deprive Rushie of the opportunity to set up his family for life by moving countries when a decade earlier I'd forsaken Scotland for England? So negotiations opened. Having worked assiduously at rebuilding Liverpool's shattered relationship with Juventus after Heysel, PBR was close to the Italians, so talks were civilised. Selling our prized striker was never the olive branch some perceived it to be. Selling him was a simple business decision, based on the prospect of £3.2 million coming in, and Rushie's desire to experience the lucrative Serie A. PBR agreed with Juventus that Liverpool could retain Rushie's prolific services for one more season, and he responded with 40 goals in 57 games, a marvellous testament to his ability, and also to PBR's skill in the trading game.

I couldn't understand why people kept arguing that Rushie's sale to Juventus signalled a shift in power away from Anfield. Exiled from Europe, Liverpool were painted as a club struggling financially, but we didn't need to sell Rush to survive. Liverpool played friendlies to cover the shortfall, competing in events such as the Super Screen Cup. As for Rushie's supposed craving for re-engagement in European Cup combat again, he never once mentioned that to me or to any of the Liverpool players. His farewell to the Kop came against Watford on 4 May 1987. Rush being Rush, he scored, threw his shirt into the Kop and departed like a hero as Anfield stood in an emotional salute. In the dressing room, everybody wished him well on his Italian adventure. Listening to the parting words from those Rushie spent so long with, I caught all sorts of comments: 'thanks, Omar', 'all the best, Tosh' and 'piss off to Italy!' Dressing rooms have always been quite cynical places and the only important people were those who remained. No ghosts could be acknowledged.

Enough respect existed for the boys to organise a surprise send-off. Rushie thought he was going for a quiet meal with Ronnie Whelan and their wives. Taking them into a restaurant, Vitch led them down some stairs to a room bathed in darkness. One of the most alert people on the football pitch, Rushie never suspected

John Barnes minus the garish clothes that enhanced his legend.

Never mind 'Fergie Time' – I started the non-existent watch routine!

As a new player-manager, I was always grateful for the wise counsel of Boot Room stalwarts Roy Evans (*centre*) and Ronnie Moran.

I made three crucial signings in 1987 – first John Aldridge (*left*) and then John Barnes and Peter Beardsley. They gave us renewed vigour.

Aldo shows how much a goal at Arsenal on the first day of the 1987–88 season means to him, as Digger Barnes and Peter Beardsley converge.

Right: Pedro, Quasi, Beardo – Peter Beardsley's nicknames were not always flattering but he shone in our charge to the League title in 1988.

Below: John Barnes was power and poise personified, rising above the vile racism of rival fans and swiftly winning over any Kop sceptics.

Left: 'This Is Anfield' – Bruce Grobbelaar touches the famous sign as we head out for another game during the run to the Championship in 1988.

Below: Being introduced to Princess Diana before our FA Cup final defeat by Wimbledon, for whom Liverpool had a strong mutual respect.

Above: Hillsborough – police inform me of the horrific events at the Leppings Lane End.

Right: Bruce Grobbelaar reads the lesson at the requiem for the Hillsborough dead.

Below: The Kop takes on a terrible beauty as the floral tributes to the victims of the tragedy in Sheffield spill over on to the Anfield pitch.

Colin Harvey and captain Kevin Ratcliffe lead Everton out alongside skipper Ronnie Whelan and me for the 1989 FA Cup final.

Bruce Grobbelaar punches clear as Dave Watson launches himself at a cross in our latest Wembley victory over our neighbours.

Ian Rush, back from his sojourn at Juventus, volleys us ahead in extra time against Everton, the first of his two goals as substitute.

Left: Arsenal's Kevin Richardson places flowers at the Kop in honour of those who died at Hillsborough, before the Championship decider in 1989.

Below: Steve McMahon falls to his knees in despair after Michael Thomas's last-gasp goal for Arsenal wrenches the title from our grasp.

a thing. When I flicked the light switch, Rushie was stunned to find the whole team sitting there, cheering, ready to bid him a boozy goodbye. Deep into a fairly alcoholic evening, Rushie suddenly appeared behind Marina, holding his farewell cake in the air. The cake was huge and covered in icing spelling out a message in Italian, not that Rushie would have understood it. Chuckling away, he looked over at me.

'Yes?' he inquired.

'No,' I mouthed back. I couldn't believe he would even think of it. Too late – BANG! Rushie brought the cake straight down on Marina's head. Assaulted by cream and sponge followed by the stainless steel salver, Marina shouted, 'Owwww.' Rushie's wife, Tracy, jumped up.

'Oh, Marina. I'll replace your outfit. I saw it in the shops.'

'Kenny said it was OK!' Rushie was laughing.

Knowing Marina, I feared for Rushie. Hell hath no fury like the wrath of a woman whose hair has been messed up and her favourite dress ruined. Marina was surprisingly calm, never uttering a word, just rubbing the bump on her head. She went to the Ladies, rinsed her hair, tied it up in a napkin and carried on with the meal. Thinking he'd escaped retribution, Rushie sighed in relief. How wrong he was.

The following Friday, we were all training in preparation for the final game of the season next day at Chelsea. While we were at Melwood, Marina drove to Anfield to wreak havoc. Her revenge mission planned with typical precision, Marina sought out Jimmy, the man who looked after the dressing room.

'Jimmy, I need to get in,' she said.

'No problem, Marina,' replied Jimmy, unlocking the dressing room.

'Jimmy, where's Rushie's bag?'

'Over there.'

Marina marched across, opened Rushie's bag and poured in the itching powder she'd brought with her. Knowing that I was a stickler for players wearing collar and tie to games, she removed Rushie's tie. On Saturday morning, Tosh phoned me.

'Gaffer, where's my tie? I'm supposed to be doing an interview for *Football Focus* in twenty minutes.'

'What are you taking about?'

'Gaffer, you know where the tie is, you'll be involved somehow.'

'Honest to God, I don't know.'

'This is out of order,' shouted Rushie, slamming the phone down.

Watching Rushie on *Football Focus*, my attention was immediately drawn to his garish tie, which struggled to match his shirt, and also his curious habit of scratching himself. The confused look on my face was replaced with a huge smile when Marina confessed. Marina is not a woman to throw herself into things half-heartedly and Operation Revenge on Rushie was not complete. Returning midway through the following season for Al's testimonial, Rushie attended a special dinner at the St George's Hotel.

'Hi Rushie, remember?' Marina remarked, immediately putting him on edge. The England team, Al's testimonial opponents, were at the dinner, most of them oblivious to the evening's subplot. Rushie sat there, watching every move Marina made. If she leaned forward for the butter, Rushie braced himself for an aerial onslaught. If she raised her glass, Rushie shuffled back in his chair, fearful of water coming through the air, but a far greater degree of sophistication underpinned Marina's mission. The seating plan had been arranged so that Rushie sat with his back to an emergency exit. When Rushie was distracted by the waiter bringing his main course, Marina made her move. I watched her nip out and then appear stealthily through the emergency exit. Suddenly, she was behind Rushie brandishing a cake. The England boys looked on bemused as the cake was smeared liberally all over his head and suit. The reaction from the England lads ranged from 'what's going on here?' to 'that's disgraceful' as all of us

Liverpool lads laughed. We knew it was just Marina getting her revenge.

Rushie's planned departure gave us time to prepare for the following season. At Christmas 1986, John Smith, PBR and I sat down for a meeting about players.

'There's money available,' said PBR. I'd come armed with a shopping list, which I then read out.

'John Barnes, Peter Beardsley, Ray Houghton and John Aldridge,' I listed, knowing the board would try their best. Ian Snodin, the Leeds United midfielder, knocked us back, going to Everton. 'Aldo' arrived within the month from Oxford United for £750,000. It grates on my obsession with value for money to admit that Liverpool could have had this prolific forward for free. Back in Shanks's time, John Bennison went round to Aldo's house in the course of doing his day-job – checking the gas meter – and Aldo's mum told him how good her son was. Benno invited the 15-year-old for a trial. Inevitably, Aldo scored but they lost 8–1 and his contribution was forgotten. Thirteen years on, and rather more expensively, PBR and I met Aldo at Manchester airport to sort out personal details. When Aldo signed, PBR rang Robert Maxwell, Oxford's owner, whose grasp of football's finer points could best be described as weak.

'That's it done, Mr Maxwell, thanks very much,' said PBR.

'Can I speak to John?' Maxwell asked. PBR put Aldo on.

'I'm really pleased for you,' Maxwell told Aldo. 'You might get a game for England now.'

'Mr Maxwell, I'm Irish.'

'OK. Whatever. Goodbye.'

Bought with the following season in mind, Aldo still managed to get a feel for the Liverpool way with 10 appearances, plus the bonus of two goals. Ludicrously, he received some stick in the papers, one belittling him as a '£750,000 misfit'. Rubbish. Having watched Aldo closely, I knew what he could bring to Liverpool. He'd scored enough times against Liverpool for us to be aware of his threat. On my final scouting trip, I admired Aldo in action for the Republic of Ireland, noting how he outstripped the centre-back. 'I didn't think you could track that quick!' I told Aldo after he joined.

His early critics ignored one thing – Aldo began the 1987–88 season on fire, having had five months to settle in. This was time enough to get used to playing for his boyhood heroes, a particular pressure I knew daunted some footballers. Liverpool born and bred, Aldo was a massive Kopite and just needed a few months to believe he belonged pitch-side of the hoardings. His stats were always going to improve when John Barnes glided into town. On the day Marina received her cake shampoo from Rushie, Barnes starred in Watford's front line against us, strengthening my desire to include his many gifts in Liverpool's attack.

'I've not got just a winger if I get him,' I told Tom Saunders. 'I've got a front man as well.' John took time and persuasion to coax north. Liverpool agreed a deal of £900,000 with Watford but John kept hesitating, hoping an Italian club would come in for him. Eventually, I set him a deadline of 8 June. Picking up a national newspaper shortly before the deadline was due to expire, I was surprised to read some unhelpful quotes from John.

'If I cannot go abroad, I would prefer to stay in London with a club like Arsenal or Spurs, and I simply cannot believe they are not interested in signing me,' John was quoted as saying. When this article appeared, causing consternation on Merseyside, John immediately phoned PBR.

'It's not true,' he told Peter. 'I've been misquoted. I know I am taking my time. I'm just thinking over your offer.' Peter relayed the details to me, immediately giving me hope.

'Right, let's strike while the iron's hot,' I said. 'Phone John straight back and tell him we'll meet him at Sandbach. We'll talk to him.'

The meeting took place and we voiced our ambition, impressing on John how he'd fit seamlessly into the attacking style I wanted.

When John said 'yes', my heart leapt. I had no doubt that 'Digger', as he was swiftly dubbed, after 'Digger' Barnes in *Dallas*, would be a sensation at Anfield. The only question mark I ever had over John Charles Bryan Barnes was his clothes. On attending pre-season training at Melwood, Digger appeared to have been given Elton John's wardrobe as a farewell present by Watford. All the Liverpool players were stunned by his flamboyance. In later years, I know Liverpool were criticised for the 1995 FA Cup final white suits, but I promise you they were a safer choice than anything John Barnes wore in 1987.

'Imagine if Digger designed the Cup final suit,' I told Al. 'The boys would look like eleven Liberaces.' Digger himself had the swagger to carry it off.

Even more recently, when his competitive instincts took him into the dangerous arena of *Strictly Come Dancing*, John continued putting on the glitz. On one programme, I thought he resembled a yellow bird, but the suit looked fine on John. He never bothered what people thought of his clothes anyway. One day at Melwood, Digger walked in looking like the fifth Beatle, wearing one of those collarless grey suits made famous by John Lennon and Paul McCartney. The boys immediately burst into a resounding chorus of 'Help!'

For all the showman streak, Digger was brought up with the right ethos by Watford manager Graham Taylor, and by Colonel Ken Barnes. John's father was a tall, straight-backed, well-presented man with a hunger for duty, a trait he passed on to his son, who worked his gaudy socks off for Liverpool. Digger was a magnificent athletic specimen, who had the determination to push himself harder and harder. That pre-season, Ronnie Moran had the players lapping Melwood and John kept shouting, 'When does this training get hard?' Bugsy grimaced. A week later, on 23 July, Liverpool were 3–0 down at half-time in Dieter Hoeness's testimonial in Munich's Olympic Stadium. Bayern were three weeks ahead of us in pre-season, so naturally fitter.

'Digger, it's just getting hard,' smiled Bugsy in the dressing room. John simply moved up another gear, joining Aldo in pulling it back to 3–2. Digger showed against the Germans why we pursued him, bringing variety to Liverpool's attacking play. We needed an outlet. If we got bogged down with our passing, here was somebody who was unbelievable at going past people, but John was so much more than a dribbling winger. He could pick a pass, playing the ball first time. Above all, John conformed to Liverpool's long-running theme of flair within a framework. A keen student of the game, John listened, learned, matured and blossomed into one of the most formidable, all-round attacking talents in the world.

Also making his dressing-room bow was Peter Beardsley, whose fashion sense I must admit differed from Digger's but whose sense of how to create and score was top drawer. I saw Peter as the perfect foil to Aldo, a second striker who linked with midfield. As a character, Peter was reserved, spending time with his head in football magazines. He was an anorak on football, impossible to beat in a quiz on the game. Before Peter arrived, I knew there was discussion in the dressing room about his teetotal tendencies, and I made sure the players were aware how highly management regarded Peter. When the Liverpool lads saw him play at close quarters, appreciating how his touch and vision would enhance the team, Peter was instantly accepted. When Aldo moved, Peter would find him, and his capacity for magnificent goals similarly endeared him to a demanding dressing room. Just before he set foot in this graveyard for weak souls, I marked the new boy's card.

'Peter, you know what dressing rooms are like, the lads have a nickname for you – "Quasi". I'm just forewarning you.'

Fortunately, his skill ensured his popularity and the lads eventually took to calling him 'Pedro'. Although needing a little time to settle, scoring in his second league game, Peter played his part as our grand new design was launched at Highbury on 15 August

1987. The cynics were watching, sharpening their knives, questioning how Liverpool would survive without Rushie and hoping we'd fail. Sorry to disappoint. Within nine minutes, Aldo scored after Peter and Digger combined brilliantly. Even though Paul Davis equalised, Barnes then crossed for Stevie Nicol's headed winner and we had the victory and display I craved.

A broken sewer under the Kop meant we stayed on the road for two more games while the repair men went about their unpleasant work. At Highfield Road a fortnight later, we ripped Coventry City apart. Nicol – christened 'Bumper' or 'Chips', which he loved – scored twice, with Aldo and Beardo also on the mark. Our 4–1 success was praised by defeated manager John Sillett as 'the best performance I've ever seen in the First Division'. That eulogy was much appreciated but I felt John was slightly biased. When I appeared on the television as a pundit for the 1987 FA Cup final, I tipped Coventry to beat Spurs. John clearly hadn't forgotten and repaid the compliment. After drawing at Upton Park, we finally appeared at Anfield and were given a heroes' reception by 42,266 punters, whose expectation levels had been heightened by the wait. Anfield came to hail the new boys and they didn't let the Kop down, both Aldo and Digger scoring against Oxford.

Opposing defences were blinded by the variety and speed of Liverpool's attacking movement. We came at them from every angle – through the middle and wide, passing and dribbling, scoring from long range and close-up. Rarely one to get carried away in front of the Press, I declared that Barnes's second in a 4–0 rout of QPR on 17 October was 'one of the greatest goals I've ever seen at Anfield'. This was the type of goal Liverpool never had in their locker before. Nicking the ball off Kevin Brock on the halfway line, John slalomed through QPR's midfield and defence before slotting the ball past David Seaman.

Aldo also beat Seaman, setting a new Liverpool record by scoring in a tenth consecutive League match. Aldo had an uncanny sense of being in the right position at the right time, but his game was so much more than instinct. An intelligent striker, he played the percentages, targeting the areas of most opportunity, such as the near-post run. So quick to melt away from defenders, Aldo could lose a marker in a phone box. He turned goalscoring into an absolute art-form, creating masterpieces that could have hung in the Walker Art Gallery. Plaudits were bestowed on many Liverpool players that season, and Digger and Beardo were constantly hailed, but neither contributed more than Aldo. Liverpool's exuberant form in the League could not have been possible without our clinical No. 8.

Comparisons were made between Rushie and Aldo, a newspaper mania that I felt to be lazy journalism. Aldo, Rushie and, more recently, Robbie Fowler, who joined Liverpool as a schoolboy when I was manager, were all different, all equally as effective. Aldo was the ultimate poacher, feeding off scraps and rebounds. He'd stand by the keeper, then suddenly drop off as the cross came in, making a yard for himself to meet the ball unmarked. Rushie's movement was even better, a touch quicker, running through and finishing left or right foot, and always more creative than Aldo. Robbie had the most skill of the three, conjuring up some magic by nutmegging a defender or dribbling past someone before shooting.

Two days after that QPR game, Liverpool drove to Dundee to play a testimonial for their defender George McGeachie. As we relaxed in our hotel on the eve of the game, I received a call from a photographer at the *Dundee Courier*.

'Mr Dalglish, would it be possible to take a picture of the Liverpool players eating?' the snapper asked.

'I don't like pictures being taken of the players eating. That's bad manners. But come in before dinner and take a picture before they eat.' The picture was duly taken and just before I went to bed, my phone rang again.

'Mr Dalglish, it's the *Courier* again. We've taken the picture and we don't know who one of the players is. Dark hair, quite short.'

'That'll be Ray Houghton. We've just signed him today. I forgot to tell the Press.'

Ray was tough as well as talented, bringing an extra energy to our midfield. When Ray came in, that was as entertaining a side as I'd ever seen at Liverpool.

Shortly after the Dundee game, Liverpool met Everton in a Littlewoods Cup tie at Anfield on 28 October. Even now, 23 years later, I find myself shaking my head at the memory of grown men throwing bananas and racially abusing John Barnes. His colour seemed to have been an issue for many people except those at Liverpool. 'He's not a black player,' I kept reminding the Press. 'He's a player.' We just laughed about this obsession with the colour of John's skin. In one team meeting at Melwood, I explained a certain tactical shape I wanted by moving figures around a magnetic board. Ten of them were red and one was black. 'That one's you, Barnsey.' Everybody laughed. Digger certainly did.

What happened against Everton was no laughing matter, and some of their fans' treatment of John Barnes was a disgrace. However strong John was, the vile abuse must have hurt him. He must have felt isolated out there on the pitch, unable to avoid hearing the monkey chants. When Digger arrived at Liverpool, some offensive graffiti appeared on the walls outside Anfield. Everyone within the club suspected the handiwork of Everton supporters, a feeling given greater credence on that shameful day in October. John and I never discussed the racism issue because I knew he had the personality to rise above such pond-life. Digger hardly needed reassurances from me about how fully supportive I was. He knew I was colour blind and interested only in building a good side, regardless of colour, race or creed. I bought him, which said everything to John about my belief in him. He had joined a club where staff still spoke in awe of Howard Gayle's

destruction of Bayern Munich six years on, and he lived in a city
with a huge black population. If some Neanderthals lurked
among Everton's support, Digger just needed to lay waste to
their defence, punishing them with the ball. Liverpool fans loved
him. Once they'd seen him play, it wouldn't have mattered if
Digger was green. One joke doing the rounds highlighted the
affection for Barnes. 'If I caught John Barnes in bed with my
wife, I'd cover him with a blanket,' one punter said to me.

The match with Everton proved a watershed. Even the media
behaved responsibly, tackling the racism subject strongly. Radio
Merseyside and Radio City were flooded with calls decrying the
abuse. Letters poured in to the *Post* and *Echo*, recording similar
sentiments. Action was needed fast, because the clubs were due
to meet in the League four days later. PBR and Jim Greenwood
put their heads together. Everton's chairman, Sir Philip Carter,
sent a message to supporters, appealing for restraint, and when
a murmur of abuse began towards John, everybody booed the
racists and the insults tailed off. We won again.

I loved watching this team, enjoyed seeing how much pleasure
it gave the Liverpool fans. On 16 January, against Arsenal at
Anfield, Liverpool scored a goal that even the great Michel Platini,
commentating for French TV, raved about. Digger unleashed
Macca, who sprinted to keep the ball in play, putting his foot on
top of it to stop it running out. The Kop roared. Macca's
momentum kept him going but he used the advertising hoarding
as a springboard to push himself back on to the pitch. He shuffled
his feet and slipped the ball through to Peter. Another roar. John
Lukic got a hand to Peter's shot but there was Aldo, right man,
right place, tapping home. A massive roar. Afterwards, one of
the reporters asked me if Platini would get in Liverpool's team.
'No chance,' I laughed. 'He's not good enough! If I can't get
into the side, nor will he!' I still swelled with pride that Platini
was so moved to praise my players.

Although records never excited me as much as trophies, I

must admit to eyeing up the challenge of going through the season unbeaten. Having equalled Leeds United's record of 29 games, we visited Goodison Park on 20 March. Predictably, Everton were incredibly fired up to prevent Liverpool making history in their back yard. Gwladys Street left Howard's players in no doubt what was expected of them. When Bruce dropped the ball, Wayne Clarke pounced and that was our unbeaten run up in smoke. Usually restrained in the dug-out, at the end of the game I screamed in anger and kicked a bucket of water. To Goodison's complete joy, the plastic bucket compressed, sending the water upwards in a jet, soaking me. Water dripped down my face, off the end of my nose, drenching my clothes. I paddled over to congratulate the Everton bench.

'Well done Howard,' I spluttered. 'Well done Colin, well done Terry.' Howard somehow managed to keep a straight face, unlike Colin Harvey and Terry Darracott, who shook with laughter. Afterwards, I went to Howard's office for a drink.

'Take us through what happened with the bucket!' Howard smiled. He, Colin and Terry were great people, powerful adversaries but respectful, too. I had a drink and a joke with them, but I was seething inside.

Further disappointment followed with the departure of Lawro, victim of the Achilles injury that accelerated his passage into management and then, especially successfully, the television studio. Lawro was a magnificent defender in his prime, brilliant at reading the game and so quick to rescue situations. He was king of the recovery tackle, sliding in to nick the ball back. Lawro was good in the air and composed enough to push up into midfield. Even from centre-back, Lawro would break out, play a one-two, keep going and occasionally score, such as the two against Southampton in 1982. Bob, Joe and I all gave Lawro the licence to go forward – pass, move, carry on the run and in on goal.

Lawro's exit triggered many deliberations about Liverpool's greatest centre-halves, and many within the club argued that Lawro and Hansen were the best partnership in the club's history. Tommo was a superb centre-back, who read the game like a book, and Emlyn Hughes was rightly hailed as a legend of the Liverpool back-four. Tommy Smith and Yeatsy were redoubtable sentries, barring the road to goal, but, for me, Lawro and Hansen were the best.

Highly popular within the dressing room, Lawro even had us laughing after he left. Appointed manager of Oxford United that March, Lawro reported to the *Mirror* offices to see Maxwell. The cameras followed as he strode confidently towards the door. He pushed and pushed but the doors were locked. 'You can never have got the sack because you never got in!' I told Lawro later.

Liverpool's dressing room lost others, too, and Ipswich were interested in taking John Wark back. 'Look, you've been brilliant for us,' I told Warky. 'If you want to go and get yourself some money, I'll not stand in your way.'

Shortly afterwards, PBR came to see me in my office. 'We need some money, Kenny,' Peter said. 'Would you mind if we sold somebody? The work on the Kop has hit us a bit. It's not desperate but have a think about it.' Paul Walsh was an obvious candidate, particularly when Spurs offered £500,000. 'It's a great opportunity for you,' I told Walshy, 'but I know you'll come back to haunt us.'

The wee man could play but he was never going to get in ahead of Pedro and Aldo. Liverpool were unstoppable and I wasn't going to meddle as this red wave flooded across the land, sweeping Forest away 5–0 on 13 April in one of the most memorable games ever staged at Anfield. The quantity of goals was staggering enough but what took the breath away was the quality. Ray set the ball rolling, cutting through the middle, playing a one-two with Digger, before firing past Steve Sutton. Beardsley, really flying now, maintained the pressure by lifting a pass over Forest's defence, ushering Aldo through for a brilliant finish, dinked over Sutton. It rained goals. After a short corner, Gillespie lashed in the third. Digger nutmegged Steve Chettle before setting up Beardo. Poor Chettle. He'd made the mistake a week earlier of claiming in a newspaper that he would have 'Barnes On Toast', and Digger kept twisting the dagger. Even as good a side as Cloughie's had no answer to Liverpool's precision passing. Nigel Spackman combined with Ronnie Whelan, Aldo sidefooted the fifth and the Kop went wild. Along with the five goals, we hit the woodwork five times and Sutton pulled off at least three world-class saves.

Forest left Anfield in chastened mood with Chettle having learned his lesson. Cloughie never said anything. On hearing the verdict of the great Tom Finney, my pride deepened. 'It was the finest exhibition I've seen in the whole time I've played and watched the game,' was Finney's reaction. 'You couldn't see it bettered anywhere – not even in Brazil. I've never seen skill at that pace.'

In the dressing room, I dished out the compliments. 'Different class, brilliant,' I kept repeating. At magical moments like that, I knew that unfettered praise was the correct response. If I'd picked out a mistake, I'd have risked losing the players. It was a time for acclaim, but for all the tributes, I knew the players wouldn't get carried away.

The title was soon ours and the only question was who would be voted the No. 1 player of the year by the Professional Foot-ballers' Association and Football Writers' Association. We feared the vote might be split because there were so many Liverpool players to choose from! Aldo top-scored with 29 goals in all competitions, Beardo got 18 and Digger 17, while Macca had been a driving force in midfield. In the end, Barnes's irresistible attacking from the opening minute of the season earned him the PFA and FWA prizes. As we celebrated those titles and assorted individual honours, Digger offered Beardsley a swig of bubbly.

'Come on, Pedro, get some Champagne down you. This is Liverpool. This is what you came here for.' Beardo refused.

'Try a bar of chocolate,' I whispered to Digger. Pedro adored chocolate.

The hope now building in my heart was that Liverpool could land a second Double in three years, which would be an unbelievable achievement. We'd been in great form in the FA Cup, knocking aside Stoke, Villa, Everton, Manchester City and then Forest in the semi, when Chettle's ill-judged 'Barnes On Toast' remark indicated to me just how terrified he was of Digger. Now Wimbledon stood in the way, but a series of unfortunate incidents troubled us up Wembley Way. A reporter whom Bob knew went round to his house to do a piece on his years at Liverpool. Bob thought the interview was over, Jessie fetched the tea and biscuits, and Bob maybe said a few things about players he didn't expect to be printed. On reading these, Aldo retaliated, defending himself. I was furious that Bob had got strapped up by a newspaper, and I saw how this incident seriously affected his health and confidence. Bob Paisley was the least controversial manager. He thought he was talking to a friend. Bob deserved more respect, and I didn't want distractions on the eve of the Cup final. Eventually, Aldo and Bob posed for a picture, shaking hands, and an embarrassing episode for the club ended.

On the Tuesday night before the Cup final, our self-inflicted wounds intensified when Gary Gillespie and Nigel Spackman clashed heads in the hurly-burly of a game against Luton. Liverpool's medical men patched up the pair but it was hardly ideal preparation for the aerial onslaught promised by Wimbledon's John Fashanu.

Another problem invaded the Liverpool camp, causing a particularly difficult challenge to my management skills. After his sister Faye suffered an horrendous accident, Craig's mood darkened almost to the point of depression. He had been becoming disillusioned with football anyway, and Faye's woes simply accelerated him towards the exit. On 12 May, two days before the Cup final, Craig revealed in an exclusive article in a tabloid newspaper that he was leaving: 'I hate being a footballer – I quit.' On reading the piece, I hit all points of the emotional compass. I was livid at the timing of the story and the very real possibility of it being an issue in the dressing room. Craig compromised Liverpool's Cup final preparations. Of course, his plight provoked sympathy. Faye needed her brother and he responded selflessly. Privately, what deeply annoyed me was that I'd contacted all the Fleet Street editors, requesting they avoid running stories about Faye's accident, but now I had to contend with his outburst splashed everywhere. A temptation presented itself to rid Liverpool of this problem immediately by sending Craig Johnston packing. Wembley was daunting enough for the fully focused and I felt that his attention clearly wasn't on the game. However, determined to avoid a rash decision, I concentrated on the cold, calculated argument of what was best for the team. Craig was never going to wear a shirt numbered from 2 to 11. The bench was always the limit of his ambition and I was weighing up between Craig's energy and the variety of options Vitch gave me in midfield.

'If this is going to be Craig's last game, he could come on and bang one in,' I said to Old Tom. Growing in my mind was the image of the fairy-tale ending, of Craig coming off the bench, and scoring the winner for Faye. That reaction was unprofessional, weak in management terms, but for once I found myself looking at the FA Cup through a romantic prism. 'And Vitch is struggling in training,' I reminded Tom. I'd come to a decision but, unfortunately, it proved to be the wrong one. I should have had Ronnie Whelan in reserve, not Craig. Apologising is not my style but I've since acknowledged to Vitch the error of my ways. Omitting him was cruel. He'd had a poor week in training, and was still hunting form after injury, but I overlooked that Ronnie was also the man for the big occasion. Vitch enjoyed scoring goals at Wembley. When I told Ronnie he wasn't even on the bench, his mature, restrained reaction simply reminded me that he was the ultimate professional. A lot of footballers would have chosen the moment to begin launching toys from the pram. Not Vitch.

The one sustained light note heard on the eve of Wembley was our Cup final song, 'The Anfield Rap', written largely by Craig and recorded in a studio in Bootle. As Mersey beats go, Liverpool's effort was never going to embellish the special legacy handed down by the Beatles, but 'The Anfield Rap' did contain some memorable lines –'I come from Jamaica, my name is John Barn-es; when I do my thing the crowd go bananas.' Digger was good at rapping but otherwise the musical merits of the squad were limited. Macca fancied himself as Bobby Darin, launching into 'Things' at every opportunity, but the rest of us couldn't hold a note. We all loved a singsong at the Christmas party or on a day out at Aintree, but the musical world never promised a second career. 'The Anfield Rap' was fun, though. Making a record is part of the unique nature of the FA Cup, an event that is so much more than a game. Wembley imposed many demands – do the song, get tickets for family and friends, measure up for the suits, get the shirt and tie, polish the shoes and, by the way, as a thousand phone-calls made clear, don't forget tickets for family and friends. Everybody loves a day out at Wembley.

Many myths attach themselves to FA Cup finals and none more so than the climax of the 1988 competition. To my eternal frustration, it has become accepted wisdom in footballing circles that Liverpool, despite our imperious form in the League, lost the Cup final in the tunnel because we couldn't handle the intimidation handed out by Vinnie Jones, John Fashanu and the rest of the self-styled Crazy Gang. All the shouting and posturing done by the Wimbledon players before kick-off was solely for their own benefit, to psyche themselves up, not to threaten Liverpool. On stepping from the dressing room and witnessing what can only be described as a war-dance, my instant reaction was that Bobby Gould's players were terrified. No one genuinely calm and collected would shout and bawl like that. Wimbledon's antics were utterly predictable as we'd played them before. We weren't naïve and we knew the script.

Wimbledon operated differently from Liverpool. Their players were incentivised for individual achievements while I always refused players goal bonuses in their contracts. Why would I pay somebody a bonus when that might make him decide to try for goal himself when a team-mate was better placed? Wimbledon's direct, uncompromising style did not fit into my vision of how football should be played, and I wouldn't watch them on television, but I admired their dogged attitude. The embodiment of Wimbledon's philosophy was Vinnie, a muscular, tattooed ball-winner who occasionally crossed the line. When Wimbledon visited Anfield that March, the ball broke between Vinnie and me in the middle of the pitch. I knew instantly this was the type of situation where bones were broken and seasons ended. Vinnie would never pull out, so as he went in for the ball, I angled my challenge to protect myself, catching him on the leg. Vinnie was poleaxed, for once a victim and a furious one. Climbing to his feet, Vinnie stared me in the eyes and snarled, 'If you'd broken my leg, I'd have stabbed you.'

'Do yourself a favour,' I retorted, 'get lost.' This was the rhetoric and behaviour of the schoolyard, almost guaranteeing that bad blood continued to flow. A minute later, Vinnie and I found ourselves in a similar position, contesting a bouncing ball near the halfway line. With the temperature having risen following our previous altercation, I sensed an appointment with Vinnie's elbow. Before he could make contact, I nudged his elbow, knocking him off-balance and leaving his elbow swishing through thin air rather than my nasal passages. To my great private delight, the referee penalised Vinnie for a foul, increasing my amusement by bringing out a yellow card and waving it in his face.

'Don't you worry,' the ref said to me, 'I'll look after you.'

'Don't you worry,' I replied, 'I can look after myself!'

The only retaliation Vinnie managed was via the headlines on the following Monday, and words were never going to hurt me as much as elbows. One piece had Vinnie promising 'to rip off Dalglish's ear and spit in the hole'. Charming. Such statements can return to haunt people, as Vinnie learned to his embarrassment one evening in the piano bar in La Manga. Walking into the room, Marina and I spotted Vinnie sitting at a table with his wife, Tanya, enjoying a quiet drink. Vinnie came over.

'I think he's got lovely ears,' Marina said to Vinnie. 'Kenny's ears are nice. Why would you want to twist them off and spit in the hole?' Vinnie froze, not knowing how to react.

'Marina, Marina, I didn't say that,' he stuttered, trying to change the subject by asking, 'Have you met my wife?' Marina and I laughed.

We were only winding Vinnie up and shared a few drinks with him and his family. No animosity coloured my thinking towards Wimbledon's old enforcer in La Manga, nor during the 1988 Cup final. The simple, frustrating truth about that game is that Liverpool played beneath the high standards that characterised our thrilling League campaign. Similarly galling was the fabrication that Wimbledon outwitted us. Don Howe, Gould's assistant and a coach steeped in the game, had the foresight to move Dennis Wise across to help Clive Goodyear combat Digger, but doubling up on John Barnes was hardly a new concept in a season when many teams tried every trick in the tactics book to deal with the Footballer of the Year, usually unsuccessfully. Just as it was unadulterated fiction that Liverpool were terrorised in the tunnel, it was an even greater fallacy that Wimbledon's tactics were in any way original.

The Cup final story line could have been so different if the referee, Brian Hill, had shown more common-sense, applying the advantage rule when Peter rounded Dave Beasant, Wimbledon's keeper. To groans from everybody associated with Liverpool, Hill instead brought the play back for a free-kick to us. Compounding that error, Hill then awarded Wimbledon a free-kick when Stevie

Nicol challenged Terry Phelan fairly. Our defending was still poor, allowing Lawrie Sanchez to steal in, reach Wise's ball and flick it past Bruce. All my annoyance that Hill had made a wrong decision was forgotten in my anger about our failure to defend. Gary and Nigel had to take on the big Wimbledon guys. Anyone donning the Liverpool shirt was immediately made aware of the requirements that go with the strip. A major trophy was up for grabs and a minor head wound was no excuse.

We were thrown a lifeline when Aldo was brought down by Goodyear. As Aldo addressed the penalty, the reassuring memory of his 11 previous successful conversions that season calmed my nerves. Even when Wise engaged in some very obvious sledging before the kick, my money was still on Aldo sticking the ball past Beasant. Aldo was no stranger to opponents attempting to ruin his concentration, such was his feared reputation from 12 yards. When Aldo's kick was saved by Beasant, no blame could be laid at the door of Liverpool's distraught No. 8, whose goals and commitment helped get us to Wembley, nor any credibility given to the effect of Wise's bad-mouthing. Sometimes I just had to note the brilliance of a keeper and Beasant had done his homework. Wimbledon's keeper reckoned that if Aldo checked during his run-up, he would put the ball to his right. If he flowed without pause towards the ball, Aldo would place the kick to his left. Aldo actually took a decent penalty, which was prevented from reaching its destination by a great save from a well-prepared keeper.

Our conquerors showed great dignity in victory, Vinnie and Fash moving among the fallen, wishing us good luck for next season. The Press slaughtered Wimbledon for their physical style, but Liverpool always had a great relationship with Vinnie and Fash. They respected Liverpool because we respected Wimbledon. We never felt superior to them. Football's big enough to accommodate contrasting philosophies.

Up in the Wembley gantry, the BBC's John Motson was

concluding excitedly that 'the Crazy Gang have beaten the Culture Club'. That line has gone down in commentary folkore and it was impossible to argue with Motty's *bon mot*. Wimbledon loved being called the Crazy Gang and Liverpool were a cultured club, although Boy George might not be too happy. Anyway, I couldn't care how Liverpool's demise was described – defeat prompted only sorrow, however eloquent the commentator. After all the beauty of our football throughout the season, after all the garlands draped around the necks of my players, Wembley was an unmitigated disaster and it hurt badly.

My mood began to lift later that summer, during a trip to La Coruna for the Herrera tournament against Atletico Madrid and Real Sociedad. Just after landing in Spain, PBR pulled me to one side.

'Kenny, would you like Rushie back?' he asked.

'Peter, behave yourself,' I replied.

Having stayed in discreet contact with Rushie, I'd gained the definite impression that he wasn't completely happy with life in Italy, but he was doing well at Juventus. A falsehood has grown over Rushie's time in Serie A, depicting him as a failure when actually his strike-rate of eight goals in 29 appearances was a good return in such a defensive league. Craig having fixed me up with satellite television, I tuned in to Rai Uno to watch Rushie. My Italian ran to 'oggi' and 'domani', today and tomorrow, so at least I knew when the match was on. The commentary could have been in Greek for all I knew but I didn't need any words to explain Rushie's performance. I saw all the hard work he put in, the closing down of defenders, and shared his frustration at his being largely isolated in attack. I also knew PBR was still in contact with Juventus.

A couple of days after PBR first mentioned it, he and I were enjoying a very pleasant lunch with members of the Merseyside press, John Keith, Colin Wood and Mike Ellis, good men to have a good meal with. Halfway through the meal, the waiter came over to inform PBR that a call had come through for him. As Peter walked back to the table, his smile signalled a momentous event. When the journalists were distracted by some line of jocularity, Peter leant across and whispered, 'Kenny, we've got him, he's coming back. We've agreed it with Juventus, he's coming back.' Somehow I managed to maintain control, not spill my coffee in the excitement and not mention anything that the Press lads might pick up on. How we kept Rushie's return quiet was a miracle.

On 18 August, I drove to Manchester airport to meet him. PBR and I joked about my providing a personalised taxi service to make sure Rushie didn't run. In truth, Rushie was delighted to be home. When I was asked by the *Irish Times* what Rushie had told me about life in Italy, I replied, 'He said it was like playing in a foreign country.' This quip became accepted as coming from Rushie himself, and I happily take the blame for that! Where I can plead total innocence is for Rushie's remark when he arrived at Turin airport to be met by 10,000 cheering Juventus fans, beseeching him to say something. Rushie stood at the top of the plane steps and declared, 'Welcome.' People say Rushie is not the brightest but he was a bloody Cambridge don at football and, for me, that's all that mattered. When I hear him on TV now, Rushie always impresses me with his thoughtful comments, a world away from the shy 'Omar'.

'Rushie is back' Liverpool fans chanted when the returning hero appeared at the Charity Shield game at Wembley. We'd met Bugsy's demand of qualifying for this meeting between champions and FA Cup-winners. Our next visit to Wembley was to prove the most emotional in Liverpool's long history.

14

HILLSBOROUGH

RETRACING the steps and memories of Saturday, 15 April 1989, is a soul-destroying task that fills me with pain and anger. Twenty-one years have passed but I can hardly bring myself to write or say its name – Hillsborough haunts me still. Drawn to face Nottingham Forest at the home of Sheffield Wednesday for the second FA Cup semi-final in succession, we drove across the Pennines on the Friday after a brisk morning training session at Melwood. We arrived at the Hallam Towers Hotel mid-afternoon after roadworks on the M1 slowed our journey, a frustration I noted with a shrug, little realising the devastating consequences of all the cones and contra-flow.

As a manager, I trusted the authorities to get the team safely and securely to the ground, expecting them to do the same for supporters who travelled 24 hours behind us. Having experienced the roadworks, I assumed the police would make allowances for the fans' journey to Hillsborough. Planning was done weeks ahead, meaning ample time was available to notify everybody, including the FA, about delays. I strongly feel that the descent towards disaster at Hillsborough began with the lack of communications between the police forces of the various counties. Why didn't they talk? Why didn't South Yorkshire police contact their colleagues on Merseyside and tell them to advise punters to leave early? Lines of communication existed, as was verified on the Monday, when we returned from Anfield to visit the injured in hospital, a trip requiring the input of three separate police forces. We were given an escort by Merseyside police, then Greater Manchester police and finally South Yorkshire police. Radio contact eased the relay through the counties. If communication was in place for the Liverpool team, why not for the Liverpool supporters? Somebody screwed up.

Holed up at the Hallam Towers, we were cocooned from the gathering storm. In the morning, a bright sunny day, I took the boys for a stroll, giving them the chance to stretch their legs before the pre-match meal. Everything was normal, just another match-day shaped by long-established routine. Just before 1 p.m., I talked to Ronnie and Roy about including Al against Forest. Injured at La Coruna at the start of the season, Al had been back in training for just a few weeks, so this was a gamble. 'It's a semi-final, a big game, and I need Al's experience,' I explained. They nodded, the two of them having faith in Al's ability to step back in without trouble. I sent Roy upstairs to find Al.

'Look, we're going to play you,' I said to Al when he appeared.

'Oh, I can't play. I'm not ready.'

'It's not your problem, Al, it's mine. I'll take responsibility. You're playing. You're not going to be captain. It's not fair on Vitch. He's been captain all season while you've been injured.'

'No problem, Gaffer.' With that, we climbed on the coach for the short hop to the stadium.

I used to enjoy visiting Hillsborough, old-fashioned and atmospheric with its giant Kop, steel girders across the middle of one stand and slope on the pitch. Before 15 April 1989, whenever I set foot there, Hillsborough reminded me of the lengthy history of English football. Along with Villa Park and, occasionally, Elland Road, Hillsborough was a traditional semi-final venue, a stadium trusted by the FA, but I knew from internal discussions at Anfield that Liverpool were unhappy about being given one particular stand, the Leppings Lane End. Liverpool's feeling was that the Kop was more suitable, providing sufficient space to accommodate our bigger support. Forest were loyally followed, passionately so, but not with the same numbers as Liverpool. Giving us 24,000 tickets for the Leppings Lane End, as opposed to the 28,000 handed to Forest for the Kop, was blatantly wrong, patently failing to reflect the respective size of supports.

I understand that, in mitigation, the authorities pointed to the same system and allocation being in place the previous season with no tragic outcome, although even then PBR requested the Kop for Liverpool, just as he did in 1989, because he felt the FA's logic was flawed. Anybody who has dipped into the history books will have seen it chronicled that crushing was reported at Hillsborough in 1981, during a semi-final between Spurs and Wolves. I strongly believe that Hillsborough was an accident waiting to happen.

According to the authorities, the reason behind Forest being granted the Kop was simplicity of travel plans. From my frequent experience of trekking to Hillsborough, I dispute the argument that it was easier for Forest fans, arriving from the south, to access the Kop. Both sets of supporters were instructed to approach Hillsborough the same way, coming off the M1 at Junction 36 and being funnelled along the A61 towards the Kop. Whether fans were coming south down the motorway from Liverpool or driving north from Nottingham, traffic flowed inexorably towards the Kop. Reaching the Leppings Lane End, or West Stand as it was also known, was complicated whichever direction fans were coming from. Liverpool supporters, delayed by roadworks, faced a race against time to make Leppings Lane before the 3 p.m. kick-off.

Even early on, the police could have seen the usual match-day flow of people was merely a trickle. From their own evidence, the police acknowledged that by 2 p.m. only 12,000 fans had entered the ground, 8,000 fewer than at the same time a year before. The West Stand pens 1, 2, 6 and 7 were nearly empty but 3 and 4 were filling. In his subsequent report, Lord Chief

Justice Taylor was critical of the fact that Liverpool fans had only 23 turnstiles through which to enter their areas while Forest had 60. I'm no architect or engineer but there seemed to be a serious design flaw, particularly as those Liverpool fans with tickets for the North Stand could access it only via the Leppings Lane. I know. My son Paul was in that area.

The configuration of Hillsborough should have been a concern – and problems had arisen in 1981 – despite the 1988 semi-final passing off without issue. But whatever the stadium's imperfections, nothing can deflect me from my steadfast opinion that the Hillsborough disaster was rooted in bad management. Nobody could have anticipated such a tragedy but when problems materialised, when Liverpool fans began arriving late through no fault of their own, those in charge should have reacted better. Unfortunately, the police officer running operations at Hillsborough that day was doing his first game. Much of the blame for the tragedy must lie with Chief Superintendent David Duckenfield. A policeman's job in any crisis is to think on his feet, yet Duckenfield froze.

By 2 p.m., and aware that fans were still stuck on the motorway, Duckenfield should have contemplated telling the referee, Ray Lewis, to delay kick-off. The tie wasn't live so there was no fear of upsetting the broadcasters, and neither team would have minded waiting another 15 or 20 minutes. A few players would have muttered, 'what's going on?' but the decision would have been accepted. Ray, a good man and a very good referee, wouldn't have objected, and the FA couldn't have argued either. The fact that a Tannoy announcement was made at 2.15, requesting fans in pens 3 and 4 to move forward, indicated that the police knew they had a problem, but why not take more substantial measures than a few words over the public-address system? The kick-off should have been put back there and then with information relayed via BBC radio to fans still on the road. Police outside the Leppings Lane could have told supporters they needn't rush. As I learned from the Taylor Report, the police discussed delaying the kick-off shortly before 2.30 but then ruled out the possibility, and this terrible indecision was to prove fatal.

When the boys went out to warm up at 2.25, they were oblivious to the tragedy unfolding on the Leppings Lane. I stayed inside the dressing room, mulling over whether I'd forgotten any instructions, flicking through the programme, answering nature's call, before slowly changing into my match-day attire of tracksuit and boots. Looking back now, thinking of the peace and quiet in that dressing room at 2.30, it is shuddering to realise that Liverpool fans were already suffering on the Leppings Lane End. Since then, I have spoken to many parents, including Trevor Hicks, an impressive man who lost his daughters, Sarah and Victoria. He told me he was in one of the side pens, which were relatively empty. Sarah and Victoria were in the central pens, which the Taylor Report proved were full by 2.30. The police had CCTV, they knew they had a problem, and yet they hesitated. I will never waver from my belief that Duckenfield lacked the experience to deal with a game of this magnitude. I don't believe he understood how to manage a crowd, or realised how fans surge. The one decision he did make had catastrophic consequences.

Duckenfield had two areas of congestion to contend with – outside the Leppings Lane and inside it. Authorising the exit gates at the top to be opened at 2.47, Duckenfield unwittingly released a torrent of people into a stationary block of other Liverpool supporters. Anxious to reach the terrace, the fans charged into a tunnel beneath the West Stand, and I read in the Taylor Report that the flow was judged by the police to have reached 2,000 people flooding through in five minutes alone, the majority of them hurtling towards the densely populated central pens. With fences at the front and the side restricting movement, pen 3 turned into a slaughterhouse. Having attempted to alleviate the pressure outside, Duckenfield accidentally intensified it inside. I still cannot understand why the police didn't think, when they opened the gates, to tell fans to turn left or right and not pile on down the tunnel. All it needed was for somebody to say, 'Sorry lads, this pen's full, go to the side.' I still don't understand why they didn't open the gates earlier, before the bottleneck built up. The police must have known those who'd reached the ground had tickets.

Liverpool fans were treated like cattle, shepherded into pens 3 and 4. Even the word 'pen' suggests herding cattle, and that said everything to me about the authorities' approach to supporters back then. For people used to entering the Kop at Anfield, and moving towards their favoured spot, arriving under the unfamiliar West Stand at Hillsborough made them even more likely to go in the same direction as everybody else. Swarming into the central pens, this wave of humanity caused the crushing down at the front. Some fans managed to climb up the fence only to be forced back by the police. This was the Eighties when hooliganism was the English disease, so most people outside the Leppings Lane would initially think fighting had broken out. The reality that fans were trying to escape a crush just wasn't in the mind-set.

What I still don't comprehend, even now, is the reaction of some of the police standing between the fences and the pitch. They must have been tuned in to their radios and heard all the communication about problems at the top, demonstrating that this wasn't hooliganism. Some unscrupulous characters claimed that the baggage of Heysel still accompanied Liverpool fans, and that the police could be forgiven for thinking it was hooliganism because of what happened in Brussels. That's not credible. The police were present the year before, overseeing that FA Cup semi. They would have based their view of Liverpool fans on the evidence of that day, when no problems arose. People did not instinctively think 'there's going to be a riot here' when Liverpool were playing. Liverpool fans had a reputation for being lively, enjoying a few beers and a singsong. Not all of them were angels, but they never went seeking violence.

The players first became aware of the problem at 2.54 when Bruce Grobbelaar took some practice shots off John Barnes at the Leppings Lane End. Going to retrieve a ball, Bruce saw the huge number of fans shoehorned into the central pens. 'Get the bloody gate open,' Bruce shouted at the police.

Liverpool fans screamed at the police to open the gates, to save them, but the police on the spot needed permission. Looking at the situation from their perspective, I partly understood their unwillingness to respond. If one constable opened a gate of his own volition, and people lost their lives in the fight to squeeze through the entrance, he'd be culpable. Again, the constables lacked direction from their superior officers, and particularly Duckenfield. If no guidance was forthcoming from the top, what on earth could the police on the ground do?

I felt sympathy for the policemen down on the Leppings Lane, who must have seen terrible sights, witnessed people having the life squeezed out of them, but couldn't act. In all the inquiries so far into Hillsborough, nobody has explained the level of communication between Duckenfield and his police down at the front.

And so, with people dying yards away, the game kicked off on time. When the first whistle goes at matches, there's usually a real buzz, a sudden burst of noise, but at 3 p.m. on 15 April 1989, the atmosphere was so different. The mood was noticeably subdued, shorn of the usual excitement, and even when Peter Beardsley hit the Forest bar at the Kop end at 3.04, the roar lacked intensity. A fan ran on the pitch, pleading with everybody to stop the game, and thank God he did because he probably forced the authorities to act quicker. Again Bruce shouted at the police to 'get the bloody gate open'. The scale of the disaster was now becoming apparent. Bruce recalled fans pleading, 'They're killing us, Bruce, they're killing us.' Just writing those words chills me. At 3.06, a policeman finally strode on to the pitch to tell Lewis to stop the game.

'Come on,' Lewis shouted to the players, 'everybody off.' When we'd gathered in the dressing room, Lewis popped his head around the door. 'Keep warm. The police have informed us that it's likely to be five minutes, ten at the outside,' said Lewis. 'I'll keep you informed. You'll have the opportunity of doing a warm-up before restarting.'

Any chance of the game being played disappeared in my eyes when I briefly went back on the pitch, stepping 10 yards over the touchline and witnessing what seemed a scene from a war-zone. Although I never realised then the extent of the loss of life, the full gravity of the situation began hitting home. Liverpool fans were ripping up advertising boards to form makeshift stretchers, tending to the injured and dying. When these fans climbed over the fences, some police feared they were about to attack the Forest end, even forming a line across the pitch. Forest fans cottoned on faster than the police what was really happening. At the beginning a few shouted 'hooligans', but when they realised it wasn't that, they quickly became supportive, clapping them for the work they were doing. Those Liverpool supporters had only one thought in their minds and that was to save their mates and relatives who'd been crushed on the Leppings Lane. They were the heroes of Hillsborough.

Responding quicker than the emergency services, Liverpool fans rushed to save lives in a stadium where the medical provision was woefully inadequate. I couldn't believe that only one ambulance was there to deal with the emergency when the game was stopped at 3.06, when the police knew from 2 p.m. they had a potential disaster on their hands. The mismanagement at Hillsborough was a public scandal. Why did they not bring in more medical people and equipment, or at the very least put them on stand-by? Every second wasted meant Liverpool fans caught up in the crush edged closer towards asphyxiation. Only one oxygen cylinder was available, so when one policeman, Superintendent Peter Wells, stepped up to the fence, and began giving oxygen to those fighting for air up against the wire, what happened to those fans lying on the grass? Wells did what was right, trying to keep alive those pressed at the fence, but more lives might have been saved if Hillsborough had had more than one oxygen cylinder. I stress over and over again that Hillsborough was a disaster waiting to happen.

I'd gone on to the pitch looking for Paul, who'd attended the game with Roy Evans's son, Stephen, and Alan Brown, a friend of ours who was involved with the Liverpool European Supporters' Club. The three of them had developed a ritual with the Cup, beginning with the third-round trip to Carlisle United. They'd made a day of it, stopping for lunch on the way. When Liverpool won 4–0, they made up their minds to go to every game in the Cup. As soon as I began to realise the extent of the problems at the Leppings Lane End, I became frantic with worry. Paul, Stephen and Alan had to go through the Leppings Lane to reach their places. If they'd arrived late, they could have got caught up in it.

Suddenly seeing Paul walking across the pitch with Stephen and Alan, my heart leapt. Thank you, God. I never said anything to Paul, just greeting him with a huge hug that communicated my feelings. I was lucky, and Paul was lucky, because all around us, people were dying. Thank God the three of them passed through the Leppings Lane before 2 p.m., before those central pens began trapping fans. They wanted to be there early for the singing, and that meant they escaped the carnage. I think Paul knows how fortunate he was. I've still never talked with Paul about Hillsborough. I just can't. The emotion is too raw. I just can't imagine how I'd have coped if my son had died, so I try to block out the awful thought. Like Paul, Stephen knows he was lucky. So does Alan. Just imagine how Alan would have felt if he'd taken the sons of two friends to a game and never brought them home? Fortunately, they survived. Leading Paul back to the main stand, I pointed him up to the directors' box where Marina was waiting with Kelly. I caught Marina's eye and we realised how blessed we'd been. We could have lost our wonderful son.

When I returned to the dressing room, the police asked Brian Clough and me to make an appeal for calm. They led us through the bowels of the main stand, through the kitchens, where a radio was on and scores were being announced, a weird reminder that life was going on outside the hell of Hillsborough. On reaching the police control box, we discovered the mike wasn't working.

'Hold on, we'll try to get it fixed,' said a policeman.

Cloughie shrugged. 'I'm off,' he said and left. Giving up on the mike, the police guided me to the DJ's studio, housed in a Portakabin adjacent to the Leppings Lane, from where I made my announcement.

'Could you calm down, please, there's been some problems,' I said. 'We really respect the fact you're trying to be calm. Let's remain calm and do the best we can for the people who are injured.' As I walked away, I saw two guys clapping me. Just as I reached the dressing room, some fans came up the tunnel, screaming abuse at the police. 'It's a disgrace,' I heard one of them say. Stepping through the dressing-room door, the place was utterly silent. Sensing the nightmare outside, the players had hardly moved. They were just sitting there, slumped on the benches. A couple of minutes later, Lewis entered the room.

'The game's off,' he said, and the players began showering and changing. Even then, with the game cancelled and having seen some of the scenes outside, I didn't realise the enormity of what had happened until we went upstairs and started watching the television. 'There's been a tragedy at Hillsborough,' Des Lynam reported. 'There are many dead.' I was anticipating the worst, perhaps four or five fatalities, but when Des mentioned that it was feared 75 had perished already, I couldn't take it in. Seventy-five? There was no conversation, nothing. Nobody could say anything. Forest's players were also in the lounge and my heart went out to them. Cloughie's men were the forgotten party in all this, witnessing those emotive events.

I met PBR and another director, Tony Ensor, the club's lawyer, who'd been up to check on the gates at the top of the Leppings Lane. They'd heard that the FA chief executive, Graham Kelly, had been told by Duckenfield there'd been a forced entry by Liverpool fans, an allegation that PBR and Tony swiftly realised to be false. Downstairs, the gym was being used as a medical station and, when that failed, as a morgue. Adding to my anger over Hillsborough was the realisation that the doctors did not have the necessary equipment or medicine. Once again, the lack of management of this disaster was shocking. The emergency services should have arrived quicker, bringing in more supplies of intravenous diamorphine and drips, a point raised in the Taylor Report. The moment they knew people were being crushed, the ambulances should have loaded up at the local hospitals with all the items required for dealing with asphyxiation.

At 5.30, we climbed wearily into the coach for the journey back to Liverpool, probably passing distressed parents speeding towards Sheffield. Throughout my years at Liverpool, the bus was a place of noise and happiness, filled with banter as we headed to training or returned from a successful expedition with a trophy on the dashboard. Not now. Silence and misery were our companions. Collapsing into my seat, I asked the driver to keep the radio off. Nothing should disturb the quietness, no music, no scores, no meaningless chatter. After what we'd just experienced, everything else seemed irrelevant. No one talked. No one wanted to. Every player was lost in thought, searching for answers. I just sat there numb, holding Marina's hand, thinking of my family and wondering whether I knew any of those fans now lying in that morgue at Hillsborough, or in the emergency ward of a Sheffield hospital. From the television reports, everybody on the Liverpool coach knew about the horrendous number of deaths but we wanted names. As a club with deep roots in the community, with a strong bond between team and terrace, everybody feared having lost a friend.

Briefly, I thought back to 1971, to the Ibrox disaster, when 66 Rangers supporters died in a crush on stairway 13. The game was against Celtic and, as a Celtic player, I was there, but only as a spectator, and fortunately down the other end. Ibrox had different causes. The overcrowding on the stairway occurred when departing fans heard the roar for a late goal and turned back up only to be swept away by those racing out. Unlike Hillsborough, Ibrox had nothing to do with bad policing.

Back at home, I couldn't watch *Match of the Day*, couldn't bear to see the scenes again. After hugging my children, I went to bed but sleep didn't come easily. The state of despair continued in the morning, and I was stirred into action only by the phone ringing at around 10 a.m. It was PBR, ever the club's servant, ever the man thinking of others.

'Kenny, there's a lot of people come up to the ground so I've decided to open the gates, let them come in, give them somewhere to be,' said Peter, adding details about plans for a service at St Andrews Cathedral that night. Shortly before 6 p.m., I entered the cathedral, clutching Marina's hand tightly, walking past grieving people sitting in the pews, their lives ripped apart by the indecision of a few police officers on the other side of the Pennines. My respect for Bruce Grobbelaar, already immense, grew even more as he bravely read from the Bible, his voice quivering with emotion, trying to provide some comfort for those in mourning. I knew Bruce was badly affected by what had happened, having been so close to the Leppings Lane End and heard the fans' cries for help. I also knew he would be steadfast when Liverpool Football Club needed him most, giving succour and strength to a distraught community. I knew, too, that I had to stand up and lead, take a more public role and speak to the Press, something I was uncomfortable with. I acted spontaneously, honestly and straightforwardly, dropping my guard and talking as a parent, not as a manager under scrutiny for his tactics. The reason I responded was because the people of Liverpool were, and always will be, part of my family.

My desire to help hardened when I heard that Graham Kelly, having been asked about the immediate future of the Cup, stated that he felt the FA would be loathe to 'abandon the competition'. I had some sympathy for Graham, who was responding to journalists' questions at Lancaster Gate, but the FA should have been more sensitive. For the FA to make a judgement call at a time when Liverpool fans were lying in morgues and hospital beds, the death total rising grimly, was disgraceful at worst, tactless at best. The FA needed to be more mindful of the families' feelings, and also aware that some people pointed the finger of blame at Lancaster Gate. It required a disaster on the terraces for the FA to start taking advice on grounds. They chose that ground, they paid the police to control that tie, so I felt they needed to answer questions on both decisions, rather than pontificate on the future of the FA Cup. The FA's self-declared role as custodians of the game rang hollow at that time.

Leaving London to its selfish stance, Merseyside rallied round the stricken. On the Monday morning, Marina telephoned all the wives, discussing how they could help. I contacted the players, saying a few words about how we needed to respond towards the relatives. 'They've always supported us and now we must support them,' I said. 'That's what families do and this club is a family.'

The players knew anyway. My words just echoed their thoughts. They were good boys, very approachable people who understood the club and its place in the heart of the community. Adversity casts light on a man's true character and I noted with quiet pride that Liverpool's players demonstrated dignity and compassion in abundance during that difficult time. That team will always have a special bond because of what they went through then.

On the Monday, they couldn't wait to get up to Anfield to

help. PBR flung open all the doors, letting everyone come in to lay floral tributes on the Kop while the Salvation Army band softly played 'Abide With Me'. I'd already left a tribute from the Dalglish family. Early that morning, Paul and Kelly gave me their teddy bears, which I tied to the goalposts. The sea of flowers and scarves on the Kop grew and grew as more and more people visited. The relatives were ushered into the Candy lounge where Marina and the girls set up a tea-urn on the bar at the back. May and the cleaning ladies were busy helping out. It was in the aftermath of Hillsborough that it became even more apparent to me exactly how strong the relationships were inside the club. The closeness of the staff, from cleaning ladies to players, was really important. It's different now, sadly, with the staff split between Melwood and Anfield, and I fear Liverpool has lost some of its identity.

Anfield became a place of solace for the families, a haven for them to come to talk and grieve. The families were so strong, often dealing with the tragic circumstances by making wry remarks about their lost loved ones' obsession with Liverpool. 'He'd be gutted if he knew we're in here,' one relative said to me. 'He's a miserable sod but he'll be happy now that he can look down from heaven and watch every game for nothing,' another said. Visiting Anfield was an incredibly therapeutic experience for them. The families knew they were surrounded by people who cared, who understood their loss. At that stage the parents didn't have a body to grieve over – many of the bodies were not immediately returned to the bereaved, an unbelievably inhumane decision by the authorities that still rankles to this day. They'd seen their loved one's body through glass in the morgue, in that gym at Hillsborough. The police even retained clothing and personal effects. Why would they keep the clothes? So many questions have still to be answered about Hillsborough.

Standing in the lounge, trying to comfort the relatives, I listened to so many heart-breaking stories, hearing from Trevor Hicks about his Sophie's Choice. Should he go with his daughter in the ambulance, or stay with his other daughter, lying on the pitch? No father should go through that hell. I just couldn't take in the sheer horror of the stories being related in the lounge. The relatives talked of the desperate search through the bodies lined up in the gym, and the anger at not being able to take them home. Post-mortems, police investigations and bureaucratic red-tape made them feel the Establishment was against them, and as a result they turned even more to Liverpool Football Club for support.

'Just tell us if there's anything we can do in any way, shape or form,' I said to Trevor and the rest of the relatives. Some wanted an item of Liverpool kit, so we raided the kit room, giving everything to the relatives. Some wanted a book, an old programme, some keepsake, anything with Liverpool's Liver Bird on it, so we emptied the store-room. Some of the lads recorded messages for the fans lying in comas in Sheffield hospitals, saying a few words the medical staff felt might trigger a positive reaction. 'Come on, you great lump, you can't lie in bed all day,' was one message from Macca.

The players were all shocked by the newspaper photographs of fans with their faces squashed against the fences, particularly the picture of two girls, Debbie and Lisa, who used to stand outside Melwood asking for autographs. We knew them, waved to them and to see them in this terrible crush was unbearable. Somehow, and I just don't know how, Debbie and Lisa survived that death-trap.

Emotionally drained, I retreated to my office, sat at my desk and knew there were calls to make, particularly to Ray Lewis. People overlooked that Ray was in the middle of the tragedy, that he'd witnessed events that would psychologically scar any man. Ray was from a village called Great Bookham, which I always found rather appropriate for a referee, so I looked up his number in Surrey.

'Ray, it's Kenny Dalglish. I'm just calling to see how you are,' I said. Our conversation was short because neither of us wanted to relive what we'd seen but I gained the impression that Ray appreciated Liverpool were thinking of him and his welfare. We all had each other at Anfield. Ray had nobody, so it was important I made contact, showing some compassion.

The phone started ringing, everybody offering support. Ian Woosnam called, offering to raise money by playing for birdies at Hillside Golf Club. Woosie's from Oswestry, quite close to Liverpool, and he wanted to help in some way. Calls buzzed in from all over football. Craig Johnston rang from Australia, saying he was flying back. Other managers called, knowing that Hillsborough could so easily have happened to their fans.

'Anything you need, Kenny, I'm here for you,' said Alex Ferguson. Then he made an inspired suggestion. 'I'll send some fans over to pay tribute.' The rivalry between followers of Manchester United and Liverpool runs very deep, and is often very bitter, so it was a marvellous idea of Fergie's to get some of his fans to come across and stand shoulder to shoulder with Liverpool fans in their hour of need. As long as I live, I'll never forget Fergie's exceptional gesture. It didn't surprise me, though, because Fergie is absolutely magnificent in any crisis. He's famous in football for being straight on the phone, offering assistance or advice.

Fergie's start at Old Trafford coincided with my time as manager of Liverpool and, inevitably, we were depicted in the Press as existing with daggers drawn. Of course, the rivalry was strong, and Fergie was somebody I wanted to beat, somebody I stood up to when he said something I disagreed with. We were competitors but that didn't mean we fought all the time. We'd have a drink after games, share pleasantries, talk about our shared roots on Clydeside. Alex hailed from a similar background to me. He came from a strong Glasgow family and that gave him principles for life, including 'look after your own and look after other people'. Alex had his brother Martin working at United, doing a fantastic job scouting for players.

Marina's family was also old-fashioned Glaswegian, also a tight unit. Her father went out to work, her mother brought up the kids, and was really supportive of everyone in the family. If anybody needed help, she was the first to offer. Marina just headed to Anfield, talking to the families all day, her strength of character proving a constant source of warmth. It was not only the bereaved she talked to – 766 people were injured at Hillsborough and some of them came in with their relatives.

Later that Monday, leaving the wives to their healing work, the players boarded the coach for the sad return to Sheffield. At three o'clock, we arrived at the North General Hospital in Sheffield for an experience that was strange, humbling and distressing. I saw one kid, Lee Nichol, only 14, hooked up to a life-support machine. I stared at him, not understanding why somebody without a mark or bruise on him could be clinically dead. Not a mark on him. Not one mark. It just didn't make sense. The medical experts explained that this is what happens with asphyxiation. The brain becomes starved of oxygen and just cuts out. Lee was pulled alive from the crush on the Leppings Lane End but had already slipped into a coma. He died later, the ninety-fifth to pass away. Hillsborough was Lee's first away game. Shocking.

Moving between the wards, struggling to comprehend, I was guided for part of the way by Dr David Edbrooke, a consultant anaesthetist. Leading me to the bedside of 20-year-old Sean Luckett, Dr Edbrooke explained that Sean had come off the ventilator but was still in a coma. Sean's mother sat anxiously by her son's side. Nodding to her, Dr Edbrooke and I stood by Sean.

'Sean, here's Kenny Dalglish to see you,' said Dr Edbrooke. 'It's Kenny Dalglish.' Suddenly, Sean's eyes opened. Amazing. I couldn't believe it.

'Hello, Sean, I know you're going to make it through,' I said. Sean was stirring now, waking from this coma. Mrs Luckett let out a cry and leant forward over her son.

'Listen, this is a special moment for you, I'll leave you to it,' I said and hurried from the room. A mother reunited with her son was a private moment.

When the story went around, some people credited me with having an influence on Sean's recovery. I know the mind works in strange ways, and some medics argue that, in a coma, it reacts to words, but I thought it was just coincidence that Sean woke up then. Whatever the cause, I was just happy Sean was back with us. Before we left the North General, I popped back in to shake his hand. Another boy, Paul Johnson, a 15-year-old, improved while the team were wandering through the wards. Even if none of the kids had woken up, it was right for us to go.

All of the players found the visit difficult, particularly those with young children. 'What would I be like if my son or daughter was lying there' was the thought thudding through everybody's head. The trip raised so many questions and emotions. One of the guys in the hospital was lucky. He'd been crushed a bit but was OK and was well into recovery. 'When are you making your comeback?' he asked Al. That comment meant he'd missed the team announcement, the warm-up, the players coming out and the six minutes of play, an indication to me of how early the crush began at Hillsborough.

With all this emotion going on, I was horrified to hear the FA set Liverpool a deadline of 7 May for playing the semi. Play or withdraw. How callous could they get? Get over your grieving by 7 May or you'll be expelled. That craven statement was made without consultation with Liverpool, who were still reeling from the disaster and would never, ever be railroaded by a bunch of uncaring administrators in London. Graham Kelly should have been more discreet, working behind the scenes with Liverpool, communicating with PBR, mentioning the importance of the competition continuing without being seen to deliver ultimatums. I had no issue with the FA in general, or Kelly in particular, more with some of the unsympathetic officials within the organisation. Kelly, a spokesman in many ways, was only making public what the FA decided in their committee rooms and so was undeserving of all the bile poured over him. Some of the other officials within Lancaster Gate, particularly those on the FA board who seemed so impatient to get on with their precious Cup, should have shared some of the flak aimed at Kelly.

Uefa didn't cover themselves in glory, either. Their president, Jacques Georges, described Liverpool fans as 'beasts waiting to charge into the arena', a despicable, provocative comment that brought more pain to the families of those who died at Hillsborough. Georges' words brought shame on him and embarrassment on Uefa. As the man whose organisation decided the sub-standard Heysel was suitable for a European Cup final, who ignored pleas to move that game, Georges made some atrocious decisions in his career, didn't he? Maybe that's why Uefa's president took the opportunity to divert blame on to others. In Georges' eyes, Liverpool fans had a bad reputation but his testimony was tainted beyond credibility.

Even worse than Jacques Georges, if that were possible, was Kelvin MacKenzie, newspaper editor. When Marina and I drove into Anfield on the morning of Wednesday, 19 April, first checking on the Kop, which had even more flowers and tributes, we found the staff and the families enraged by a piece in the paper. Its infamous front-page headline, 'THE TRUTH', caused hurt and outrage by accusing fans of pick-pocketing the dying and urinating on the bodies. Just unbelievable. Liverpool punters went ballistic, some of them burning the paper on the news-stands, others coming up to Anfield to talk about their anger. The following day, MacKenzie rang the club. Anfield's receptionist, Karen, buzzed me.

'Kenny, it's Kelvin MacKenzie on the line.'

'You'd better put him on to PBR, Karen.'

'Peter says you have to speak to him.'

'Thanks! Put him through.' MacKenzie came on the line.

'Kenny, we have a bit of a problem,' he said.

'Aye.'

'How can we resolve it?'

'See that headline you put in, 'THE TRUTH'? Just have another one, as big: 'WE LIED. SORRY'.

'Kenny, we can't do that.'

'I can't help you then,' I replied and put down the phone. MacKenzie simply didn't realise the offence he'd caused to a grieving city. A few minutes later, the governor of Walton Prison phoned.

'Look, Kenny, the inmates are getting really restless with the stuff that's been in the papers. Can you come up to the prison and speak to them?'

'OK, I'll be there at nine tomorrow morning.'

What was I doing now? Going into a jail? But I had to. Liverpool was a city in ferment and I had to do everything to bring some calm and hope. If there was a threat of a riot in Walton Prison, I had to go there.

Driving to Anfield early on the Friday, I made a detour via Walton. Looking up at the big door, I whispered to myself, 'Bloody hell. What am I doing here?' Entering the prison was deeply unsettling. I heard the door slam shut behind me, the clank of keys as the warder turned the lock and then the polite instruction to follow another guard. I heard the quiet words of prisoners, working on the lawn, hoeing the grass. 'How you doing Kenny?' they asked. Badly. This experience of incarceration was awful, the feeling that there was no escape, that the outside world was blocked off. Passing through more gates, hearing them close behind me, I understood how prison sent some people mad.

One final door opened and I was led into the chapel. The inmates sat there, totally silent, their heads turning to see me. Suddenly, they began clapping, which startled me. It seemed to me they just wanted to demonstrate their respect towards Liverpool Football Club and the way the club were trying to deal with Hillsborough. The governor took me to one side.

'Kenny, they've all seen the paper so anything you can say to pacify them would be magnificent. If you can just reassure them.' I tried.

'Listen,' I said to the inmates, 'what you've read is not "the truth". That never happened. Please, I know it's difficult for you in here and you want to be with your loved ones outside, but please stay calm and know that Liverpool are working night and day to help the families.' I explained how the relatives were coming up to Anfield, how they were being looked after by the players and their wives. I told them how Anfield was now a shrine, a fitting tribute to the fans who died.

When I finished talking, I couldn't get out quickly enough, through all the clanking gates and out into the fresh air and freedom. I almost ran. But being inside Walton Prison emphasised the damage wrought by one newspaper's lies. Their vile insinuation emanated from the word of an unidentified policeman. Well, if they had information, why hide it? If they or the police had proof of mass drunkenness, show the world the evidence. They couldn't because the claim was fabricated and was comprehensively dismissed by Lord Chief Justice Taylor. In his report, I noted one particularly damning sentence that read: 'I am satisfied on the evidence that the great majority were not drunk. Some officers, seeking to rationalise their loss of control, overestimated the drunken element of the crowd.' Taylor's judgement was spot on. The police tried to divert attention from their own mismanagement. Some Liverpool fans would have had a couple of pints, the usual match-day convention with friends, and a few might have been inebriated but not many. As the gruesome succession of autopsies revealed, some of the bodies contained some alcohol but not enough to impair judgement. Remember, a good proportion of the fans were driving. As an area, Hillsborough wasn't packed with pubs while the few local off-licences told Taylor they'd not sold huge amounts.

As the paper was making its deceitful comments, Liverpool began burying its dead. One of the club's directors, Noel White, organised a rota to ensure each funeral was attended by a representative of Liverpool Football Club, whether that was me, a player or one of the player's wives. The boys travelled everywhere, mainly across Merseyside but some went down south. From helping at Anfield every day, most of the players had formed some attachment with different families. Even though those people wanted them at the funerals, the players were very conscious of not wanting to be the focus of attention. We were there to pay our respects and didn't want publicity. Wherever the families asked us to sit in church we did, whether at the front alongside them or at the back, more discreetly.

The last funeral I attended was as difficult as the first. Familiarity with the service, and the ritual of saying farewell, did not lessen the emotion. As I sat in another church, looking down the aisle towards another coffin, I simply didn't understand how the relatives had the fortitude to keep going, but they did. They were so strong. The first funeral I went to was for Gary Church, a 19-year-old, in Crosby. John Barnes and Gary Ablett carried a wreath with the message: 'We brought you back in our hearts'. I listened to John Aldridge read from the scriptures and then the Reverend Ray Hutchinson say some words: 'The message of caring and of wanting to share your burden has been marred by some distasteful reporting by the media. But on Merseyside, the message is loud, clear and all the stronger as again our city has to show its resilience to yet more pain and suffering.' Reverend Hutchinson was right. Resilience defined Liverpool, still does. A great community spirit united the city in the aftermath of the Hillsborough tragedy, everybody sticking together and protecting each other. At one service, one of the players looked through the window behind the altar to see a photographer from MacKenzie's newspaper being chased by four people. That summed up the mood of Liverpool people defending the community.

Every dawn brought preparations for more funerals. Marina and I went to four in one day, needing a police escort to make sure we fulfilled our pledges to each family. At Lee Nichol's funeral in the cathedral, the service felt particularly poignant, having seen him lying in that Sheffield hospital, not a mark on him. Like most of the services, Lee's funeral finished with the congregation singing 'You'll Never Walk Alone' but I was too emotional to do anything more than mouth the words.

Returning to Anfield, I saw the Kop now covered, and flowers spreading towards the halfway line. So many people visited, the queue snaked around the block and down the road, a silent line of people shuffling forward to pay their respects. Some politicians jumped on the bandwagon, coming along to have their pictures taken, but one really impressed me. Neil Kinnock arrived with no warning, no fuss, just queuing, leaving some flowers and then departing. Alerted to his presence on the Kop, I had a brief chat with him and he struck me as genuine, very different from some of the politicians.

Scarcely had I settled back in my office after talking to Kinnock, when there was a knock on the door. A lady I'd never seen before walked in, sat down and introduced herself as a stress counsellor.

'Oh, listen, do me a favour,' I told her, 'go and see Peter Robinson. He might be able to help you.' So she trooped off and I counted down the time until my phone rang – about 90 seconds.

'Thanks, Kenny!' Peter said. 'I don't need any counselling.' I understood.

Acting with extreme sensitivity, PBR quietly gauged the mood of the families over what should be done with the shrine at Anfield. It was agreed there would be one final service before we tried to return Anfield to normal, if such a state were possible after Hillsborough. On the Friday morning, I paid a private visit to the Kop with Paul, Kelly and Marina's dad, Pat. Walking carefully through the wreaths, scarves, shirts, football boots and scribbled messages of sorrow, I appreciated fully the powerful hold Liverpool exerts on people. 'Why did it happen to us?' asked Paul, speaking as a fan, as somebody who understood Liverpool's place in the hearts of the people. Anfield was their second home, their second place of worship. Until then, I never understood that fans on the Kop always stood in the same place, creating a little community within a community. In remembrance of happier times, somebody left a couple of oranges, recollecting a ritual he'd shared with a friend or relative who went to Hillsborough but never returned. Somebody else left a Twix bar, a reminder of something they shared. Talking to the Press, I remarked that the Kop was 'the saddest and most beautiful sight I have ever seen', a comment that drew much discussion. 'Why beautiful?' people wondered. Why? Because the tributes came from all over the world, from fans of other clubs and from people who'd never before set foot in Anfield, holding it was against their beliefs. Evertonians entered Anfield for the first time to lay flowers, and to behold that outpouring of love and respect was beautiful. The messages propped against the railings on the Kop were beautiful. To visit early in the morning with Anfield deserted, and to smell the thousands of flowers was the saddest and most beautiful experience.

Moving sights were everywhere on Merseyside. On Saturday, 22 April, scarves were tied between Goodison and Anfield, the last two being joined up by Peter Beardsley and Ian Snodin, symbolising the connection between the clubs. I drove to Tranmere Rovers' ground, Prenton Park, for a service there, everybody standing in silence at 3.06 p.m. The players stayed at Anfield for the service there, some of them, including Stevie Nicol, standing on the Kop. Anfield then closed the gates after an estimated two million people had passed through, showing what a fantastic idea it had been from PBR.

Many of the players were due to report for international duty but some simply couldn't stomach the idea of playing football. John Barnes withdrew from England, Stevie Nicol from Scotland and Ronnie Whelan and John Aldridge from the Republic of Ireland. All their countries showed real compassion, never complaining about some of their best players not turning up, although the FA were still on to us about playing again. On Tuesday, 25 April, the FA chairman, Bert Millichip, mentioned it again, but it could never be their decision. Only the Hillsborough families could decide. Talking to them, PBR and I found the relatives keen for the Liverpool players to get their boots on again. So, with the families' approval, we returned to Melwood for the first training in a fortnight and I couldn't believe the ferocity of the tackling, as if some players wanted to purge the anger and frustration. The lads needed the work-out. We'd organised a tribute match with Celtic to raise money for the Hillsborough families on the Sunday. Before we set out, I made a worrying discovery – we'd no strip. All the Liverpool first-team kit had been given away to the families, so the manufacturers rushed some more over.

Celtic Park has a special place in my heart and never more so than on Sunday, 30 April 1989. The place was packed, all the fans holding aloft green-and-white and red scarves as they sang 'You'll Never Walk Alone' before that wonderful moment when Celtic supporters chanted 'Liverpool, Liverpool'. For the players, the game was part of the healing process. Aldo, who'd been painfully affected by the tragedy that hit his city, didn't want to play, so I put him on the bench and sent him on for the second half. Privately, I knew Aldo was considering jacking it all in. Finding the enthusiasm to kick a ball was beyond him, it all felt so meaningless and I understood his despair. Even when he scored twice at Celtic Park, John never celebrated, just turned away and headed back to the halfway line. Knowing John, I'm sure he was just thinking about the Hillsborough victims. I'm sure, in the end, John played on because he knew that was what the families wanted.

After the match, we went to a great restaurant, The Rotunda, for a private party for players and wives, giving everybody a chance to let off some steam. While making sure we weren't being disrespectful to the families, I felt the players needed to let rip after so much strain and stress, helping them on the road back to normality. We were joined by Marti Pellow from Wet Wet Wet. In the restaurant, there was this wee guy playing very sombre songs on an electric organ.

'It's like being back at the funerals,' I whispered to Marina.

'Have a word, Kenny,' Marina said. So I went over to the organist.

'Excuse me, thanks very much, take the rest of the night off, there you are,' I said, slipping him a few quid.

Marti took the microphone, and as he sang the mood started to lighten. An almighty singsong broke out, everybody joining in. Back at the hotel, the fire alarm went off. By that stage of the evening, I was struggling to focus straight and my last memory was of seeing a fire engine.

'You were embarrassing last night,' Marina said in the morning.

'What do you mean?'

'You asked the fireman if you could ring the bell.'

'I don't believe you.'

'Well, what's that then?' said Marina, pointing to a fireman's helmet by the side of the bed.

Marina had had a lively night as well, intervening in a tiff between Aldo and his wife Joan, which culminated in John telling Marina to 'fuck off'. John knew he was out of order. Emotions were running high so everybody soon forgot about it.

Marina, Joan and the rest of the wives went home to Liverpool while the boys went to Blackpool on the Monday, preparing for the resumption of competitive football on Wednesday, 3 May against Everton. We could not have picked more fitting opponents as the city sought to recover from Hillsborough. Goodison Park crackled with an amazing atmosphere, 45,994 Scousers screaming themselves hoarse as Liverpool and Everton tore into each other. Capturing the city's unity, nothing could divide these famous neighbours and the game finished 0–0. At the time, the dropped points didn't feel important. What felt good was for the boys to be playing again, particularly with the Forest semi now arranged for 7 May at Old Trafford. This was a tie we couldn't lose.

Apart from Forest fans, the public willed Liverpool to reach Wembley to honour those who died at Hillsborough. I sensed the emotional momentum building behind Liverpool, the boys feeding on the energy of the huge roar that marked the end of the minute's silence. They quickly swept Forest out of the way to set up a final with Everton, again fittingly. The situation cannot have been easy for Cloughie, who knew he was up against the whole nation, but I appreciated the Forest manager's magnanimity in defeat. 'Good luck in the final,' said Cloughie, 'you deserve it.' For all his famous unpredictability, I respected Cloughie, a strong disciplinarian who always insisted his players showed respect to referees, a quality I admired.

My players were ready for Wembley, relaxing in training at Bisham Abbey on the Friday with an hilarious game. Macca flicked the ball up, Bruce caught it in on the volley and if he beat Beardo in goal, Bruce would do a backflip. Pally Blue was no fool – he picked Beardo because he was the smallest, so there was more of the goal to aim at. Bruce duly did his flips, easing the tension before the big day.

At Wembley, the players wanted to get out early on the pitch, feeling the unique atmosphere of an all-Merseyside final, joining in when Gerry Marsden powered memorably through 'You'll Never Walk Alone'. After the traditional rendition of 'Abide With Me', a moving minute's silence fell over Wembley. It was like the world stopped turning for those 60 seconds. Everything was so still. The FA got one decision right, removing the fences for the day, and the fans sat among each other.

Fate decreed it would be Liverpool and Everton, helping the healing process, and fate also knew Liverpool must win. A final weighted with such emotional significance proved a classic. Fittingly, two Scousers combined for Liverpool's first, Macca squaring to Aldo, triggering a seesaw game. Stuart McCall equalised and it was 1–1 at 90 minutes. Rushie immediately put us back ahead before McCall levelled. At 2–2, I was stunned, wondering which way the final would go now. A policeman walking past the bench reassured me by saying, in a broad Scottish accent, 'Don't worry wee man, you'll still win.' Digger soon embarked on a run, putting in a cross for Rushie to head the winner, and the PC strolled back. 'You're all right now, wee man,' he said. I had to laugh. A Scottish guardian angel had been sent to watch over me.

At Joe Worrall's final whistle, I hugged Ronnie and Roy. Seeing the punters on the edge of the pitch, streaming towards us, I said quickly to Bugsy, 'I'm off. It might take some of them away and then you can get on with the lap of honour.' I dashed to the tunnel, gaining a Celtic scarf on the way, to be met by Liverpool's security chief, Tony Chinn. Tears rolled down Tony's face. This Cup meant everything.

'I can't be tough all the time,' said Tony before suddenly snapping back into hard-man mode. 'Who hit you, Kenny?'

'What are you talking about, Tony?'

'Your eye's cut.'

'Where?' I put my hand to my face, felt a trickle of blood and remembered I'd clashed heads with a punter while running through the throng to the tunnel.

'It's worth it.' It was.

'This is the best one for me,' I told Ronnie and Roy when they reappeared in the dressing room, having abandoned all hope of a lap of honour. And it was the best. Even now, the Hillsborough Cup final was the trophy that meant most in my career, above even the European Cups. This trophy was for the 95 who had died and for their families, who bore the tragedy with such dignity. It cannot have been easy for the relatives who travelled to Wembley, feeling the sadness amid the celebrations, knowing their loved one would have been there to see Ronnie lift the Cup. If only the FA had thought of saying to Liverpool: 'We'll get a new trophy, you keep that one.' Such an act of generosity would never have crossed Lancaster Gate's mind. They got the FA Cup final played on the day scheduled, so what else mattered? But Hillsborough changed everything.

Liverpool's return to Hillsborough on 29 November was really difficult, really distressing. The whole occasion of the League game was very solemn, with wreaths laid before kick-off. We couldn't get in and out quick enough. The players hardly covered themselves with glory and Wednesday deservedly won 2–0. I understood why the players' hearts weren't in it. They couldn't stop thinking about what had happened the last time they were here. I sensed their discomfort before, during and after the game. The Leppings Lane End was empty and that made the atmosphere even more eerie. We fulfilled our obligations, took the defeat and sped home. I was in a car with Hansen, Stevie and Eleanor Nicol.

'Gaffer, can we get some chips?' asked Stevie, who loved chips.

'Not tonight, Chico,' I replied. 'I just want to get home.'

Hillsborough continued to dominate our thoughts. When the Taylor Report recommended all-seater stadia, I understood why, but I also feared the working-class man might be priced out of football. Fans nowadays enjoy greater access to hospitality, more comfort and, touch wood, they feel safer, but all that comes at a cost. Somebody has to pay for all those magnificent facilities and it is the fan. Stepping through the turnstiles is an expensive move and football must be very, very careful that it doesn't lose generations of supporters. When I was at Blackburn, we failed to sell out Ewood despite the team doing well, so the club, intelligently, let in local schoolkids for a quid. Anfield, Old Trafford and the Emirates do get sold out, so they don't have the opportunity to do this. I worry that the younger generation will get out of the habit of going to the game and will go elsewhere.

My view of the police changed after Hillsborough. As a child I was brought up always to respect the police. My parents taught me the police were there to safeguard society, that they were good people doing a vital job and I should listen to anything they said. At Hillsborough, I felt no animosity towards the police as an institution, solely towards individual officers, including Duckenfield, who made mistakes and have still failed to admit responsibility for their calamitous decisions on 15 April 1989 and to apologise. The final death toll rose to 96 when Tony Bland's life-support machine was switched off in 1992.

Everybody was scarred by events that dreadful day, some more deeply than others. Some policemen received compensation for stress suffered, but they never lost a loved one. They never went through the harrowing experience of having to identify their precious child's lifeless body. It was wrong that only the police had their emotional wounds dressed when the families suffered more. When BBC *Grandstand* went live to Hillsborough that afternoon, the families were traumatised by the scenes they'd tuned in to. They were looking at the television pictures, searching for their sons, seeing them lying on the pitch, friends desperately trying to revive them. How shocking was that? Sitting at home watching was more distressing than being there at Hillsborough, where at least you could do something.

I still cannot understand why the authorities felt the police should get preferential treatment when it came to reparation. When somebody joins the police force, he or she must know and accept that stressful circumstances will be encountered. When somebody enters a football ground, that does not imply acceptance of possible threats to life and limb. The Establishment tried to protect itself. Any other club might have let it go but never Liverpool. The people have held on because they want closure, want somebody to hold up their hands and acknowledge their guilt. If the police accepted responsibility, the floodgates would open for compensation and that's the big issue, the Establishment's fear that the families will claim off the state. So the Establishment is going to block them. Trying to discover whether there was a cover-up has seemed an impossible task.

In the summer of 2000, Duckenfield was brought to court along with Bernard Murray, another police officer from Hillsborough. Murray was cleared of any wrongdoing while Duckenfield had no verdict against him. Any hopes of a retrial were scuppered by the judge. I always felt it was unfair that just two people were called to account. The whole system stank to me. Nobody had a personal vendetta against Duckenfield but the buck stopped with him. As the person in charge at Hillsborough, he had to face the wrath. The judge ruled that Duckenfield had suffered enough trauma, a verdict that wouldn't have brought much sympathy from the families.

On the twentieth anniversary of the tragedy, Government minister Andy Burnham was heckled during the memorial service at Anfield, an incident that said everything about the enduring resentment on Merseyside over the authorities' failure to alleviate the families' suffering. I felt for Andy, a politician of principle, a local man and an Evertonian who understood that Hillsborough was a national scandal needing tackling. Andy was always part of the solution, not the problem within Government. Since Hillsborough, the grieving families were let down by politician after politician until Andy Burnham came along, promising justice and a proper investigation.

Later on that day, Andy spoke at the Town Hall, where the Hillsborough families were being inducted in the roll of honour for the City of Liverpool.

'I have it on my agenda to get you access to the records earlier than you should,' Andy told the families. At the time, Andy was minister for Culture, Media and Sport, giving him the power to release classified details of reports given to the first Hillsborough Inquiry.

That night at the Town Hall, Andy confided to me that some of the reports left a lot to be desired. 'They are quite embarrassing,' he said.

'Andy, you spoke brilliantly and if you get those files opened for the families, I know how much it would mean. They just want to find out if there was a cover-up.'

Andy kept his word and it would be nice if he comes to the next Hillsborough memorial, in 2011, so people can apologise to him. In the spring of 2010, thanks to Andy Burnham, a panel was formed to examine these reports, a huge step forward in the fight for justice for the 96 who died at Hillsborough.

15

LEAVING HOME

DEALING with Hillsborough took a toll on me, physically and mentally. I can never say definitively that the tragedy was the reason for my resignation as Liverpool manager on 21 February 1991, but it played a part. Others suffered far more than I did, but I did feel incredibly drained. Stresses and strains dogged me during that period, tensing me up so much inside that my body broke out in blotches. Bottling up my emotions was deeply unhealthy. I never addressed issues, storing them up until eventually my system overloaded.

The pressure started building a year before Hillsborough, with the shock of the FA Cup final defeat by Wimbledon, and intensified some six weeks after the disaster with the game against Arsenal on Friday, 26 May, the last day of the 1989 season. When people talk about that remarkable match at Anfield as an epic moment in the history of football, I struggle to feel any pride or pleasure. I just feel pain. Anfield played host to a packed crowd of 41,718, tickets were like gold-dust and I was sure the television producers were licking their lips at the likely bumper viewing figures.

Privately, I was deeply unhappy about Liverpool being ordered to play on that Friday. The fixture had been scheduled for several weeks earlier, but the fixtures had been rescheduled and re-ordered after Hillsborough. I understood Liverpool–Arsenal offered the perfect showdown, a dream for ITV, but it was unfair on us. The League and ITV contributed to Liverpool losing the Double because they made our run-in too difficult. We beat Everton after two hours of draining football in the Cup final on the Saturday, grabbed a breather on the Sunday, took the Cup around the hospital in Liverpool on the Monday to show to those injured at Hillsborough, and then played West Ham on the Tuesday. Running on empty, the boys somehow summoned up enough energy to win, although the 5–1 scoreline was deeply misleading. Liverpool hadn't won at a canter. Defeating West Ham was a real struggle. The lads were magnificent but there's only so much a human body can take. We were shattered by Hillsborough and by the intense demands of an unforgiving final week.

Standing in the dressing room before kick-off against Arsenal, I caught a look of weariness in some eyes. Having gone through so much, some of the players just closed down. I tried to rally them for one final push. 'Just go out and win,' I said. Even a 1–0 defeat would give Liverpool the title, but it was never in the club's mentality to play cautiously. Sensing their exhaustion, I urged the players to take the game to Arsenal, knowing a goal would kill them off.

Down the corridor, I learned later, George Graham told his players that 'Liverpool will fall apart under the pressure. They will not be able to breathe out there for the weight of expectancy.' It seemed to me that George was trying to build Hillsborough into the equation but that pressure had gone. After Hillsborough, our mission was to win the Cup for the families and we never buckled in fulfilling that vital duty. Liverpool players were long skilled in the art of handling heavy expectations.

As the players left the dressing room, I felt it was all so surreal that in a year of so much trauma Liverpool were within 90 minutes of the Double. I filled with pride that my players, who'd gone through a storm, were so close to another momentous footballing landmark. The heart was willing but I feared the legs might be weak.

When they came out on to the pitch, the fatigue slowly seeping into the players was a contrast to the vibrancy of the Kop. Liverpool's fans greeted the visitors with 'boring, boring Arsenal', a reference to their style of play under George. Arsenal's back-four of Dixon, Bould, Adams and Winterburn was the strongest part of the team, a formidable barrier that loved an offside. I never criticised Arsenal for their approach because they enjoyed great success, and I also really liked George, a thoughtful foot-baller I'd known from our days with Scotland. George had a great managerial career, starting at Millwall, and was obsessed with football. I could imagine George and Terry Venables sitting at the dinner table, lining up pepper pots, empty coffee cups and wine glasses in formations as they debated tactics long into the night.

Just as I greatly admired Arsenal's manager, so mutual respect defined relations between the clubs. To Anfield's eternal appre-ciation, Bould, Adams and the rest of George's players paid their respects for Hillsborough, handing out flowers to the fans. It crossed my mind that this could have been a psychological ploy. I know some people genuinely thought Arsenal were trying to push Hillsborough back into Liverpool minds with all the flowers. Personally, I felt they were a touch of class from a classy club. Hillsborough was always in our minds anyway, so we didn't need our memories jogged.

The game unfolded in a blur and, looking back, it's still like peering into mist. I can just about make out the outline of certain events, such as Arsenal's first goal, an indirect free-kick that Alan Smith claimed he got a touch to, diverting it past Bruce. I can see the referee, Dave Hutchinson, talking to the linesman, checking the goal's validity before pointing to the centre circle. What I recall most about Arsenal's decisive second goal was the criticism of John Barnes for trying to take the ball past Kevin Richardson and losing it. Even now, newspapers pass critical comments about Digger for not knocking the ball out, or keeping it down by Arsenal's corner-flag. I resented this condemnation of Digger. Why shouldn't John attempt to go past Richardson, who was hobbling? John had been racing past people for fun for four years at Liverpool, and I'd never slam somebody for expressing themselves – that's what I bought Digger for in the first place. All our success and our enjoyment came from Digger attacking, Rushie and Aldo trying moves in the box and Ray Houghton gliding forward. Why change them? I'd never question my players' instincts nor Liverpool's historic obsession with attacking. When Barnsey waltzed past three QPR players and knocked the ball in the top corner, nobody ventured the view that he should have played it safe because Liverpool were already ahead. John Barnes was a wonderful, creative footballer who tried moves that sometimes didn't come off, but that never altered my belief that Liverpool were incredibly lucky to have him.

I once watched a clip of that Michael Thomas goal and heard that great commentator Brian Moore say: 'Dalglish just stands there.' I did. The shock froze me to the spot. I was numb, the fuel gauge showing empty as dejection set in. Doing the Double would have been a fairy tale, an unbelievable achievement after what Liverpool had endured. When some feeling returned to my body, and I shook hands with George, I acknowledged that Arsenal deserved so much credit for their display. Arsenal had been under pressure, too. George was very respectful and I admired Arsenal players for not going over the top in their celebrations. Liverpool had laid on some Champagne, which simply got rerouted to the away dressing room. It was one of those evenings when everybody conducted themselves impeccably, and I'll never forget the Kop's applause as Arsenal received the trophy. Even in defeat, Liverpool showed dignity. On the way off, I did check with the referee about Arsenal's first.

'Are you sure about the goal?'

'Kenny, I'm sure,' replied Dave. 'You go and check.' I did. Dave was right – it was a goal. So I went to the referee's room with a bottle of Champagne.

'OK, Dave, no problems, you'd better have this.'

I'm not normally that obliging with officials, but Alan Smith had touched the ball. I believe the absence of sensible communication between managers and referees has become one of the banes of the modern era. If a manager seeks out the referee afterwards and speaks to him in a reasonable tone, what's wrong with that? They can have a dialogue, discuss any controversy and understand each other's positions. Unfortunately, some current referees are stand-offish, almost arrogantly ignoring the managers, whose livelihood they threaten. If a referee occasionally admitted to making a mistake, they'd be treated with greater respect.

After that loss to Arsenal, the pressure was on us to deliver the title in the 1989–90 season and we didn't disappoint. Liverpool always reacted to adversity. One of the secrets of Liverpool's success was their togetherness. When the team struggled for form, Al would shout, 'Full dog day, tomorrow.' This was a glorified bonding session, involving clear-the-air arguments, alcohol, pizzas for the boys and jerk chicken for Digger. Such sessions were vital for camaraderie. When Jose Mourinho managed Chelsea to back-to-back titles, it didn't surprise me to hear that his captain, John Terry, organised get-togethers for the lads at his house, hanging out and playing computer games. At Liverpool, I certainly encouraged the full dog days. As long as none of them ended up in jail, it was all right. Sometimes the boys had a day out at the races, going to Chester or Aintree.

Racing was a major interest in the Liverpool dressing room. We always prayed we would be playing at Anfield on Grand National day – kick-off in the morning, bus revving up outside after the game to take us and the wives to Aintree. On 8 April 1989, we beat Sheffield Wednesday at a canter, winning 5–1, then sped to the course, all the boys piling into a hospitality tent for a raucous afternoon to celebrate the victory and the Grand National's 150th birthday. By the time Jimmy Frost raced home on Little Polveir, I'm not sure too many of the lads were focusing properly. Those days were special because they strengthened team morale, and also made the wives feel part of Liverpool. I'm sure that's why the dressing room reacted so strongly after Hillsborough. Wives of the Liverpool players had always got on royally. When the singing started, it was often Tommo's missus, Marge, leading the way through all the Liverpool songs. When Marge and Tommo started courting, Tommo must have romanced her with Kopite tunes because she knew every word, every verse even to 'In My Liverpool Home', which goes on for days.

Using that camaraderie, we tore into Crystal Palace on 12 September 1989, putting nine goals past them. Aldo was leaving for Real Sociedad, so when we got a penalty, I told him to get off the bench, get out there and score it – a hugely emotional moment for him and the Kop.

Rushie's return had inevitably placed pressure on Aldo, yet it surprised me that Rushie initially attracted some critical headlines, including one that read 'Rush's Best Days Are Behind Him'. Newspapers' capacity for ignorance never ceased to amaze me. 'Pay no attention,' I told Rushie. 'It's all bollocks. I brought you back. I have faith in you and that's all that matters.' Aldo was playing well and I briefly considered using Rush behind him. Rushie could see a pass and could have put Aldo through, but Beardo was doing brilliantly for us in there. Rushie and Aldo played together briefly and successfully, but when Sociedad showed an interest, I informed Aldo.

'I'm doing you a favour, Aldo,' I told him. 'If you want to go, you can go. You're at a premium now and can cash in.'

It was a really difficult decision to let Aldo go, because he made a huge contribution to Liverpool Football Club. Before he left, Aldo gave the Kop a typical farewell gift – that penalty goal against Palace. The next day, I dropped Palace's manager, Steve Coppell, a supportive letter, just saying it was a freak result and I knew they'd go on to have a good season. When Palace beat us 4–3 in the Cup semis on 8 April to scupper our chance of a

Double, I did look back and think that sending that letter was not one of my wiser decisions. Palace were very defensive in the Cup, Coppell almost ordering a man-to-man marking job on each Liverpool player out of fear of another thrashing. Palace won because of their set-pieces.

I was furious and brought in Ronny Rosenthal for the next game, against Charlton Athletic in the League at Selhurst Park. With Rushie out injured, Ronny readily accepted the challenge of a first start, scoring the perfect hat-trick – head, left foot and right. Ronny had come on trial from Standard Liege and did so well we signed him. His single-mindedness about goalscoring stood out a mile and, although Ronny understood he might be a sub, coming on rather than starting, I liked the way he picked up the game quickly. Many people unkindly remember Ronny's stay at Liverpool for that miss against Aston Villa in 1992, when he hit the crossbar after rounding Nigel Spink. For me, I'll always think gratefully about Ronny's goals that pushed Liverpool past the winning post in the spring of 1990.

A date that should be inscribed on the conscience of all Liverpool fans, players and managers is 28 April 1990 – the last time this great club won the title. We'd just beaten QPR 2–1 and needed Villa to drop points against Norwich City. When word came through from Carrow Road that Villa had drawn, there was an almighty roar. 'Champions, champions,' chanted the Kop, even being so gracious as to sing my name.

On 1 May, we were presented with the First Division trophy after defeating Derby County at Anfield. For the first, and last, time in my career, I pulled rank. I put myself on the bench, even though others offered more, and brought myself on for Jan Molby with 19 minutes left. I wanted my last-ever game to be a special occasion, and winning the title was certainly that. If my joy at reclaiming the trophy was immense, so was my delight in the manner in which we'd conducted the campaign. Digger was flying all season, so was wee Peter, and Ray Houghton more than played his part. Ray was a really underestimated footballer, but I rated him so highly for the way he read the game. Ray's astute positional play was a real asset to Liverpool.

I was particularly pleased for Al, who was able to hold the League Championship trophy up in front of the Kop, and was reminded of the extraordinarily competitive nature of the people in the Liverpool dressing room by his reaction – he collected his eighth title-winners' medal that year but banged on about the 1985–86 championship. Still does. 'The record books claim Nealy got one more title medal than I did,' Al tells me on frequent occasions, 'but I don't think he got a medal that year. He left in October. He needed twelve appearances.' Hansen was as competitive as they come.

Playing alongside him was the hugely experienced Glenn Hysen, who had chosen Liverpool over Manchester United. Glenn brought authority in the air during onslaughts from opponents such as Wimbledon, even Arsenal when Alan Smith was up there. Sometimes he played a bit too deep for us, defending on the 18-yard box when we were used to pushing up, but the likeable Swede soon settled.

When I reached the dressing room after the win over QPR, all the boys were celebrating, and the emotion of the occasion certainly got to Bruce, who threw me in the communal bath, drenching my lovely Candy coat.

'I'll be looking to sell you now, Bruce,' I joked with him.

The truth was so different. The only person's future preoccupying me was mine. Almost exhausted, I was very frank when PBR and the new chairman, Noel White, called me in to discuss a new contract before summer.

'I need a break,' I told Peter and Noel. Surprised, they talked about how vital I was to Liverpool, how I'd feel refreshed after the summer holiday, and I agreed to think it over. Liverpool was home, a huge part of our family life, and Kelly and Paul were big fans. They loved going to matches and being around Anfield.

So I decided to carry on, hoping the dark cloud hanging over me would blow away.

'All right, I'll have a go, but at least you know about my reservations,' I informed PBR and Noel at the second meeting. 'But I don't want to take money under false pretences, in case I leave. So please don't give me money. Give me shares in the club. That's me showing my loyalty to Liverpool, being a shareholder.'

'We can't give you shares,' PBR replied.

'Look, I don't want to take the money because I don't know if I can carry on,' I replied. 'If I can't and I have shares, then I will still have an affiliation with the club, even for the kids.'

'We can't,' repeated PBR. That was that. I couldn't argue, but I found the board's intransigence disappointing.

'Get yourself a good holiday,' PBR said as I left. 'You'll be fine for the start of the season.'

However churned up inside I felt, I returned to work determined to bring more trophies to Anfield. Liverpool enjoyed a storming start but the newspapers decided it was my turn in the public stocks, particularly having a pop over my signing of Jimmy Carter for £750,000. They never understood. Liverpool's defence had a healthy respect for Jimmy because he had a real good game on the wing against us for Millwall. Ray and Digger were doing brilliantly but we needed a bit of cover out wide. Some newspapers speculated I hadn't spent more because the transfer budget had been slashed. Anfield teemed with surveyors and builders, transforming the Kemlyn Road at a cost of roughly £4 million, but in all the boardroom meetings I attended nobody ever refused me money to strengthen the squad. Jimmy was what I felt we needed. He had pace, could go right or left, and people forgot he had a great start, being Man of the Match in his first two games, against Villa and Wimbledon. Jimmy was made to feel very welcome by the lads and it saddened me and the boys that he couldn't maintain his form. I think Liverpool were just too big for him. In the end, Jimmy felt inhibited by Anfield, which was a disappointment because he could have given us an extra dimension.

Liverpool were blessed with the Footballer of the Year in Digger and a striker of the quality of Rushie, and we still led the League, yet the newspapers had the nerve to call us negative when we went to Arsenal on 2 December 1990. For the record, and for the education of those who claimed I picked a cautious team, we lined up: Grobbelaar, Hysen, Burrows, Nicol, Whelan, Gillespie, Ablett, Venison, Rush, Barnes, Molby. And that's defensive? How could I go for a draw with Molby, Digger and Rush starting, players who amassed 53 goals between them that season? My side at Highbury was designed for victory. Arsenal won 3–0 because they were good and we were poor on the day. One-off embarrassments happen to even the best. 'Dalglish gave us negative virtues and his side paid a heavy price,' ranted the *Daily Mail*. What did they want? Ten forwards? Peter Beardsley had shin splints so I couldn't call upon him, but we still had two attackers on the bench, Ray and Ronny, who both came on, yet I got slaughtered.

I felt some people were out to get me, that an agenda existed against me. Liverpool were top and I was getting panned. Explain that. I knew the Press often found me awkward but I resented being labelled 'boring', 'miserable', 'sulky', even 'prickly'. Prickly? Of course I was prickly defending the people I worked for and protecting my family. If somebody upset me, I stood my corner. The 'dour' perception emphasised how ignorant the papers were – anybody who played alongside me would laugh at that image.

We were sitting on top of the League, so why weren't all the managers below me getting stick? People queued up to give me a kicking. 'What we've got now is a very imbalanced Liverpool team,' moaned Jimmy Hill. 'The great stylish midfielders of Liverpool will be turning over in their graves to see the orthodox and very average way in which they are performing.' What unbelievable nonsense. My opinion of Jimmy Hill was never shaped by that historic Scottish antipathy towards this opinionated Englishman. I respected Hill for his achievements as a football administrator, particularly with the Professional Footballers' Association, but not his football philosophies. If Hill sat and talked to me about football, it wouldn't educate me. I'd accept criticism from people I respected for what they'd done in the game. If I had a constructive conversation with Fergie, Arsene Wenger or Terry Venables, I'd take note if they made a suggestion, but I didn't take much notice of somebody paid to pass comment on TV, radio or in the prints, saying things they couldn't really substantiate. Shanks's advice that 'newspapers are tomorrow's fish and chip wrapping' has always stayed with me, but I must admit to great sympathy for the modern manager, with so many media outlets spouting opinions.

Even Bertie Mee had a go, saying I should use Peter Beardsley more, and he should really have known better. Nobody knew my players better than I did. I knew very well who was best suited to face physical sides such as Millwall, Wimbledon and Arsenal. It was easy for people to criticise – perhaps they thought it might wind me up, maybe even unsettle the players. I don't know – but this perception that I deliberately used Beardsley sparingly was just plain wrong. I never tried to flex my muscles in a show of strength over Beardsley. I wasn't so arrogant that I'd sacrifice a result just for my selfish benefit. I explained to Peter he was being omitted against Arsenal for tactical reasons.

'We've got to play some big guys, Pedro. Arsenal are a big, physical team and we have to make sure we can match their physique with ours.'

'I'm not happy,' Peter replied. 'I think I should be playing.'

'I'm the one who makes the decision. I never made a bad decision when I asked you to come to Liverpool Football Club, did I? If you put your trust in me when you signed, you must trust me now, even if you don't necessarily agree a hundred per cent. At the end of the day, Liverpool Football Club and the result is more important than any one individual, and that includes me and you.'

Paul, in a Juventus top, with the League Championship trophies in 1990.

I bowed out as a player after we beat Derby *en route* to another title.

Coaches Ronnie Moran (*left*) and Roy Evans had as little idea as I did that the title would become so elusive for Liverpool.

My judgement was questioned when I signed David Speedie – yet he scored three times in his first two games for Liverpool.

Chairman Sir John Smith joins me at a press conference to announce my resignation as manager – I felt my head was exploding.

A 'well done' from Robbie Fowler after
Blackburn took the title – at Anfield.

More congratulations from Steve
McManaman on Rovers' red-letter day.

Holding the Premier League trophy with captain Tim Sherwood was a wonderful feeling,
although my heart was still at Liverpool.

In training for the Hillsborough Memorial Match are (*back row, left to right*) Gary Ablett, Jan Molby, Paul Harrison, Gary Gillespie, Mark Lawrenson and (*front row, left to right*) Jean-Paul Sproson, Ronnie Whelan, me and Ian Rush.

Kelly interviews the old man for TV after the memorial game.

Rafa Benitez bids farewell to Anfield, looking wistful as he realises his Liverpool days are over, but he left with warm memories and a Champions League triumph to his name.

Chatting to Christian Purslow, the chief executive, who has played an important part in stabilising Liverpool in difficult times.

Roy Hodgson, pictured with Steven Gerrard, earned his chance at Liverpool, but issues over the ownership of the club meant he worked against a backdrop of uncertainty.

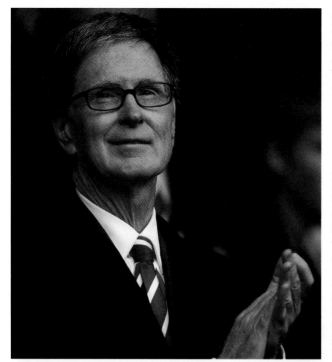

Left: John W. Henry became Liverpool's principal owner in autumn 2010. He and fellow American Tom Werner arrived with a background in baseball – the Red Sox, naturally!

Below left: The timing of Fernando Torres' transfer to Chelsea wasn't ideal, but the club is bigger than any individual and we moved on with the signing of Luis Suarez and Andy Carroll.

Below right: Maxi Rodriguez scored two hat-tricks in three matches for us early in 2011, a richly deserved reward for the intelligence and professionalism he brings to his game.

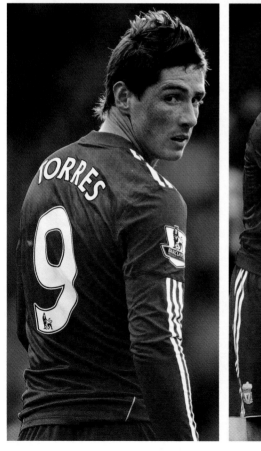

Luis Suarez (*left*) was our record signing for an hour and a half after joining us from Ajax – until we landed Andy Carroll from Newcastle, and unveiled them both to the media.

Dirk Kuyt responded to my recruiting new forwards with a hat-trick against Manchester United and goals in five consecutive games, including this penalty against Newcastle.

At Buckingham Palace to receive my MBE with Marina, Paul and Kelly in 1985.

A proud moment as Prince Charles awards the MBE to Marina.

Another family affair at Buckingham Palace with Lauren (*left*), Lynsey and Marina's mother Martha present for the investiture.

I still understood Peter's frustration because he loved playing. I would have been surprised and disappointed if Peter had done cartwheels. Of the rivers of nonsense flooding through the columns of newspapers, one of the most ludicrous involved the allegation of animosity between Peter and me, even between Marina and Sandra Beardsley. Just because Peter didn't play every game, the papers concocted an image of neighbours at war – the Beardsleys lived two doors away from us in Southport. What garbage. Paul popped into Peter's to fix his video. Whenever I saw Sandra pushing Drew in his pram down the street, I'd stop and chat, find out how Drew was doing. Recently, when Drew visited Liverpool's Academy with the Newcastle lads, I sought him out, had a word and wished him well in his career.

Peter featured regularly enough even when I brought in David Speedie from Coventry City on 31 January 1991. Again, my judgement was questioned in the newspapers, some people claiming he wasn't 'a Liverpool player', but what the hell did that mean? They said John Barnes wasn't 'a Liverpool player' and he was magnificent. I always felt it was good to have different styles, different characteristics. 'Speedo' could drop back to be an attacking midfield player if we wanted, although he was not much use defensively. Scarcely 5ft 7in, he was still brilliant in the air, and he was aggressive, bringing a spiky impetus to our attack. We needed a bit more fight at that stage.

'If he's in the penalty box scoring goals for Coventry, he'll do even better with the service he'll get here,' I said to Old Tom. 'I know he's never been anywhere with the magnitude of Liverpool. He's never played at the top. He's got decent abilities but I know it's a punt.' Speedo was a gamble but he scored three goals in his first two games, one at Old Trafford and two against Everton, so that vindicated my decision. Some gamble! Speedo was effective wherever he went, and when I managed Blackburn, with his goals he did more than anyone to get us promoted. He left Liverpool because of a personality clash with Graeme Souness and newspapers banged on all the time about Speedo's short fuse. He was strong willed and spoke his mind but was never a problem in the dressing room when I was there. The guy just wanted to win and that's what the game's about.

For the FA Cup replay at Everton on 20 February, I brought Peter back for Speedo, so that killed the anti-Beardsley theory. The decision was easy. I felt Peter's greater subtlety on the ball would trouble Everton more than Speedo's directness. Five hours before kick-off, I came to a far harder decision. Whatever happened at Goodison, I made up my mind I'd be in to see the chairman, telling him I had to leave. I just had to go. The pressure was too much. Driving home in the car after games, I was nipping away at Kelly and Paul. When Kelly said something, I'd snap, 'Shut up.' I'd instantly regret it, thinking the kids didn't deserve a father in a mood as bad as this. The atmosphere at home wasn't nice and I was to blame. My tense state of mind was unfair on the kids, I was upsetting them with my behaviour. I was a mess. The previous December, I'd come out in big red blotches all over my body. I went to the office staff Christmas party covered in these huge blemishes. Al still winds me up about it now.

'It was your Jimmy Carter rash,' says Hansen. 'You were allergic to him!'

Liverpool sent me for an allergy test but all that showed was a 0.0001 intolerance towards fish. To calm the rash down, the Liverpool doctor pumped me with Piriton at Anfield every other day, alternating the cheeks on my backside, so that within a fortnight I felt like a pin cushion. As Piriton made me drowsy, Old Tom drove me home and I'd fall through the door, stumble across the hall to the living room and slump into a deep sleep on the couch for a couple of hours.

I wouldn't have said I was an alcoholic but I found a few glasses of wine took the edge off me. Having stopped playing, there wasn't the professional necessity to stay in and stay fit. I'd been at work all day, so it was nice to go out at night, sit down and have a bit of food and a drink.

The nation's amateur psychologists subsequently claimed it was the stress and strain of that extraordinary Cup tie at Goodison that tipped me over the precipice. It wasn't. My nerves were shredded long before 20 February 1991, an evening inevitably seething with tension. Just heading into Goodison, I was vilified by Everton fans, but I shrugged it off. I'd have been more surprised if they'd serenaded me. Everton punters cared passionately for their club and certainly got behind the players that night. Recalling the seesaw sequence is distressing. Liverpool kept taking the lead, through Peter, twice, and Rushie, but Everton kept equalising, through Graeme Sharp and then Tony Cottee in the 89th minute. It was madness, like watching a car-crash and not knowing which emergency service to call first. When Digger curled in a fourth after 102 unbelievable minutes, I thought that might be that. Job done.

'Let's shut up shop, Bugsy,' I said to Ronnie. 'Let's stick Jan back to sweeper.'

'Hold on,' said Ronnie.

'Just leave it,' I shrugged.

At that instant of indecision, I knew the emotional conclusion I'd reached that afternoon was justified. I should have put Jan back there but I froze. Time to go. When Cottee again exploited our defensive disarray, my failure to shift Jan back was fully punished. In the dressing room afterwards, the mood veered from frustration to fury. Some of the players were screaming about the defending. Having gone in front four times, it was criminal to let the lead slip four times. I was speechless, helpless really. At least the pain would soon end. The dressing-room storm went on around me and I was there in body but not mind. The process of leaving had begun.

The following morning at 10.30, I drove into Anfield for a routine management meeting with PBR and Noel White. Peter was shuffling some papers, mentioning the first item up for discussion when I interrupted him. I couldn't delay.

'I want to resign as manager.'

'Pardon?' Noel said.

'I've had enough. I need a break. I just feel as if my head is exploding.' They were shocked.

'Why?' Peter asked.

'It's the pressure. It's incredible. I've been feeling this for some time now. You knew last summer the reservations I had. I've soldiered on but no more. My health is suffering. I want to go now. Today.'

There was a stunned silence. Peter and Noel needed time to collect themselves, so I went downstairs to the office. Old Tom was there, scrutinising *The Times* crossword, and I explained what had happened.

'Are you sure you're making the right decision, Kenny?'

'There's no going back, Tom. You see what I'm like now. You share the office. You drive me home. You see the injections. You know something isn't right.'

'You just need a long rest, Kenny. Get away from football, spend some time on the golf course and come back refreshed next season.'

'I have to go, Tom.'

PBR came in for another attempt.

'Are you sure you don't want to take a sabbatical?' he asked.

'Of course I don't. I'm out. I'm shot. I've got to go. I have a position of responsibility at this football club and I can't make decisions. I don't deserve to be here. And you don't deserve me to be here.'

Liverpool's solicitor, Tony Ensor, walked into the room. PBR and Noel had sent him to have a word.

'Kenny, I'm talking to you as a friend. Peter's right. Why not have a sabbatical? Take some time off and then come back.'

'Tony, how can I go on holiday and know I'm coming back? It wouldn't be a holiday. I can't walk out on a club, leave Ronnie and Roy to take the team for Saturday, not knowing whether I would be fit enough to return. How can that be beneficial for me or Liverpool Football Club? That leaves everybody in limbo. It's the middle of the season, we are top of the League, still in the Cup, with a replay with Everton, so how could I have a sabbatical? It wouldn't look right for the players. My mind's made up. I need a clean break. It's over.'

Tony sighed and looked at me.

'OK, Kenny. Now I have to talk to you as the club solicitor. If you go, first you have to read this and sign it.' He pushed what looked like a contract across the table, to cover Liverpool for compensation if I pitched up elsewhere.

'Tony, I'm not even going to read it. I'll sign it because I don't care what the conditions are. I've just got to go. Look, if I'd had an agenda, I'd have had representation in here.'

After Tony left with the signed paper, I phoned Ronnie. He deserved to know quickly.

'Bugsy, I'm resigning.'

'Are you winding me up?

'No. I've got to get a break, get away and get rested.' Ronnie wasn't happy but he respected my decision.

At 4 p.m., Liverpool held an emergency board meeting at which they reluctantly accepted my resignation with the stipulation I attend a Press conference in the morning and then I could go. Later on, I read a very sorrowful comment from PBR who said that 'watching Kenny Dalglish walk out of Anfield was the saddest moment of my life'. Well, I wasn't best pleased either. Nor were Kelly and Paul when I got home. Sensibly, Marina had kept them back from school.

'I've resigned,' I told them. They burst into tears and so did I. The kids were distraught that I'd turned my back on the club I loved, and they loved. Paul had turned 14 three days before and I felt so bad. Happy Birthday, wee man, you can't go back to Anfield. Telling the players was almost as hard. In the morning,

I reached the ground at 10 and headed straight to the dressing room where the players were getting ready for training.

'I'm finished here. I'm just going upstairs to announce it. Thanks very much.' With that, I turned and walked away. What more could I say? All I could think of was getting out of Anfield as quickly as possible. Al knew what was happening. I always kept Al abreast of my situation. He told me later how after I left he went into the dressing room and said, 'I'm the new manager – and there are going to be big changes.' The players looked at him, perhaps a few wondering if they'd be bombed out. 'Only kidding,' said Al.

Upstairs, I was forced to go through the nightmare of a Press conference. A few journalists had got wind of my resignation but most in the room thought it was some announcement that John Barnes was on his way to Italy. The papers had been full of speculation about Digger. They were shocked when Noel White opened up and I'll never forget his words.

'With great regret I have to say that Kenny Dalglish has requested to the board of Liverpool to resign as manager,' Noel said. 'I would like to assure our supporters we did everything in our power to change his mind, and persuade him to continue to do the job which he has done with such conspicuous success during the last five years or so. However, he has made it clear that he was determined to give up active participation in professional football and he has also assured us that we could do nothing to alter his decision to resign.'

I sat there, listening to all this, not understanding why I had to be there. Liverpool were just prolonging my agony. Noel could have announced it and I could have been away somewhere, heading to a beach with Marina and the kids. Everybody in football knew I'd rather be in front of a firing squad than the Press. My ordeal deepened as I spoke.

'This is the first time since I came to the club that I take the interest of Kenny Dalglish over Liverpool Football Club. This is not a decision that I just woke to. The worst thing I could have done was not to make a decision at all and just carry on until the end of the season, knowing I was not happy. The main problem is the pressure I put on myself because of my strong desire to succeed. The stress that comes right before and after games has got the better of me.'

Honesty underpinned my every word, and I even openly admitted that I felt 'my head would explode', but the Press still hunted alternative motives, and I found that truly hurtful. If I'd continued pushing, pushing and pushing myself, I wouldn't have recovered. Walking away was the right decision for everybody, the responsible decision. Some joker ventured the idea that I couldn't live up to Liverpool's huge expectations. How ridiculous was that? I'd helped raise those expectations as a player and a manager. Think of the trophies that had come into Anfield during my 14 years.

My microphone torture over, I raced to Hillside Golf Club, so often my refuge, for a round with Ron Yeats. A photographer tried to snap a picture but fell over, got spotted and thrown off. Everybody seemed to be talking about my resignation, every radio station seemed to be discussing every crackpot theory over why I'd left. Eventually, unable to contain my anger, I rang Radio City.

'I sat there at that Press conference and told the truth. I've been manager for five years and always told the truth, so why would I make up a story now? I've left because of the pressure. There's no conspiracy.' I was touched to read an appraisal of my time as Liverpool manager by Matt Darcy of the *Daily Star*. 'The most honest manager I have worked with,' wrote Matt. That meant a lot. I might have been awkward at times but I never lied.

Inevitably, the fancy columnists weighed in, trampling over my reputation. Michael Parkinson berated me in the *Sunday Telegraph*, claiming I knew nothing about pressure. 'Pressure is something that nurses know about, or people who grind out a living in a factory, or men who dig a coal mine underground,' Parkinson wrote. 'Pressure is being poor or unemployed or homeless or hopeless. What it's not is being paid £200,000 a year to manage one of the world's greatest football clubs.' Parky talked crap. The money was irrelevant and the profession was irrelevant. What mattered was the nature of the person. Some people are more prone to pressure, some people had jobs where they could take time off, but I couldn't. Managing Liverpool was relentless. Did Parky work every day of the week? I don't know. What did Parky want anyway? For me to carry on grinding myself down? For my kids to have a stressed-out father? I just thanked God that I got out in time to rescue my health.

Corroboration for my decision came on the Saturday morning when a doctor friend came over to our house in Southport. When he heard my whole story about the blotches and dithering over decisions, his response was simple: 'You've done the right thing.' A week later, on 4 March, Marina organised a surprise party for my fortieth birthday. All the boys from Liverpool turned up with Ronnie and Roy and we had a good old drink. I'm not sure they felt that life began at 40, and a few of them joked I was finished at 40, but it was great to see them again, a reminder that life went on.

The kids' tears soon dried. 'Can we go to Disney?' Paul asked. So we did and it felt good to focus on the kids for once. They are so special and I'd neglected them because of my obsession with Liverpool. Old Tom stayed in touch with Marina while we were in Orlando.

'Just leave him, Tom,' said Marina. 'Just ask him in a couple of weeks and he'll come back.'

She was right. If Liverpool had asked me to carry on as manager the moment I returned from Florida, I'd have jumped at the chance because I felt my head had cleared, and my batteries were recharged. Sadly, Liverpool never asked. During our stay in Orlando, I received a phone-call to tell me Graeme Souness had got the job, and I felt a twinge of regret. Liverpool were my club, my job, my home. Now somebody else was in. The blow was softened only because the torch had been picked up by Graeme, my old room-mate. Having impressed as a manager at Rangers, revamping Scottish football with David Murray, Graeme was the logical choice. Liverpool stuck with the tradition of promoting one of their own, in Graeme's case a former captain and distinguished player. On returning from Orlando, I made sure I stayed out of the road. Anfield was now Graeme's place, not mine any more. The stories of Shanks getting under Bob's feet were very much in my mind. I knew I'd be made welcome at Anfield, but I didn't want to cast a shadow.

Graeme was busy imposing himself on the dressing room. Among those heading out of the building were Speedo, Peter, Macca, Gary Gillespie, Steve Staunton, Gary Ablett and Glenn Hysen. Over the years, a fallacy has spread like poison ivy that Graeme inherited a Dad's Army squad off me. After I left, some people claimed I jumped ship because the team were ageing. The figures certainly don't give any credence to such an allegation. Hansen was 36 and he packed it in because of his knee, anyway. The next oldest were Glenn Hysen and Gary Gillespie at 31, an age when many defenders were at their peak. The next group comprised Beardsley, Nicol, Whelan and Rushie who were still the right side of 30. So the balance was good, particularly as I'd stocked up with good kids who were beginning to come through. A production line had long been in place.

The first guy I got in as Director of Youth was Malcolm Cook, a professional with Motherwell, Bradford and Newport County, and coach with a few clubs, including Doncaster Rovers. Malcolm left after two years when I happened to bump into Steve Heighway at a game in 1989. I knew Steve was working in the States.

'What are you doing?' I asked.

'I'm director of coaching at the Clearwater Chargers.'

'You don't fancy a job here do you?' He did.

Steve came back and his strong personality was exactly what Liverpool needed to get the kids coming through. Michael Owen was nurtured by Steve. Jamie Carragher was already in the system. He'd left to have a go at Everton and returned under Steve Heighway's wing. Carra trained with my son Paul in the evenings at Netherton and I'd go down and join in. Carra's developed into one of the top centre-halves in Europe but he started as a striker, a good one, with Bootle Boys. I was so committed to signing up these good kids I had the best ones brought to the office. Steve McManaman came in with his dad to speak to me and I convinced them to sign. Robbie Fowler trained at Melwood in the evenings and one day came in with his dad. Again, I persuaded him to commit himself to Liverpool at 16, so no one can question the quality of my legacy.

One day in 1990, I was driving out of Melwood and spotted Robbie, then a 15-year-old beginning to make a name for himself in the youth team. Robbie was standing at a bus-stop with his dad.

'Where are you going?'

'Into town,' Robbie replied. 'The Dingle.'

'Jump in.'

'But you live in Southport, the other way.'

'It's not far, Robbie, hop in. I'll give you a lift.' Having deposited them in town, I turned round and sped back up to Southport. On seeing Robbie at Melwood the following morning, I asked, 'Did you get home all right?'

'Yeah, no problem, but my dad was gutted.'

'Why? I dropped him off where you wanted.'

'No, no. Not that. That was great. Ta.'

'So why was your dad gutted?'

'None of his mates saw him coming out of your car!'

I went out of my way to recruit good young talent. Jamie Redknapp came up from Bournemouth to train at Melwood when he was 16 and I'd have taken him there and then because he had this great presence. Even at that young age, Jamie took control of games. With Harry as his dad, Jamie's good breeding showed on the pitch. I pleaded with Harry to sell him but he wouldn't, arguing that Jamie was too young to leave Bournemouth. We just had to wait until Harry was ready to let Jamie go. Our patience and quiet persistence was rewarded and Liverpool landed a gem in Jamie.

I kept refreshing the squad. Mike Marsh was spotted by Tommo on a public pitch up in Kirkby and he was starting to get involved. I made sure Marshy quickly became familiar with the first team, encouraging him to be on speaking terms with Rushie, Digger and Peter, all of whom he revered, being a Liverpool fan.

'I know they're your idols,' I said to Marshy. 'But now you are coming to play with them, don't let yourself down by being overawed. If you make a mistake, it's how you react. Enjoy yourself. I'm including you because you're good enough.'

Gentle initiation helped those boys settle in, so it wasn't too much of a culture shock when they were promoted from the reserves full-time. That was the Liverpool way, building for the future. We brought Nicky Tanner for £20,000 from Bristol Rovers. Nicky played 32 League games the season after I left, so that was a good inheritance for Graeme. Steve Harkness came from Carlisle, having impressed when playing up front against Liverpool in an FA Youth Cup tie at Anfield. Big Don Hutchison came from Hartlepool. They were educated in the art and craft of football and didn't do too badly.

Graeme's time as manager of Liverpool wasn't a huge success, because, I believe, he made too many changes too quickly. Finishing sixth, Liverpool's lowest placing since 1965, was a development that never gave me any pleasure. I had too much respect for Graeme and Liverpool to say that I'd recently won the League. Leaving Anfield never stopped me loving Liverpool.

16

EXILE

THE call was a pleasant surprise, a welcome reminder of my Liverpool home. It came through from reception at Ewood Park to inform me that Peter Robinson was at the ground, picking up tickets for the Liverpool game the following day, and he wanted to say 'hello'. The date was 2 April 1993 and I'd been manager at Blackburn Rovers since October 1991, enjoying the task of rebuilding this famous old Lancashire mill-town club. Driving into Ewood, I saw PBR standing there, and all the Liverpool memories raced back, the European Cups, League titles, open-topped bus rides and non-stop banter.

'Hop in Peter, I'll give you a lift back up to the car park,' I said. When he'd settled in the passenger seat, PBR turned to me and asked, 'Kenny, when are you coming home?'

'What do you mean?'

'When are you coming back to Liverpool, Kenny?'

'Peter, you just have to ask.'

'OK,' he said.

'It's up to yourselves,' I added. 'You just need to phone.' PBR nodded, climbed out of the car and walked across to his.

Liverpool never phoned, though, and regret has been my constant companion ever since. My hopes were lifted and dashed. I'd have leapt at the chance to rejoin Liverpool. The people at Blackburn were special, really unassuming, but Anfield was home. Ewood never felt like home. I had total respect for Rovers, and deep admiration for their benefactor, Jack Walker. Jack made the dream possible, supplying the finance, reconstructing the stadium, but I disagreed with Jack after Rovers were promoted in 1992 when he questioned one of the players I wanted to bring in.

'Convince me, Kenny,' Jack said about my transfer target.

'What?' I replied, my blood beginning to boil.

'Convince me.'

'I'll not convince you and you can stick the job. If it wouldn't be an embarrassment to me to walk away from you, I'd be off, so forget it.' My assistant, Ray Harford, was in the meeting and grabbed me outside.

'Kenny, what are you doing?'

'I'm not managing like that,' I told Ray. 'It's not irresponsible, the money we're spending. We're not indulgent. I've always told Jack I'd spend his money as if it were my own, and I have done so far. The boys who've come in haven't been greedy. I shouldn't have to convince Jack if I feel the player is right for Blackburn Rovers. I never had to convince the board at Liverpool. They trusted my judgement.'

From that day on I was just serving my time at Ewood. I thought of Liverpool, of how PBR and the board always backed my judgement, never putting obstacles in my way. Some people might suggest it was rash to have that defensive train of thought so early at Blackburn. Not for me. I was livid. At least I honoured my contract.

On leaving Liverpool, I'd had a range of offers. The chance to take over Sheffield Wednesday was briefly presented to me but I couldn't have sat in the dug-out, knowing the Leppings Lane End was to my left. I just couldn't have looked towards that goal, knowing what I'd seen in 1989. Bernard Tapie called, offering me the Marseille job, and I agreed, but then the agent who'd been involved in the deal phoned, telling me what he required as his commission. Even I know the French for no. 'Non,' I told him. I never heard from him or Tapie again.

Believing that Liverpool might not come back in for me, I settled on Rovers. The early days reminded me of when I started out as a player, washing the kit, putting up the goalposts and checking the training ground at Pleasington for dog mess. Melwood it wasn't. A road ran through the middle of the training pitches towards the crematorium. The club received letters from the council, saying: 'Will you kindly refrain from shooting when a hearse goes past.' I tried to instil some of the camaraderie we had at Anfield. Graeme Le Saux was a wee bit different because he read books and was into art, unlike Alan Shearer, Mike Newell, Tim Flowers and David Batty, but, in the main, the lads got on. Graeme and Batts had their scrap in Moscow but that was just frustration over the poor performance spilling over. Otherwise, the team spirit was good and the sound of their laughter took me back to Anfield. Before kick-off the Blackburn lads used to play a game of keepie-uppie in the temporary dressing room we used while the main stand was renovated. I'm sure the chairman wasn't chuffed because, inevitably, the ball got banged against the ceiling and the sound-proofing tiles came down. I didn't approve of the damage but it made us strong and I approved of the sort of Liverpool-style togetherness.

The mood on the bus echoed Liverpool. At the back of the bus on the way to away matches, the players had a game with the emergency exit, which they took in turns to tap with a hammer. One day, they actually smashed the window, so I came storming down the aisle.

'What's that? Have some of those idiot kids been throwing bricks?'

'Oh, yes, Gaffer, must have been,' said the players. 'Terrible.'

I discovered about the emergency exit game later from reading Batty's book. Inwardly, I loved their comradeship because it reminded me of Liverpool.

On 15 September 1992, I returned to Anfield, a strange experience akin to finding people had moved into my home while

I'd popped out to the shops. Everybody was very welcoming and there were familiar faces everywhere. Karen was in reception. 'Hello, JR,' she said. Karen always called me JR because she felt our house in Southport resembled Southfork. Fred was still on the door of the players' entrance, the stewards were the same, cleaning ladies the same. Anfield felt as homely and special as ever.

I wasn't going back for a party, though, I was going for three points with Blackburn. Walking into the away dressing room felt very odd, although I'd been quartered there when Scotland played Wales. Coming out of the tunnel, I leaned across to shake hands with Ronnie and Roy. Bugsy took my hand and kept hold, trying to pull me into their dug-out, my old Liverpool home. I laughed away, perhaps hiding some of the emotion inside. All the triumphs, all the reminiscences of the great nights, came rolling back. Even though I was annoyed by our 2–1 defeat, at least I took away the uplifting memory of the Kop reminding me how good my time at Liverpool Football Cub had been. I wouldn't have disagreed with them.

Fate kept me in contact with Liverpool in the shape of David Moores, who'd become chairman in September 1991. The following summer I bumped into him in Marbella, and we went for a Chinese meal. The next year, I'd taken a break on the Orient Express with Marina, and David was down the dining carriage. He sent a wee box containing an orchid for Marina. I scribbled a note back.

'Don't try to chat up my missus,' I wrote. 'And when are you going to use joined-up writing?'

'Didn't Marina like the flowers?' came the message back from David.

'The last time my wife asked me for flowers, I spent two million quid,' I wrote.

David never replied. Rovers had beaten Liverpool to the signature of Tim Flowers from Southampton. I knew Tim wanted to come to Rovers because of his friendship with Alan Shearer.

When I heard Liverpool were in for Tim, I told him, 'Tim, if you want to speak to Graeme Souness, you're only going to tell him you've no interest in going to Liverpool. I think you should treat Graeme with respect and get your manager to tell him you don't want to go there.'

Before the start of the 1994–95 season, a year that was to climax so gloriously for Rovers with the Premier League title, the chairman, Robert Coar, called me into his office.

'We want to give you a new contract, Kenny,' Robert said, pointing out that my current deal expired in October 1994.

'No, I'm not signing.'

'Why?'

'I'll honour my contract to October, but I'm not staying.'

'OK,' said chairman. 'You can take some gardening leave until October.' I felt he was challenging me, not believing I'd stand down.

'Aye, no problem,' I said and walked out. My time at Blackburn looked over. The next thing I knew, Ray Harford was on the phone, sounding nervous.

'What's going on?'

'Well, Ray, my contract is up in October and the board have asked me to sign a new one. I told them I'll honour the contract I've got but I'm going no further.'

'You can't do that,' said Ray, shocked.

'I told them I'll honour the contract, Ray. Just leave it.'

My hope was that Liverpool would come in for me. They'd have to move quickly, getting me in for pre-season and paying Rovers compensation to October. When I was on holiday, I got a phone-call from Liverpool.

'Will you come and speak to us?' PBR asked.

'Of course.'

'We just want to know whether you would be interested in coming back to the club,' Peter said.

'Of course I'm interested.'

I couldn't pack fast enough, jumping on a plane and, once back in England, hurtling up to David Moores' house. PBR, Roy Evans, Tom Saunders and David were already there. Scarcely had I sat down when Peter announced, 'We don't think the time's right for you to come home.' I was taken aback.

'What?' I said.

'We just don't think the time's right.'

'Why phone me and ask me to come back if you don't think the time's right?' I was furious. 'I want to come back to Liverpool. I wouldn't be sitting here now otherwise. I did a good job the first time. When you gave me the job, the person who came in to help me was Bob Paisley, the most successful manager you will ever see, with six titles in nine years. I wasn't intimidated by Bob. I was grateful he was on my side. You've asked me to come back and now you say the time's not right. If I'd been bad at my job, would I be sitting here? I don't think so. If I was a dud, would you be saying the timing was right?'

Liverpool couldn't give me an answer. Their logic baffled me then, and still does now. Never before in all my life have I felt such anger. My stomach was churning as I got in the car and sped off to Anfield, of all places, because Paul was playing some game for Liverpool reserves. I sat there, fuming, thinking this could have been such a pleasant experience, watching my son play, and looking forward to a return to the dug-out just down there. I'd have quit Blackburn. The pull to Liverpool was always strong, so what was the board playing at? Why lead me up the garden path and then shut the gate in front of me? So I returned to Robert.

'Chairman, look, I'll tell you what I'll do,' I offered. 'I'll sign a contract extension to the end of the season and that's me finished.' And that's what happened.

Leading Rovers to the title was special, and it felt very fitting to lift the trophy at Anfield on the final day of the season. I know all about the history of managers winning the title with two different teams – Herbert Chapman did it with Huddersfield and Arsenal – but wallowing in self-admiration was not my style.

As the years passed, I still thought of Liverpool, still occasionally returned to Anfield for the annual Hillsborough service. When Liverpool brought in Gerard Houllier to work as joint-manager with Roy Evans in 1996, I wished it had been me. Why didn't they approach me to help Roy? I'd have gone and assisted him, just as the board appointed Bob to give me any guidance I required. If it had worked with me and Bob, why not with me and Roy? Liverpool's decision to recruit Houllier was a surprise. There were no lines of demarcation. Nobody knew whether Roy picked the side or Gerard did. Nobody knew who was responsible for signing players, Roy or Gerard. Who set the blueprint for training? The players were asking Roy and Gerard the same question and sometimes receiving different answers. Two equals never works in football. Players will always play one off against the other. There could be only one leader, one person making the calls and taking responsibility.

If it had been Roy and me, I'd never have tried to undermine him. Having been manager of Liverpool, knowing the pressures of the job and having enjoyed such support from Roy and Ronnie, I could have made the relationship with Roy work. I'd have kept my counsel, just chipping in when Roy asked. I'd have been loyal, doing anything to make Roy's time in the job a success. Good players abounded at Melwood, some of whom I'd signed. Steve McManaman, Jamie Redknapp and Robbie Fowler were all coming on, and Liverpool could have challenged for trophies. Roy's joint-managership with Gerard was doomed, so I wasn't totally surprised when it broke down. Roy was incredibly honest, telling the board it wasn't working, making a brave decision to walk away from the club he loved. Many people would have thought 'last in, first out' and waited for Gerard to leave.

After Blackburn, my career took me to Newcastle and Celtic,

both fantastic clubs. My CV may be dominated by Liverpool, but my time with them represents much more than the mere passage of employment. I was delighted to be at St James' Park and back in Glasgow. But I always thought of Liverpool.

17

COMING HOME: LIVERPOOL 2009–10

M Y RESPECT for Rafa Benitez will always run deep, partly because he invited me back to my Liverpool home in 2009. It took a strong man to allow a predecessor back into the building. Although the main part of my role keeps me in the Academy at Kirkby, there was the possibility of a shadow being cast, so I admired Rafa for not worrying about the past and simply doing what he felt was best for Liverpool's future. I'm not sure many managers would have done the same. My job title is Academy Ambassador, which means if anybody on the youth-development side needs any help, I'm there. If it's advice, I'll raid the memory bank for any experience that might assist. If the commercial department requires somebody to promote Liverpool Football Club to a sponsor, I'll put on my smartest suit and best smile and go and meet people. Turning up for home matches is also part of the role, and one I love fulfilling, and I've taken in many Liverpool away games as well.

Despite my unequivocal support for Liverpool, I cannot dispute that the 2009–10 season was incredibly disappointing. Back in August 2009 anticipation and confidence, at Anfield were high because the team had just come second, as close as ever to winning the Premier League title, with a fantastic head-to-head record against United, Arsenal and Chelsea. Xabi Alonso was a loss because the previous season the Spanish midfielder had looked a great player, but Glen Johnson and Alberto Aquilani came in, so we were all right for numbers. The frustration gripping all of us at Anfield was due to the inability to hold on to results, particularly in the Champions League against Lyons and Fiorentina, and then Atletico Madrid in the Europa League. Some Liverpool fans might consider such late lapses unfortunate, but we never considered it lucky when we scored in the dying seconds. We called it persistence.

Rafa was not to blame for Liverpool's plight. He's a good coach, very stubborn in his implicit belief that his way is the right way. Rafa's tactical presentations to the players are famed within football. He tells the team every significant detail about the opposition. When it comes to dodging responsibility, many footballers are the worst offenders and some really needed to look in the mirror. It was always somebody else to blame. Had they done everything correctly? When I look around football, I find it no coincidence that the very best teams accept responsibility for their errors, players and managers, in the bad times as well as plaudits during the good times. Strong characters such as Stevie and Carra show an honesty that others should match.

What I still cannot comprehend about Liverpool's failure in 2010 is that Rafa's best players were as good as anybody else's. When I sat in the Main Stand, watching them line up, admiring the quality of Pepe Reina, Glen Johnson, Javier Mascherano, Fernando Torres, Carra and Stevie, I just thought these were top names who'd shine in the Premier League. Take Pepe. What a fantastic goalkeeper he is, as good as anybody in the world, if not better. Liverpool can't improve in goal, and I don't think they have had a better defender than Carra for a decade. He'll put his foot in, head the ball, and it riles me when critics disparage Jamie's passing. It's not the worst passing around by a long chalk. Newspapers say the reverse about Glen Johnson, banging on about 'he's really good going forward but terrible defending'. Everybody has a weakness but Glen isn't a bad defender and he's fantastic at attacking. When Glen pushes on, Carra makes sure the right-back space is covered, another sign of how well he reads the game. As well as being a brilliant defender, Carra's a great leader who talks to players, encouraging them and criticising them when they deserve it.

Carra's a real student of football, a bit of an anorak actually, but I never discussed Liverpool games with him when we bumped into each other last season, because that would have been unfair on Rafa. I was brought up to respect the position of Liverpool manager. Even if the manager changes, as it has now with Rafa's departure and Roy Hodgson's arrival, my principle of respecting the office has never altered.

When Carra voiced his interest in management, I understood why because he's just so taken up with the game. I don't think many of the top players from the modern era would want all the hassle of management, particularly as they are financially secure, but Carra's different. He's certainly been a top player but he's also got the hunger and football brain to do well in management. He's already taking his coaching badges. When I read Carra's book, it was creepy because many opinions he had about the Academy system chimed with mine. Some people suggest Carra might step up one day at Liverpool. The appointment from within can work brilliantly but it's more about the person than the principle. The individual has to be right. Carra will know if management suits when retirement beckons. That's the day of reckoning.

Stevie Gerrard's more noticeable than Carra because he scores goals and you can see him driving forward, but I feel Carra's contribution has been just as important for Liverpool. I hope that Stevie, like Carra, plays for as long as possible at Anfield. He's a fantastic asset and what I like most about him is his humility. He never, ever chases the limelight. Stevie's never comfortable being showered with praise but he deserves all the accolades. He fulfils his obligations as Liverpool captain superbly. When I listen to him being interviewed, he comes across as level-headed, intelligent and a responsible ambassador for the club. Stevie's just a really good footballer who appreciates the money he's getting and the life he's leading. He's not one of those who pushes his fame and fortune in punters' faces.

As a player, he's been truly fantastic. So many times Stevie's lifted Liverpool by the scruff of the neck and dragged them back into games. It brings a smile just thinking about the match against Olympiakos in December 2004, when he rescued Liverpool with that stunning strike in front of the Kop. The punters were magnificent in Istanbul in May 2005, singing their hearts out. Stevie also inspired Liverpool, stirring the players at 3–0 down. When he got the first goal against AC Milan, Liverpool got back in the game. Against West Ham in the 2006 FA Cup final, Stevie conjured up a wonder-strike. The greatest compliment I can pay him is to say that he's the man for the big occasion, who treats adversity with contempt. With that commitment and eye for goal, Stevie would have been welcome in any of the teams under Bob, Joe and me. Lawro once described Stevie as 'Souness with pace', which I thought was a fantastic tribute. Anybody who gets mentioned in the same breath as Graeme Souness has done well. Stevie certainly has.

Mascherano is far more defensively minded than Stevie, and I wouldn't rate too many other players around the world higher than Javier for breaking up attacks. Opposing teams know a dog of war guards Liverpool's back four. Mascherano possesses all the qualities required for a top ball-winner – he's tough, mobile, quick, reads the game brilliantly and puts his foot in. I love the way the Argentinian puts in a really strong shift every time, getting around the pitch, nicking the ball, never stopping, and competing hard until the final whistle. Nobody can claim to have seen Mascherano play and not give 100 per cent effort for Liverpool. His many other virtues far outweigh his passing, but I've also seen how he could send Stevie or Fernando away with a simple ball.

Fernando's endeared himself to Liverpool supporters, not just because he's the best centre-forward around, but by making an effort to understand the club's culture. When I spoke to Fernando, I was impressed by how quickly he assimilated the principles and history of Liverpool Football Club. As a striker, he's unstoppable when he goes one-on-one, isolating the defender so brutally I almost feel pity for them. Almost. I felt for Fernando last season. It was an unfortunate, stop–start year for him, yet he still bagged 22 goals – that demonstrated his class. One injury after another plagued him, and my long-held belief is that Fernando has been overworked. Spain's leading striker has not had a break for three years. His summers have been filled up with Euro 2008, the Confederations Cup in 2009 and the World Cup in 2010. Those constant demands have definitely taken their toll. Fernando is a thoroughbred footballer and nobody would exhaust a race-horse like that. All that relentless football caught up with him and Liverpool paid the price in 2010. People say players get a rest when they're injured but that's rubbish. Recuperating from his injuries, Fernando was hardly on holiday. He was in rehab, in the gym, in the treatment room hour after hour, day after day and that's no rest. His unforgiving schedule suggests, I think, that Fernando's problems will continue and I fear for him this season.

Whenever I take my seat in the Main Stand, I passionately hope Alberto Aquilani will show his true qualities. Liverpool resigned themselves to Alonso leaving for Real Madrid, so Rafa had plenty of time to pick a midfield replacement, and Aquilani was his choice. Unfortunately, he arrived from Roma with an ankle injury, a frustration for him, Rafa and everybody at Liverpool. Whenever I've observed Aquilani, he seems quite alert, seeing a pass. I saw his excitement when scoring at the Kop against Portsmouth and Atletico Madrid, a reaction that proves how desperately he wants his transfer to work out. I believe he has a real desire to show people he's better than they imagine. He cannot complain, though. It's the nature of football for there to be criticism if somebody arrives for £20 million and struggles to deliver in his first season. Sympathy was always going to be in short supply for Alberto. I heard people whisper, 'why did Liverpool pay that for him? Look at the state of him.' I felt that to be unfair because, after all, he was returning to fitness after an operation. Missing pre-season was especially damaging, particularly for a new signing from abroad, unfamiliar with the frenetic pace of English football. So I'll reserve judgement on Alberto Aquilani until well into this season. If he has an injury-free run, Anfield can judge Aquilani properly.

A squad is only as good as the weakest player and that fact has held Liverpool back. Liverpool don't have the financial riches of Manchester City or Chelsea, so I knew the thinness of the squad would be exposed. I can understand why Liverpool have failed to land a title in the 21st Century. Rival clubs have poured heavy investment into salaries and transfers, and the competition is stiffer now than when I was managing, but what mystifies me is Liverpool's lack of League success right through the Nineties. I simply cannot believe that subsequent Liverpool managers did not build on the solid foundation. Blackburn have lifted the title more recently than Liverpool. People said it was Jack Walker's cold, hard cash that made it possible, but money was no guarantee of success or is it ever. Rovers finished fourth, second and then first, as we slowly shaped a team capable of winning the title.

Among the many excuses bedevilling my beloved club in 2009–10 was that matches were overshadowed by fans' venting their spleen at Tom Hicks and George Gillett, the American owners. Actually, I thought the Kop were really good, giving tremendous backing to the boys and Rafa while making their point about Tom and George. The Americans were unfortunate that the global economic crisis complicated their re-financing of Liverpool. High finance would not feature high on my picks as a specialist subject on *Mastermind* but I'm sure there were an awful lot of people borrowing money to buy assets at that time. So George and Tom ran into a blizzard of difficulties, which would have been exacerbated if they hadn't brought in Ian Ayre as commercial director, Christian Purslow as chief executive and Martin Broughton as chairman. All are excellent people, doing important jobs to safeguard the club's future.

I understand the Kop's frustration at the waves of embarrassment that have washed over Liverpool, but plenty of positives have happened off the pitch. Ian helped increase the commercial side by 83 per cent and sponsorship money is up as well. Liverpool's success in the Seventies and Eighties attracted millions of fans around the world, who are passionate about the club, and, finally, Liverpool are tapping in to our huge global support. In Singapore last year, I saw a man whose back was tattooed with the club's honours. He loved Liverpool yet had probably never set foot inside Anfield, let alone on Merseyside, but he was still a diehard Liverpool fan. The club must cater for men like him around the world.

Where I understand the punters' anger is that Tom and George promised a new stadium, with a spade going into the turf of Stanley Park within 60 days, and it hasn't happened. Building up supporters' expectations and then smashing them is a recipe for trouble. Once an owner makes a pledge to fans whose life is Liverpool Football Club, they never forget. Rafa was given £220 million to spend on players over five years. As a fan, the transfer budget is never enough but Tom and George couldn't give more because of the borrowings. But for all the gloomy headlines, I honestly don't believe Liverpool are financially poor.

When I think about how Liverpool's future may unfold, I'll admit to a concern about filling a new stadium every week. It's assumed we'll sell out but that will depend on how well the team are doing. In the first season, I'm sure Liverpool will pack out a 60,000-seater stadium, because everybody will want to experience Liverpool's new home. Once that first rush is over, and curiosity has been satisfied, the fans will turn up in numbers only if Liverpool are prospering. Otherwise punters will pick and choose games. Liverpool must be competing for silverware to make the new stadium work. I've read all the figures stating that an awful lot of people are on the waiting list, and the passion and loyalty of Liverpool fans can never be questioned, but it's one thing being on the waiting list and another being asked to part with money. If all the season tickets aren't taken up, I'd like to see Liverpool set aside tickets for some games for school-kids. I often worry that we risk losing the next generation of supporters through availability and cost of tickets.

I know I'll be accused of nostalgia, even stupidity, but I'd prefer Liverpool to pour resources into extending the Anfield Road end upper tier, and re-configuring the Main Stand, to increase capacity towards 60,000. I honestly feel the best scenario would be to keep the Kop, the most famous stand in sport, and build up around it. That's my personal wish but I understand it is unlikely ever to be fulfilled. The big question eating away at me is why should Liverpool and Everton both spend hundreds of millions of pounds on a new ground each? Purely from the perspective of raising funds, perhaps it would make sense for Liverpool and Everton to share. The only way that would work is for the Council to step in. I'm sure the Council could build a magnificent new structure as a thank you for how well both clubs have served the community, and then charge them a rental fee. For Liverpool and Everton, a shared facility would be fantastic financially because neither would have the burden of forking out fortunes.

Of course, many obstacles stand in the way of this shared dream becoming reality. What happens if Everton or Liverpool cannot afford the rent? Which colour should the stadium be, red or blue?

And what about the rivalry? The animosity at Derby games now is unacceptable. Stevie gets abuse when he takes corners near the Everton supporters, although insults have always flown. Evertonians sang that I was homosexual while Marina was sitting at home with the kids. David Johnson used to get terrible, merciless stick because he played at Everton. Souey was always slaughtered by Everton punters but that was hardly special. Most clubs' fans had a pop at Graeme. The atmosphere at Derby matches has definitely darkened over the past few years, though. Maybe a shared stadium wouldn't work. In fact, the more I consider the options between Liverpool and Everton, the more I feel it's better for the two neighbours to continue living apart.

I know there are many clouds on Liverpool's horizon but important steps are being taken to build a better future. When Rafa received his new contract in 2009, he reorganised the Academy at Kirkby. An awful lot of staff lost their jobs as Rafa replaced them with people of his choice. Rafa put Frank McParland, a good man, in charge of the Academy and brought in a Spanish technician, Pep Segura, as Academy Technical Manager and Rodolfo Borrell as coach of the Under-18s. Rafa wanted to restart the conveyor belt of talent, educating kids in the skills and mindset they'll need for Liverpool's first team. People keep saying the Academy hasn't produced a player for many years but many have emerged to earn a decent living elsewhere. Stephen Warnock went on to Blackburn Rovers, then Aston Villa, and made it to the World Cup with England. Stephen Wright went to Sunderland, David Thompson to Coventry and Neil Mellor moved on to West Ham, Wigan and Preston. These Academy graduates are not where we'd like them to be, in Liverpool's first team, but a couple are on the fringes, including Martin Kelly, Jay Spearing and Stephen Darby, and a good few are on loan. If they have the ability, they'd be in.

I love being at Kirkby. My office has huge pictures of Liverpool fans celebrating in Istanbul. The Academy is a special place, strengthened by coaches such as Rodolfo, who has an amazing record of working with kids, including Lionel Messi and Cesc Fabregas, at Barcelona.

'I could have stayed at Barcelona but I wanted to come and work here because Liverpool are a great club,' Rodolfo told me. Quite rightly, Rodolfo demands so much of our young players. 'If you don't share my ambitions, don't stay here,' Rodolfo tells them.

'Having good facilities doesn't mean you'll be a good player,' I tell the youngsters. 'You have to want it enough to be a professional footballer. No hunger, no chance. We'll help you with your academic education, because there's no guarantee you'll make it as a footballer. There's a safety net.'

I know many people worry about youngsters' hunger, but when I look around the Academy, I see kids equally as ambitious as I was. When I was growing up at Celtic, I played with kids who were probably better than I was but lacking the dedication to make it as a professional. I believe it's even more difficult to break through now, because of the demands on the first team. Managers have a responsibility to stay in the Premier League because of the damaging financial repercussions of relegation, so many play it safe, ignoring the kids and relying on more experienced players from abroad. At Sunderland, Steve Bruce has been brave with two midfield players, David Meyler and Jordan Henderson, who look promising, but Steve started playing them together last season only when Sunderland were safe.

When I spend time with our Academy kids, I also admire the desire and dedication of their parents, who must show a real commitment to bring their sons training four nights a week. Parents are passionate about their kids, praying they will become football stars, and at some clubs that can cause problems. Liverpool's Academy players understand the honour of playing for the club, having been taught the club's history by their mums and dads, uncles and aunties. That's the Liverpool way, the passing down of club traditions from one generation to the next, and some Liverpool traditions are known about all over the world. A German kid arriving here will know all about 'You'll Never Walk Alone'.

Here at the Academy, there are pictures of Rafa in Istanbul, of Fernando Torres, Michael Owen, and they even managed to squeeze in a picture of Al and me with a trophy. Tradition lies down every corridor. The meeting room at Kirkby is called the Tom Saunders Theatre, which is only fit and proper given Old Tom's contribution to Liverpool Football Club. I've trained a few times with the 13s, 15s and 16s and sometimes I'm convinced they think I'm just a stupid old guy trying to get a kick of a football. Actually, having got to know the kids, I've discovered most are Liverpool fans anyway, and know exactly who I am. At the start of last season, I was watching the Under-9s when the ball rolled off the pitch. I side-footed it back and one of the Liverpool boys shouted, 'Kenny, you've not lost it, have you?' Respectful Scouse humour from the wee boy.

My Liverpool family may not appreciate the sentiments but I strongly believe that many clubs should look and learn from Alex Ferguson's early years at Manchester United – the way he came in and had a right good look at the youth side. Fergie needed a few years before he was properly up and running but the foundations he put down were deep and gave United a great platform. He employed some people from Manchester City and got hold of local boys, including Ryan Giggs, Paul Scholes, Nicky Butt and the two Nevilles. He didn't gauge their progress in terms of trophies but through progressing their ability.

Fergie and I have had the odd disagreement down the years but I stood up for him when he first came south from Aberdeen. At one North-west football writers' dinner in Manchester, Fergie didn't turn up because he was getting pilloried in the Press. So I made a wee speech, trying to correct the wrong impression the media had of our relationship.

'You have Fergie and me in a conflict,' I said. 'I'm in competition with him, I want to beat him, but I don't have a problem with Fergie. He hasn't got a problem with me, so you are inventing the problem. And another wee thing. You are presumptious in your critical thinking about him as a manager. Fergie's a good manager and you need to take a rain check on that. Give him time.' It wasn't the greatest speech but I wanted to explain my relationship and respect for Fergie.

United's old physio, Jimmy McGregor, was at the dinner and came up to me later on.

'I'm sure the Gaffer will appreciate that support,' said Jimmy. 'He needs it.'

'Jimmy, it's only the truth.'

Given how well United have done since then under Fergie, I probably should have kept my mouth shut, but his success is no surprise to me. Fergie's got the work ethic, toughness, ability and knowledge, and he's built United the way he wants it. When I look across at Old Trafford, it's like the old days with Liverpool, bringing in two or three class acts every year. At the same time, Fergie has installed a load of promising players, such as Rafael, Macheda and Hernandez. Fergie's really clever. He develops a player such as Fraizer Campbell, gives him a few games in the first team, builds up his reputation, the price soars, and then sells him to Sunderland in a deal that could net United £6 million.

One of the more distressing developments in the modern game has been diving, which is a stain spreading across the game. I believe the influx of recruits from the Continent, is the reason diving has proliferated to the point where it is now almost routine. If a player attempts to be honest nowadays, staying on his feet after being fouled, and misses with his shot at goal, the moment he walks into the dressing room somebody will hit him with a barbed remark, amounting to 'Why didn't you go down?'

Diving has become accepted practice and I sympathise with

referees struggling to combat this curse because it must be incredibly difficult to make an instant decision about simulation. Football is so fast and the human eye can only follow so much, particularly in a crowded penalty area. If I were playing today and a referee accused me of simulation, and television evidence proved the defender had caught me, I would seriously consider taking legal action because my integrity would have been impugned. That's why I feel for Stevie, who gets accused of diving, which is laughable really. Anybody with an understanding of football – or knowledge of Stevie's personality – can see that he simply takes evasive action, riding the tackle. Technology should be introduced urgently to protect the innocent and punish the real culprits. I honestly believe that an extra official, sitting in the stands reviewing footage, would require only two or three seconds to rule on penalty calls. The game would stop until the official told the referee whether or not to award a penalty. Even a small delay is nothing in establishing something that could decide the game, or damage a player's reputation. Referees want to get decisions right and I think a screen judge would really help them.

Michel Platini's experiment with extra officials behind the goal in the Europa League in 2009–10 seemed farcical and impractical to me. There are simply not enough officials around, as people who know about Sunday League football keep telling me. Somebody should invent a fertility drug to bring some more referees into the world, and quickly. To improve standards, I'm convinced referees should be called to account for mistakes and asked to explain themselves. The authorities should not simply shuffle an errant official down to the Championship. Tell the truth, everybody makes mistakes, but clarify the situation so everybody knows and learns.

Another sadness troubling a footballing traditionalist like me has been the decline in prestige attached to the FA Cup. Winning the Cup, a trophy I always held close to my heart, used to be special, but the lustre has been rubbed away by frequent format changes, weakened teams and the lengthening shadow of the Champions League. Chelsea's positive attitude, invariably putting out their strongest XI, deserves real praise. The Football Association should encourage clubs to think more imaginatively about the cost of Cup tickets. When the third round of the Cup comes around, punters have just forked out for Christmas, have already invested substantial sums on a season ticket, and must then find the funds to afford passage through the turnstiles on Cup day. Football must beware fleecing fans in times of economic hardship. Clubs are going to the well of public loyalty too often.

The growing distance between player and supporter also troubles me. Back in the Seventies and Eighties, punters thought nothing about seeing a player out on the town, having a drink and a meal with mates or girlfriends. Nowadays, jealousy and camera-phones stalk the streets, with punters looking for someone famous to prey on. If an England international is pictured having one beer, he's automatically painted as bladdered, and the story is embellished. The modern footballer is isolated – placed up on a pedestal that also serves as a coconut shy. Players must be so careful about contact with the public. For all the images of players as prima donnas, I've never met one who believes he's above the law of the land, and he'd be very foolish to, because many a policeman would adore the kudos of arresting a star. The police love sending out a loud message that if an England player can get done for parking on a double-yellow line, anybody can. Players must be responsible, though.

I believe that society is more questioning and less sympathetic than it used to be and, sadly, that prevents footballers living a normal life. Players are easy targets for abuse from some idiot wanting to make a name for himself, who may be embittered anyway. But why shouldn't players earn millions? If clubs rake in tens of millions of pounds from the Premier League, and more in commercial deals, then Stevie, Fernando, Wayne Rooney and

Frank Lampard deserve every penny their agents can get them. Where I fear the game veers down a path marked financial madness is at clubs, such as Portsmouth, who spend money they haven't got, and everyone involved, barring the fans, deserves to suffer. Average clubs granting long, lucrative contracts to average players soon find themselves on suicide watch. Players are rewarded before delivering and that can deaden ambition. My son Paul was driven to be the very best he could be as a footballer, but when he bought himself a BMW at 21, I bristled.

'What are you doing, Paul?'

'Dad, I'm never going to be 21 again. If I can afford it, I'll have a nice car. It won't affect my training, my hunger to win. I won't be custard-pieing it in people's faces.' Paul was right, I guess. Why shouldn't he enjoy himself? I knew it wouldn't lessen his hunger, but such luxuries must be earned. That's what I tell the youngsters at Liverpool.

Disciplining players is nearly impossible for a manager nowadays because they don't fear anything. Fine them? So what? Here's an exchange I know occurred between a Premier League manager and a star player.

'Can I take Monday off?' asked the star player.

'No, you're in training. You'll be fined two weeks' wages if you don't turn up,' replied the manager.

'OK, here's the twenty grand. I'll not be in Monday.' And he wrote out a cheque!

That was a decade ago. It's even worse now. The bigger the pay-packets, the greater the player power. Stars control clubs, whispering stories to an awe-struck chairman, undermining the manager. Clubs back in my day were strong. If a player was out of order, he'd be shipped out or not paid. It's not like that nowadays.

The Bosman ruling was great for players who had genuine problems with a selfish club, but the agreement was abused by people just trying to find the exit. I loathe the Bosman rule because it has bred uncertainty and greed. A player can now negotiate with another club six months from the end of his contract but, in reality, deals are verbally agreed 18 months in advance, and that can affect the player's commitment. The whole football transfer market needs to operate with greater integrity, and some players should have more pride in their work, showing more support for the manager and more passion for the cause. Football can't just be about the next Bentley, the next Caribbean holiday, the school fees.

I hate the modern footballer who takes the money and doesn't bother whether he starts, stays on the bench or has the afternoon off shopping. An offer of 100 grand a week wouldn't stir me, not if it came without a chance of glory in the major competitions. My wages allowed me to provide for my family and that was all that ever mattered to me. How many cars can you drive at a time? Only one in my experience. As I sit in the Main Stand at Anfield, lost in reminiscence, I actually feel deeply sorry for this 21st Century over-paid under-achiever who will never know the joy I had in winning three European Cups, in playing for a team that was the most dominant in English history, gaining friends and memories for life and bringing such pride to my family.

18

THE FAMILY HOME

My Liverpool home has been made by my wife Marina, and I look back with tears in my eyes to the time I almost lost her. It was March 2003, and I was sitting in the kitchen at home when Marina came home after seeing her consultant, Lee Martin, a wonderful man who'd just given her the results of a scan.

'I've got breast cancer,' she said. 'I need chemotherapy.'

I only remember the two Cs, 'cancer' and 'chemotherapy'. The shock ran through me. A generation earlier and that was you gone, finished, no chance of recovery, but women nowadays are more aware of the threat of breast cancer. The medical people detect it earlier, giving a better chance of survival. Our family coped with that deeply stressful time with resilience and, at times, humour. After Marina underwent a double mastectomy operation, Paul visited her in hospital and was messing about, trying to lift her spirits, as sons do. Paul was tickling her feet, hiding behind the curtain and jumping out, but Marina couldn't laugh or she'd burst her stitches. Eventually, she just spewed everywhere. The kids and I knew how serious Marina's plight was but that was how we handled the pressure, with a wee bit of humour. Some people would call it black humour but it worked for us. In private, we could be more serious, but there was no point sitting about being morbid, and Marina would never have tolerated that. The most important thing was that Marina was positive she'd fight off this poison in her body. Fortunately, the doctors caught the cancer early enough.

Mr Martin, an expert in the field of breast surgery, wrote the definitive paper on breast reconstruction for the whole of Britain. He was very mindful of the psychological effects of a mastectomy, and he rebuilt Marina's breasts. She was so brave and determined. Even when the chemotherapy took her hair, she just bought these great wigs, which the kids loved messing about with.

'It's better to have no hair than no life,' Marina said. Her strength in fighting the cancer gave me strength. If Marina wasn't stressed, why should I be? I was only driving her to and from hospital for chemotherapy sessions. It wasn't me getting pumped with drugs, but it was tough. I couldn't believe this nightmare that had descended on her, but we got on with things. That's how Marina and I were brought up. Fortunately, we came out at the other end of the tunnel.

'I'd like to do something to help,' said Marina when Mr Martin finally gave her the all-clear. That was only right and proper because Marina was cared for fantastically well. Each time I visited the hospitals, whether the Clatterbridge Centre for Oncology or University Hospital, Aintree, where Marina was operated on, I marvelled at the time, patience and love the nurses bestowed on their patients. Marina and I both felt that cancer patients and their families had to do too much travelling, criss-crossing Merseyside. Marina's chemotherapy was sometimes administered at Aintree and sometimes over the Wirral at Clatterbridge.

'Some of the facilities leave a wee bit to be desired as well,' Marina said. In truth, it was remarkable how well the nurses coped.

'What can we do?' Marina asked Mr Martin.

'Well, as you know, the facilities are pretty primitive,' said Mr Martin. 'We'd really like a new chemotherapy unit.'

'OK. I was thinking of a golf day!' I said.

'We'll have a go,' promised Marina, who was already planning, already determined to make the whole cancer experience less stressful.

She started the Marina Dalglish Appeal, raising money to build a Centre for Oncology on the fifth floor of University Hospital, Aintree. When I first set foot on that floor, it reminded me of the old ward in that television drama, *The Royal*. It required so much work and money, but people's generosity was staggering and the Appeal soon passed the £2 million mark. Marina's involvement meant every penny was a prisoner, going only to the charity and not on any overheads. She got free office space from FMG, a financial services company.

The Appeal is still going strong. Marina is helped by a good friend, Diane Whalley, and our daughters all chip in. Lynsey is often in the offices – sometimes they need a younger brain to get the computer going. Kelly is used to public speaking from her TV career, so she makes speeches and presentations. Wee Lauren goes along and makes speeches on behalf of Marina if she's not there. Lauren's so young and yet she stands up in front of packed rooms and talks away. I'm so proud of all of them. When Paul's back from his coaching in the States, he mucks in as well. All the children want to help because it was their mother who suffered and survived.

With the funds in place, they gutted the fifth floor, redesigned it and when the Centre opened on 4 June 2007, it was truly magnificent, like walking into a wood-panelled spa. A curved walkway leads past large fish-tanks and flat-screen tellies, through a nice reception and waiting area, and into the patients' part. The windows were enlarged to give bigger views over Liverpool. Andrew Collinge, who owns one of the top hairdressing salons in Liverpool, gives the lady patients a pamper day once a week, doing their nails and hair. They come up from the ward downstairs and love it. The nurses are still brilliant and the level of care remains the same but the Centre offers more dignity to those being treated.

Clatterbridge then approached us about the Marina Dalglish Appeal helping them build a radiotherapy centre over this side of the Mersey. Clatterbridge had been fantastic to Marina, and it wasn't their fault they were over the Wirral. I'd talked to all these people making long journeys. 'It's too much that people going in for radiotherapy have to go through that tunnel an hour and a half each way every day, assuming they have a car,' I said to Marina. 'They go to Clatterbridge, have their treatment, come home, have a sleep and go back again. It's needed this side of the water.'

Requiring £15 million, Clatterbridge asked us whether we could raise £5 million. 'I don't know but we'll have a go,' said Marina, who loves a challenge. The Appeal had a few quid left over from Aintree and Marina threw herself again into the money-raising mission. She's still at it. We've had golf days, a ball, a buy a brick campaign that the Liverpool players have been fantastic promoting, and even a couple of matches. It's a great feeling knowing that every pound generated goes towards this amazing new Radiotherapy Centre, specialising in really innovative surgery. It's attached to the Walton Neurosurgery Centre, so the kids with brain tumours will not need to take an ambulance over to Sheffield for radiotherapy. They can just be pushed on a trolley down the corridor. It'll make life so much easier.

Marina's hard work was recognised by the Queen when she was awarded an MBE in the 2009 New Year Honours List. I know it's a fantastic accolade but I also know my wife, and Marina wasn't seeking any public honour when embarking on her charity venture. Marina just wanted to help those suffering the difficult times she endured. She has very strong family values and showing compassion for others runs through her veins. In adversity, the true personality comes out and that's how Marina dealt with Hillsborough and how she dealt with the cancer. Now she's driving through this campaign to raise money for Clatterbridge. Marina doesn't want her name up in lights and, in fact, she wanted Aintree to take her name down, but they said the sign had put too many holes in the wall. Marina's a very private person, and at the fund-raising ball for the Appeal in March 2010, her speech set a world record for brevity. Here it is in all its glory: 'This is my first public speech, so thanks very much for coming.' With that, she sat down. The whole room applauded because people respect Marina's humility and determination. She's so wrapped up in the cancer charity, she's got her teeth into this fund-raising for Clatterbridge and won't let go until it's finished.

I am forever in her debt for bringing up our four children so beautifully, teaching them right from wrong, making them understand the importance of discipline. Kelly, Paul, Lynsey and Lauren are all well-balanced, responsible, loyal people, and that's a tribute to Marina. The kids understood that just because their father was in the public eye didn't give them any right to put on airs and graces. Imbued with a strong family ethos, each of my children will stand up for me if they hear anyone being critical. They fight my corner. All my life, I've protected the kids, keeping them out of the papers. We once did an advert with Kelly, Paul and Lynsey, but I made sure it was with somebody I trusted, Gordon Shaw, who worked for Scottish Farm Dairy Foods, which is now Wiseman Dairies. We made this ad in Glasgow for Fresh and Low Healthy Milk, and the kids were very relaxed about it. They only became excited when I explained what the reward was. 'You get fish and chips afterwards,' I told them.

They consider Liverpool home, just as I do. As a family, we put down roots there quickly. From the moment Marina, Paul, Kelly and I arrived from Glasgow in 1977, we were very well looked after by Jack Ferguson at the Holiday Inn. While I was out training, Marina went down for tea and toast with the front-desk staff, who became friends. The chambermaid ended up as baby-sitter. That's the Liverpool way, everybody so accommodating. During our eight months of house-hunting, the Holiday Inn really felt like home, and Jack, a genuine character, actually sounded sorry to see us leave.

'We got Rentokil in when you moved out,' he told me a couple of months later.

'Why?'

'To clean that suede suite in the sitting room! Your kids!' That poor suite took a battering with a twenty-three-month-old and a six-month-old dribbling all over it.

As they grew, the kids knew how driven I was with my career, but also how much my thoughts were with them. When I was manager, I'd walk to the dug-out, turn round and wave up to them in their usual seats in Row 7. Paul and Kelly were treated to sweets by a lovely lady, Mrs Prince, and I often suspected that was the real reason they wanted to come to Anfield.

For all my obsession with Liverpool, being part of my children's formative years was vital for me, even if it meant rushing away from Anfield to attend an activity at school in which the children were involved. They were reassured that their father was in the audience, watching proudly. I then dashed back to Anfield. I do look back with regrets and wish I'd seen the kids more, particularly playing sports. Lauren wasn't especially sporty, but Kelly was always in swimming races while Lynsey competed strongly at hockey at county level. I never understood what was happening when Lynsey was running around with a stick but I loved being there.

Driving in to Anfield for games, I'd stop off and catch Paul playing for Crosby Schools at 10 a.m. During Paul's match, my thoughts would drift towards the Liverpool match but it was good just being there, standing on the touchline, showing my support for him. In his Sunday League matches, I loved helping put up the nets and clearing the puddles, sharing all the normal match-day chores I did with my dad.

Being the son of a well-known father cannot be easy. Paul attended Rossall School with Liam Botham, a very talented sportsman who had a choice between rugby union, rugby league and cricket. When Liam avoided cricket as a career, some people felt it was because he didn't want the comparisons with his father. I never wanted Paul to shy away from football, so when he was considering his career options, I offered some simple advice: 'You want to play football, so go and do it. If you pick a different sport because you're scared of comparisons, then you've failed twice. Look around the house. It's full of pictures of you kicking a ball, right from a young age. It's what you've always loved, always wanted to do. On you go.'

It annoyed me deeply that people compared Paul with me as a footballer, a frequent and frustrating occurrence. When he was doing well for Newcastle, Norwich and Wigan, what difference did it make what I'd done in my career? Like any player, Paul deserved to be judged on his performance, not his parentage. I must confess to finding it uncanny how similar we look on the pitch. Of the many family photographs I cherish, one of Paul particularly stands out. He's pictured in a match, pointing his fingers as he ran in exactly the same way I did. Liverpool's photographer, Harry Ormesher, caught me in the same posture. Paul and I are so close as father and son, so it was unbelievable to see how we resembled each other when caught up in a match.

Giving Paul advice about football was something I avoided, although I did talk to him about the correct way to behave on the field. I was sensitive to the idea that if I spoke to him, it might place pressure on him. I always kept in the background when Paul played. One day when Paul was playing for Celtic reserves, I travelled up to watch.

'I wish you came to every game,' said one of Paul's coaches.

'Why?'

'Paul's always brilliant when you're here.'

That felt strange. I always worried that my presence might intimidate Paul, yet it seemed to liberate him, perhaps giving him the security to go and express himself. Some kids feel inhibited when their dads are watching, some are lifted. Nigel Clough was always magnificent when he played for his father.

Like Nigel, Paul is blessed with an incredibly strong character. I take great pride in the fact that Paul never lived off my name, and his achievements are down to his own efforts. Football is such a demanding world that no manager would ever pick a player because of his parents. Paul played for 16 years because he was good. It was disappointing he never got as far as he could have done. Yet the most emotional I've ever been at a game came when Paul was playing for Houston Dynamo, who'd reached the final of the MLS Cup in Frisco, Texas, on 12 November 2006. Marina and I flew over and we were wrecks just watching our son competing against New England Revolution for this great prize in American soccer. Paul did all right but then came off. I was texting Lynsey to tell her New England had scored when Brian Ching made it 1–1, forcing penalties. I was so desperate for Houston to win that I couldn't watch. I covered my eyes. The tension was too much. Even though Paul wasn't taking a penalty, my stomach was churning. When I heard the huge Houston roar, and Marina shout, 'He's missed it,' I realised Houston had won.

It was brilliant to see Paul and the Dynamo players celebrating, sprinting all over the pitch. Deliberately, I kept out of the way. This was Paul's day, Houston's day, although I made sure I congratulated his coaches, John Spencer and Dominic Kinnear and consoled New England's, Stevie Nicol and Paul Mariner. I can honestly say I have never been prouder or more ecstatic or emotional in football. I felt a greater satisfaction for Paul than I ever did for myself in winning a European Cup. Seeing Paul's smile was my finest success in football. It helped me understand the joy my dad must have felt when I won a trophy.

Paul packed in at 31 but I knew he'd stay in the game. He loves football so much. He coached the Under-16s at Houston, worked on a big soccer camp, leading one of his teams to an all-state league title, and took his coaching badges. Paul caught the eye of Andrew Nestor, the co-owner of FC Tampa Bay Rowdies, and was named head coach in 2010. I know that Andrew has taken a bit of a gamble on Paul, who'd never been tried or tested in first-team coaching, but he started well. It helps that Paul's got a fine eye for a player, and I know he's built up a good network of people from his old clubs, who'll keep him informed on players. Paul's also blessed with an experienced number two in Perry van der Beck, who played alongside Rodney Marsh with the original Rowdies. I watch the Tampa matches streamed online and talk to Paul regularly, hearing how he does power-point presentations to prepare his players. The technology may have changed but the principles are the same. I remember when Don Revie managed England, he gave the players dossiers on the opposition. Jose Mourinho sends his players video clips.

I wouldn't say Paul's going to take over at Inter Milan, but Tampa's a great stage for him. Before even considering a return to Europe, Paul must fulfil his obligations to Tampa and loyalty to Andrew. Success at Tampa will dictate whether Paul has options elsewhere. As a father and passionate football man, I've just loved watching Paul evolve from playing his first game to see him standing on the touchline, taking a team. I understand even more my father's delight when I was named manager of Liverpool. All my children's achievements fill me with pride. So does Marina's remarkable work with her cancer charity. As I sit in my place in the Main Stand at Anfield, listening to the Kop, thinking what a special place this was to raise a family, I just thank God that I made this my Liverpool home.

19

SUMMER 2010

RAFA BENITEZ left Liverpool in the summer of 2010 knowing he'd done a good job. I certainly considered him a success. Rafa won the Champions League in Istanbul and the FA Cup in Cardiff. In losing to AC Milan in the Champions League final of 2007, I actually thought Liverpool looked better than they did in Istanbul. I know Rafa's rotation policy attracted a lot of debate. Having changed the side for 99 games in succession, he played the same team for the 100th. Rafa made changes because he thought it was right. Certainly, at the beginning, there were times when I'd be sitting at Anfield, trying to work out what the starting team was and which subs would come on. I knew somebody would be coming on between 60 and 65 minutes. Rafa's preparations were very precise.

Everybody was really looking forward to 2009–10. These weren't pipe dreams. Hopes of doing well in the Premier League and Europe were realistic because of the team's achievements the previous year. In the 2008–09 season, Liverpool had come as close as ever to winning the Premier League and had a fantastic head-to-head record with Chelsea, Arsenal and Manchester United. That's why everybody thought 2010 would be a really good year. Rafa made an excellent signing in Glenn Johnson. Xabi Alonso left but Liverpool had known for a long time that he was going. The problem was the protracted nature of discussions with Real Madrid, leaving Liverpool less time to find the right replacement. Anyway, it's difficult to replace a midfielder of Alonso's stature. Unfortunately for Alberto Aquilani, it's hard to come to a club of Liverpool's stature, especially with a £20 million price tag and also being injured.

People talked about whether Rafa had been given enough money for transfers but the Liverpool board will always give as much as it can. It's not in the club's interests to restrict the manager and the team. There's always been a philosophy at Liverpool that every asset should be running around on the pitch, not lying in the bank. All managers would like more. But I felt the board did as much as they could financially for Rafa.

I was still surprised he went. During the previous summer, he had revamped the Academy at Kirkby and was clearly thinking long-term. Rafa wanted to make the relationship between Kirkby and Melwood closer. That had long been missing. He inherited this problem and was determined to put it right. After such a good season, in 2008–09, it was a good time to tackle the youth develoment side. If the Academy kicks on and produces good players, he has left a great legacy.

Not too many people felt much resentment towards Rafa for going. The fans supported him because they support the position of the manager at Liverpool. They are loyal to the chair, especially in times of trouble. Rafa certainly wasn't disliked. Some of the critics might have perceived him as cold but every time I was with him, we'd have a chuckle, tell a few stories. Rafa's good company. It's important to understand that Rafa Benitez is obsessed with only two things: family and football. After games, Rafa was straight on to the video, analysing play on the way back on the coach. He works an awful lot and takes very little time off. Maybe he should have rested more, although the fresh challenge of Inter Milan must have felt as good as a holiday for him. Rafa is not without feeling. He made a fantastic gesture to the Hillsborough Families Support Group with the huge donation he made to help them with their cause.

It was right for everybody that Rafa left – for him and for Liverpool Football Club. There just comes a stage in every manager's career when the board says, 'You've been good for the club but we feel it would be best if you go.' Sometimes it works the same way for a manager – 'I've done my time. There's no animosity but it's time to have a go somewhere else.'

When it was clear Rafa was going, Christian Purslow asked me to get involved in the selection process for the next manager. 'I'll help in any way I possibly can,' I told Christian. They drew up a list, asked me to come and meet the candidates and then let them decide who the manager should be. In mid-June, I had to let them know my real views. I wanted the job. I couldn't miss the opportunity. One day, I was in a meeting with Christian and the chairman, Martin Broughton, and I formally put my name forward.

'We don't want you, Kenny,' came the reply from Christian and the chairman. Fine. That's their prerogative. They explained they had different plans for me, a position with greater longevity.

'We want you for a role at the club that would be for longer than the tenure of the manager,' the board told me. The job focused on player development. It wasn't management, though. Martin Broughton made that abundantly clear. People have asked me whether I was disappointed, and of course I was. I passionately wanted the job. But I would have been more disappointed if I hadn't put my name forward. I love Liverpool so deeply I felt almost an obligation to apply. This was about helping Liverpool more than reviving my management career. If another club came in and asked me to be their manager, I honestly don't know how I'd react. Liverpool's my home. There was no self-glory attached to my application. I did feel I had unfinished business with the job, though, since my previous tenure was aborted in 1991. But I was enjoying myself with the Academy, going in, helping the kids and attending matches at Anfield. I usually find it difficult to promote myself. That's not my nature.

Liverpool were experiencing hard times and I wanted to help. If I hadn't expressed an interest, people might have thought, 'Well, if Kenny Dalglish doesn't want to help, there must be big problems at Liverpool.'

When the news of my application emerged, the Liverpool punters were more favourable than not. That was reassuring. Maybe I didn't make the wisest decision in the world in going for it. By expressing my ambition for the job, the board might think that complicated life for Roy Hodgson. They needn't have feared. I fully respect Roy, a man I've known for a long, long time, ever since he was in Sweden, at Halmstads and Malmo, and he visited Melwood with Bobby Houghton. We struck up a friendship. Roy's a very honourable and decent person, and very experienced in football. He has his beliefs in how the team should be set up, but when he arrived at Liverpool, he will have known that he had to make one or two adjustments to his system, because the individuals are different at Liverpool. No manager can just impose their style. It's all right having a system but players dictate how it is played. When Roy came in, I knew Liverpool would be committed and well organised. He's the type of guy players enjoy working for. He's very honest in the way he handles players, and he speaks very well. He'll get a great deal of respect from the players as well as the fans.

Roy must know he has walked into a world of uncertainty at Anfield, and until Liverpool are sold, the situation won't settle down. Even then, people always feel uncertain when they have a new employer. What decisions will the new buyer make? Will he keep people? Will he want his own men in? Roy understands the situation. At his press conference, he was asked how he would cope when a new owner arrives. His answer was very good.

'I'm the same as everybody else. If I'm getting results, I've got a better chance of keeping my job.'

Roy knows I'll help him in any way I can. Liverpool Football Club are much more important than I am, or Roy Hodgson,

Christian Purslow or Martin Broughton. I've put aside any resentment I felt about not being considered for the manager's job. I'm focusing on the bigger picture, which is Liverpool Football Club. Roy has no problem with me being here. I have never undermined a manager. When I was given the Liverpool manager's job in 1985, I had the best guy ever as my ally, the most successful manager ever in British football history to consult. Bob Paisley wasn't a threat. He was 100 per cent on my side, and I knew that. I'll be the same for Roy if he wants it. What matters is Liverpool fighting their way back up to where they belong.

Liverpool will always be special in my eyes but they must take care. They are in danger of missing out on the support of a young generation, who've been brought up watching the Premier League on Sky. They want success. Unless Liverpool are winning trophies and keeping hold of quality players, such as Steven Gerrard and Fernando Torres, the club will struggle to pull in that generation of support. At the moment, the kids go to Anfield because of their dads and the players. That's the attraction. But that can't last forever. Liverpool have to win some silverware or lose a generation. Whatever happens, the club can always count on my support.

20

BACK HOME

'**G**o.' Marina's reaction to the call that changed my life was simple and emphatic. Just one word. We were in the bar on cruise liner *Silver Wind*, somewhere in the Arabian Gulf. It was late evening on Friday, 7 January 2011, and I'd just done a question and answer session with some of the passengers. I was relaxing, having a drink, when my phone rang.

'Kenny?' The American voice was immediately recognisable as belonging to John W. Henry. He and Tom Werner were Liverpool's new owners. I stepped away from the bar and found a quiet corner. Even though I knew results were bad and Roy Hodgson was struggling, nothing had prepared me for what John proposed.

'Kenny, would you be interested in coming back?' John asked. 'Roy's leaving and we want you back.' I tried to think straight, to keep my emotions in check. This was the call I'd dreamed of, asking me to go back to my Liverpool home, back to the job I loved.

'Of course I'll come back, John. I'll do whatever I can to help the club.'

'Good,' John replied. 'Get back quickly. We need you as caretaker. Until the end of the season. There are no targets, Kenny, just come in and do your work. Do what have you to do. Get the team playing again.'

I returned to Marina at the bar. She could see the excitement in my eyes.

'They want us to go back,' I said. 'Caretaker. What do you think?'

So she said it. 'Go.' Marina knows how much Liverpool Football Club means to me. In truth, Marina was probably happier than I was – she would be able to get me out of the house now!

Liverpool needed me. It was imperative I got home as quickly as possible. *Silver Wind* was due to arrive in Bahrain early on the Saturday morning, so Marina and I packed and grabbed a few hours' sleep. A car was waiting on the quayside to take us straight to the airport from where we flew to Dubai for the connecting flight to Manchester. In Dubai, we were delayed for an hour but eventually boarded the plane. As we started to move, I commented to Marina, 'That's good. We're getting away now.' I was amazed the story hadn't broken. Nobody on the plane had a clue. Liverpool had kept it secret. So had the cruise people on *Silver Wind* and I will always be grateful to them. I still needed time to take in this whirlwind. Then, as we taxied along, the pilot suddenly announced: 'Ladies and gentlemen, I'm afraid we have a minor technical fault and we're going back to the stand.'

'Christ, I need to get back,' I muttered to Marina.

Back in departures, phones started to ring, pinging with texts or calls. News was out. Punters kept coming up, congratulating me. In the background, I could see a screen showing BBC News with a breaking-news line about me returning to Liverpool.

When we finally got back on the plane, I settled in my seat but my mind was racing. I was so close now. I'd always hoped I would go back. When Rafa left, I had a conversation with Christian Purslow, who was managing director at the time, and I couldn't help but reflect on it. I've already aired my thoughts on the events of summer 2010, but the subject demands further elaboration.

'If there is any way I can help the club I will,' I told Christian. I hoped Liverpool would turn to me.

'You can help, Kenny. Look at this list of candidates,' Purslow said. That was not the reaction I sought. A darkening mood was not improved when I looked through the names.

'Christian, I'm not trying to be disrespectful to anybody on here. But I really think I need to promote myself. Can you put my name on the list?' I was blushing. Pushing myself forward felt awkward. This wasn't my style but I knew I had to say something. This might be my last opportunity to manage Liverpool Football Club, to address unfinished business from two decades earlier.

'Christian, when you sell the club, even if the new owners want me out of the door, I won't have a problem with that. I wouldn't stand in anybody's way. Just give me this chance now.' It was a plea from the heart.

'I'll talk to the chairman. We'll think about it.' But they didn't. The chairman, Martin Broughton, didn't want me. I asked him direct. I had nothing to lose.

'Chairman, I'd like to put my name forward.'

'Kenny, we've got reservations about you. You've not been involved in football for ten years.' That hurt. 'But you could come and meet some of the candidates.'

That just felt like adding insult to injury but I swallowed my pride. This was about Liverpool. I had to help.

'Of course I will,' I said, hiding my fury.

So I sat in on interviews, giving opinions on each candidate. When we interviewed Roy, it was like sitting in the pub with a friend having a drink. I'd known Roy for many years. Christian and Broughton asked me what I thought of him.

'He's a good manager and a good man,' I replied.

I never recommended anybody. I just talked about their attributes. I was there to give opinions, not make decisions. That was down to Christian and Broughton.

When Roy was appointed, I felt the chairman belittled me at Roy's first press conference. When asked about me, Broughton said, 'We have an important role for Kenny.' What? They never offered me anything. What was this important role? Turning up at matches and smiling?

People often ask me whether I feel let down by Broughton but that's life. He didn't think I was the right person and that's fine. But I still believe Broughton and Purslow should have handled the situation more professionally. I deserved more respect. Broughton said I'd been out of the game for 10 years. Factually he was correct, although Liverpool had given me a job, helping out in the Academy, so they must have thought I had some knowledge of the game still. Then they wanted me to help pick a manager. Again, I must be some sort of football judge to do that. But they felt I was an outsider. That was ridiculous. I was never cut off from football. I studied the game passionately, talked with experts including Al Hansen. I watched games all the time, live or on television. Football is not like technology, where you go to bed, wake up and something's changed. The skills required to be a good football manager are essentially the same now as when I started – buy the right players, organise them and motivate them. Then win.

Christian and Broughton had made their decision. As the 2010–11 season got under way, I was made very aware of the fans' dissatisfaction. Frustration had been creeping into the fabric of Liverpool even before Roy arrived. He was appointed during the distrusted regime of Tom Hicks and George Gillett so that was Roy already 1–0 down in the eyes of the Kop. The Liverpool fans weren't supportive to Roy, as everybody hoped they would be. He was caught in the perfect storm. His signings never really worked out as he would have liked, either. Roy arrived in July, so there was a wee bit of a rush to get everything sorted for the season. Up until July, Roy was buying players for Fulham. All of a sudden, he was looking for players for Liverpool and there's a difference. Also, a lot of Liverpool players were coming back in dribs and drabs after the World Cup summer, so Roy's pre-season plans were disrupted. It was difficult for him to assess them and he had to take a few youngsters off on tour. That was no way to bed in a team for the new season. It wasn't an ideal start for him.

It pained me when Liverpool lost to Northampton Town in the Carling Cup or to Wolves in the League. Before the Bolton game on New Year's Day, I called on the fans to get behind the team. People always say I cast a long shadow at Liverpool, which made it difficult for managers, but what could I do? The important thing for everyone at Liverpool Football Club was to work together for the same cause. That has always been the Liverpool way, going back to Shanks. It's what 'You'll Never Walk Alone' means. We stick together at Liverpool. Roy knew I backed him 100 per cent.

'However I can help, just say,' I told Roy. I covered games for him, looked at players. Whenever I went to Melwood, Roy and Mike Kelly always welcomed me. But I couldn't avoid the fact that the Kop were chanting my name. Losing to Blackburn on 5 January made it very uncomfortable for Roy. So John Henry called me and there I was flying back to the job I coveted most. I knew there was so much to do. One of my first tasks was to call Roy. I don't like to see anyone lose their job. Unfortunately, I couldn't get hold of him. Eventually, we had a drink when Liverpool played his West Brom side in April. We never mentioned what happened to him at Liverpool. I don't think we'll ever discuss it. Life moves on. It would probably be a wee bit painful for Roy to look back on that time anyway. The Kop wasn't happy that Liverpool weren't getting results but Roy wouldn't have been happy, either. He suffered and I have sympathy for what he endured. He's a good manager. He knows I hold him in the highest regard.

Late on that Saturday night, we landed at Manchester. Marina went home but I jumped in a car to the Hilton in town. I had immediate business to attend to. Liverpool were playing

Manchester United in the FA Cup on the Sunday. When I walked into the Hilton, Sammy Lee and the backroom staff were there.

'Where've you been?' Sammy smiled. 'Do you want a drink?'

'I've missed my dinner. I'll settle for some food.' It was good to be back. It felt so natural, just picking up the reins again.

In the morning, I saw the boys. The players seemed underwhelmed.

'Morning, Boss,' they said, and got on with their breakfast and preparations. But the big smiles from Carra and Stevie meant so much to me.

The team had been prepared by Sammy and the director of football strategy, Damien Comolli, but I took responsibility in the dressing room. It was vital I showed leadership immediately. I gave the team-talk, keeping it short and simple. 'The important thing is for all of us to stand together,' was the gist of it.

Out on the pitch, I was greeted by a smiling Fergie.

'Welcome back, Kenny. What have you done that for?!'

Little welcome could be found on the pitch. Howard Webb made a couple of exasperating decisions, giving United a penalty and then sending Stevie off. I felt I'd never been away. What was Broughton thinking of? Nothing's changed. It was the same old problem with referees: inconsistency in interpretation. I study the laws, understand the game and then scratch my head trying to work out why referees reach certain decisions. Referees will gain proper respect only if there is greater transparency. That means explaining decisions afterwards. As I surveyed the game at Old Trafford, seeing the expensive refereeing decisions, all the old adrenalin was flowing again. That competitive spirit, that frustration in defeat, never left me. Afterwards, I had a drink with Fergie. This was one of the game's many traditions I'd missed. Such is the unremitting tension between United and Liverpool that some people might be surprised to find me enjoying time with him. We're rivals but we respect each other.

After the wee drink in Fergie's office, I headed back to Melwood

with Damien. The result was disappointing but the most important event of the day for the future of Liverpool Football Club
was still to come. Once in his office, Damien produced a piece
of paper.

'It's a list of coaches,' he said, handing me the sheet. I just
needed to see the top name.

'Steve Clarke. That'll do for me.'

'Ring him then.' So I called Steve and explained the situation.

'Look, Steve, it would be fantastic for us if you came up. It's
only short term, until the end of the season. It's a fantastic opportunity. I'd love to work beside you.'

'I'll see you in the morning,' Steve replied. Brilliant! Steve was
just what the players needed. He's a good, experienced football
man who is a great organiser of teams. Steve, Sammy and I confer
before training and they put our ideas into action.

My first win back came at Molineux on 22 January. When Raul
Meireles scored with that volley, my face lit up in the biggest smile.
Some ignorant people were surprised that I could show such
emotion. Some critics still think of me as dour. When the Liverpool fans chanted my name, I waved back. That would never
distract me; my focus was always on the game but I would never
detach myself from the emotion. I may not be demonstrative all
the time, and I've certainly not got an Equity card, but I'm definitely more relaxed as Liverpool manager this time round.

As a club, Liverpool has grown enormously but managed to
keep its soul. People matter, and the staff were as good as gold
when I walked back into Anfield as manager.

'Morning, Boss,' chorused the stewards at main reception.

We had a problem with Fernando Torres. He was struggling
for goals, so I tried to give him a wee bit of reassurance. 'You're
a good player,' I told him. 'The goals will come.'

I liked Fernando, and it doesn't matter how good a player you
are, you want to hear compliments about yourself. Even super-
stars need an arm around the shoulder now and then. But for

all my attempts to gee him up, I quickly realised that he couldn't be helped. Fernando didn't want to be helped. He'd made up his mind to leave Liverpool. Of course, I spoke to him, tried to dissuade him. We had two or three meetings. After each one, I felt like I'd wasted my breath. Fernando was off. Nothing I could have said would have swayed him. Towards the end, it became a wee bit acrimonious. That was sad. Fernando wanted to speak to the staff, to explain his decision to quit for Chelsea, which I suppose was an honest thing to do. I hope he was doing it because he respected the staff. I just felt, 'Adios, Fernando, off you go,' and don't forget that Liverpool Football Club will always be bigger than any one player. We move on. Always. I never even considered addressing Torres' leaving with the players. I didn't need to with two crackers coming in.

Damien had Luis Suarez on the go before I returned, but he still wanted to know I was onside with the deal.

'You won't get any resistance from me on Suarez, Damien!'

'What do you like about him?'

'Everything. His attitude, enthusiasm, the goals he scores, the level he played at with Ajax. He went to Holland, picked up the language and captained the side. That tells me everything about his character.'

I never saw Suarez's hand-ball at the World Cup against Ghana, but I know one thing – Luis Suarez is a better goalscorer than goalkeeper. He quickly proved that with us, scoring on his debut.

Suarez's impact was also testament to the unbelievable amount of work Damien does on Liverpool's behalf. He oversees the scouting, handles the negotiations, has regular conversations with Tom and John about finances. It is a huge role. Some people might have thought I would be a wee bit old school, not liking the idea of working with a director of football, but I've never had a problem with it. It's straightforward – if I don't want a player to be here, he won't be. I get on with Damien. I don't know what he was like before but he's been as good as gold with me.

The day before the January transfer window closed, Damien said, 'What about Andy Carroll?'

'Can you get him?'

Somehow, Damien did manage to get Carroll out of Newcastle United. He did brilliantly to pull off such a deal with time running out. I couldn't believe it when some critics said we'd paid over the odds at £35 million. Suarez was coming anyway, so take him out of the equation. We sold Torres for £50 million and brought in Andy for £15 million profit. That's good business in my eyes. It looked even better business when Torres found goals hard to come by at Chelsea. I took no satisfaction from that. Torres will come good. I just focus on the value of the people we bring in. Andy was unfortunate with injuries and he did fantastically well to get back as quickly as he did, and gave the fans a glimpse of his class with the goals against Manchester City. I was grateful to Fabio Capello for handling Andy carefully in the March friendly against Ghana. Fabio played him for 60 minutes only, so that eased him back in, and scoring was a massive moment for him. Seeing Andy start for England never surprised me. He could be England's main man for years to come. I rate him that highly.

Sadly, Andy took a bruise to the knee at Arsenal in April and we shouldn't really have played him against Spurs. He's so willing; Andy always wants to play. I get annoyed when people talk about Andy's injuries. He's just had a bad run; it's a temporary thing. When people mention Andy having the occasional drink, that irritates me, too. I've not got a problem with him liking a beer, as long as it's not just before the match. Andy's not a boozer. Punters will snap a picture of him with a wee glass of beer and the photograph will be shown over and over. It's half a pint! If Andy's sensible, he's got a massive career in front of him – and he is sensible. Too big an issue is made of the odd drink. What does the public want? One minute people complain about foot-ballers being cut off from real life, the next they slam them for being in a pub having a half of beer. Andy Carroll wants to stay

normal, stay connected with the real world. He's a sociable character who likes being among people.

That game at the Emirates had one of the most amazing endings
I've ever seen. When Dirk Kuyt put the penalty in to make it 1–1,
I never realised Andre Marriner had blown for time up. I was
coming back towards the dug-out when I saw Arsene walking
along the touchline. 'Where's he going?' I wondered. Arsene was
blathering away.

'The referee's given a penalty.' Arsene sounded shocked.

'It was a penalty,' I replied, adding a wee expletive to make
my point. It was a stonewall penalty. Emmanuel Eboue clearly
barged into Lucas. As I turned away from Arsene, I saw all the
Arsenal players walking off the pitch. The game was over, so I
turned around and shook Arsene's hand. No problem. People
bang on about Arsene not having any dignity after a bad result.
Well, show me a good loser and I'll show you a loser. I have
enormous respect for Arsene and what he's done. He can lead
his life the way he wants to, as long as it doesn't interfere with
mine and as long as he doesn't preach to me. Arsene didn't invite
me in for a drink afterwards. He never does.

The draw with Arsenal was a great result and a great performance. I was really pleased for the players, and especially Lucas,
who had a terrific season. People praised me for getting the
players going again but they did it themselves. They found the
desire within themselves to push forward. Lucas has always been
a good player. He's always been appreciated within the confines
of Anfield. People outside Liverpool recognise his worth now.
Becoming a regular in the Brazil team has given Lucas even
more confidence.

I'm often asked what has changed about management. Well,
sports science has developed, I don't recognise any of the music
the players have on in the dressing room and footballers are more
powerful now. Apart from that, football will always be the same.
In any dressing room, there will be some players who draw their

inspiration from medals and others who are mercenary, finding their inspiration from money. What really impressed me was the good attitude of those players who didn't often feature. Christian Poulsen and Joe Cole, for instance, were well behaved, training hard, never an ounce of bother.

Young ones, such as John Flanagan, Martin Kelly and Jay Spearing, gave the older ones a lift. Having been at Kirkby, I knew the kids and brought some of them in when we had injuries. Not one of them let Liverpool down when they played or when they trained. That's great recognition for the work done at the Academy. I thought it was a fantastic idea for the Academy to recommend that the kids attend the annual Hillsborough memorial at Anfield on Friday, 15 April. None of the Academy boys were born 22 years ago, when the tragedy occurred, but it is vital they understand. It was a moving experience for them to be at Anfield, showing their support for the families who lost loved ones at Hillsborough. It was good to see Rafa there as well, paying his respects. Afterwards, there were a few speeches but I never really needed to express any sentiments. Liverpool fans know my feelings.

The bond with the Liverpool fans is unbreakable. I was hoping to stay on, to make the caretaker role permanent. I knew if I did well, John and Tom would ask me to stay. If I wasn't deserving of it, I'd have walked away happily. It wouldn't have been a problem. I'd never hold Liverpool back. But things were going well and I was enjoying working with John and Tom. They were as good as gold, the two of them. They are different personalities. Tom is a film producer in LA. John is more hands-on. He's really grasped football. Both are decent people and care about others. They understand what Liverpool means to the fans. Tom and John also care about Liverpool being successful. I wouldn't describe them as ruthless but they know what they want. They are ambitious to get Liverpool back to the top again.

On 12 May, after my weekly press conference finished at

Melwood and the cameras were turned off, I made an announcement.

'Anybody need a set of Callaways? I've signed. I'm staying for another three years.' Golf could take a back seat. Reporters asked me why the deal took so long. It was the owners' decision. I wasn't going anywhere! It's a fairytale for me that I was asked back. Not many people get a second chance. I left abruptly 20 years ago and now I can finish what we started. I hope it proves a fairytale for Liverpool as well. Anfield certainly seems a happier place. As far as I'm concerned, it's the only place to be. I understand the magnitude of the job I have taken on. It's not just me, though; Ian Ayre's appointment as managing director and Damien's as director of football both went down well with the supporters.

My return to Liverpool was inevitably shrouded in romance. That romance has gone now, history, evaporated into thin air. It is only right that I be judged solely on results. I'm not in short trousers any more. I know the expectations, improving month after month, year after year. A feelgood factor has taken up residency inside Anfield going into the new season. We want to start winning the League again. Liverpool's history demands it. We have to respond to Manchester United.

'Does United's nineteenth Premier League title hurt?' I was asked by one reporter.

'You mean United's twelfth Premier League win?' I replied, jokingly.

I deeply respect United's achievements. We're not resentful of the success they have had. They're the benchmark and we have to prove our worth. We won't overcome United by being jealous and bitter. They are better than us at the moment. Only hard graft will help Liverpool overtake them. We have an opportunity on the pitch to do something about it. That's a challenge we accept with hunger and dignity. I dropped Fergie a line of congratulations. I was tempted to write 'Happy twelfth Premier

League!' but thought better of it. I was upset about United
breaking our proud record but I wasn't going to admit it.

As I look back on a special season, my best moment was actually against United on 6 March. The Kop sang 'Happy Birthday',
48 hours late but still greatly appreciated. I was so touched. That
was the best birthday present ever. I'd got my old job back, we'd
beaten United 3–1 at Anfield and it certainly felt like my birthday!
Sometimes we've lifted the fans. Sometimes they've lifted us. I
also know the level of their passion from being on Twitter. I only
started on Twitter to try to win £10,000 from Absolute Radio
for Marina's charity. It was the kids' idea. I got into it and the
reaction has been unbelievable. I get so many tweets. When Marina
tweeted that she wanted a cup of tea brought upstairs, I got loads
of people telling me to put the kettle and get cracking.

Marina has been ecstatic at seeing me back doing the job I
love. She comes to all the home games. I can't say it has been
the greatest year of my life – that was the year I married Marina
– but it comes close. During the season, three new grandkids
came along. Kelly has had another girl and Paul's had twins, and
one's a wee boy, so that keeps the Dalglish name going. It's been
a fantastic year for my family. And for my football family. Instead
of sitting in the directors' box, I'm back in the dug-out. Looking
to my right, I see the Kop, the greatest sight in football. I love
being back in my Liverpool home.

21

OUR LIVERPOOL HOME

Marina's Story

WHEN we left Glasgow for Liverpool in 1977, I was a 23 year old with two babies – Kelly was 20 months and Paul was just five months. I had no idea what to expect. Moving from Scotland to England in those days was a very big deal.

We stayed in the Holiday Inn in Paradise Street in Liverpool where we were welcomed by the innkeeper Jack Ferguson and his wife Meg, which was lovely because they were good friends of my parents. I cannot thank them and their staff enough for making our move to England so easy. Kelly used to help wee Cathy, the chambermaid, clean the bedrooms and Cathy eventually became their babysitter. In fact, when Kenny wasn't around, the kids and I would eat in the staff canteen!

I remember feeling immediately welcome at my first game at Anfield. Everyone was so friendly. There was a lounge where friends and family would gather after the game to wait while the players changed. I thought this was great because at Celtic the wives would have to stand outside or sit in the car park waiting for their husbands to emerge. Mind you, I think Terry, who looked after the players' lounge at Anfield, would have been glad if I'd left Paul outside – especially when he got a bit older!

It was there I met the other players' wives. One night we decided to go to aerobics together. The occasion sticks in my mind because we failed, and it turned into a girls' night out. We had all agreed to meet at the aerobics studio at 7 p.m., having fed and bathed the children and husbands and left them looking after each other. Running late as usual, the girls decided to wear just leotards and tights to save time changing when we got there. However, when we arrived at the class, it was cancelled. At this point we made the unanimous decision to check out the new wine bar. So, in tights, leotards and coats off we went.

One glass of wine became two, at which point we felt the need to call home and tell the husbands why we were late. All the men were fine about it, apart from Kenny. He was manager at the time, and his response was: 'What are you doing taking those girls out? They're going to go home and wake up the lads. We have a quarter-final tomorrow.' He put the phone down. I relayed this to the girls who found it hilarious and we decided to phone him back. I think it was Julie McMahon who said, 'Don't worry, Kenneth, I'll sleep in the spare room tonight.' I think he put the phone down again. Thank goodness they won the next day.

Whenever I meet up with the girls now, we all agree that we would not swap the good times and lifelong friendships that we have made to be a footballer's wife today. In an industry where people move about a lot it's amazing that so many of us still keep in touch.

I clearly remember the day that Kenny resigned from Liverpool. We were all in tears watching the news conference. A great part of our life had gone. However, Kenny made the right decision for both himself and our family. His health was suffering and he was not an easy person to live with. He was given very little help to cope with the stress that he was under, although I doubt he would have taken it if it had been offered.

He could have chosen a better time to resign – I was in the middle of arranging a surprise 40th birthday party for him less than two weeks later and suddenly he was at home while I was trying to make secret telephone calls. I thought of cancelling but decided to go ahead, which was for the best as it was great for Kenny to have his friends around him.

Hillsborough is still very fresh in my memory and I will never forget the event or the 96 people who lost their lives in the tragedy. It was a great privilege for Kenny and I to be allowed to share such a private and tragic time in the lives of many. I would like to thank all of the families who allowed Kenny and I to be a part of this. I hope that one day soon the families of those who died will receive the justice that they are owed.

The Kids' Story

As we've grown older, we've really enjoyed visiting Anfield, especially because each time we go to a match we bump into the same friendly faces, many of whom have been there for as long as we can remember. They have stories to tell about each of us. Lauren was the baby whose nappy they remember changing, Lynsey was the one with Barbies, Paul was, and still is, the one causing mischief and Kelly was, and still is, the perfect child! This is why Anfield is such a special place for all of us – it's like a second home. Thank you for making us all feel so welcome.

Kelly

My memories of Anfield during Dad's time as player-manager are a mixture of the sickly sweet and the deeply sad, from the bars of chocolate that were a highlight of our trips as kids to the dreadful poignancy of the aftermath of Hillsborough.

I was nine when Dad became player-manager in 1985. Our seats were at the back of the directors' box, just in front of an older lady called Mrs Prince, who had white, set hair and was an avid Liverpool supporter. To every home game she would bring a Wispa bar each for Paul and me, which she gave us at half-time. It taught us never to be late taking our seats!

Amazingly, it wasn't until 1989 that I first stood on the Kop. It wasn't full of swinging and swaying fans that day but a sea of flowers, scarves, messages and tributes to those who had died or been injured days earlier at Hillsborough. I was with Dad and Paul, who tied his old teddy to a goalpost before looking up at Dad and asking, 'Why us?'

Another vivid memory, and a far happier one, was Dad's last game as a player. It was against Derby in the final home fixture of 1989–90, when he was two months past his 39th birthday. He'd picked himself to be a substitute, although the Kop knew better than to call for him too soon because they knew the full 90 minutes would be too much for him!

They waited until well into the second half. Then all the old songs and chants started up, urging him to make his entrance. With less than 20 minutes to go, when it was still 0–0, he sent himself on for Jan Molby. Ten minutes later, Gary Gillespie got the winner and the celebrations started for what, amazingly, is still Liverpool's last League title.

It was wonderful to watch Dad play in front of almost 40,000 people, at an age when I could properly appreciate their support rather than seeing it as a child with confectionery on her mind.

Paul

Liverpool Football Club and my family are the most important things in my life. They always have been and always will be. They are the two things that I truly love. A lot of people say supporting Liverpool is a religion. Well, to me it genuinely is. The club taught me many of the values by which I lead my life. Anfield was my Mecca, Jan Molby was my Buddha, and I was a disciple of what the great Bill Shankly created and what my dad taught and passed on to me, the Liverpool way. When my dad was at Liverpool, the team were the greatest team in the world and my dad was the King of the Kop. It would have been easy for him to have become carried away with his success, but he actually tried to stay away from the limelight and still doesn't feel comfortable taking praise. Humility, the thing that my dad always preached, was an important part of the Liverpool way. The people at Liverpool Football Club understood and embraced the responsibility that comes with living out the dreams of the fans, the people who chose to spend their hard-earned cash supporting the team. That's why the bond between Liverpool players and supporters is the closest in the world.

Despite Liverpool being the greatest team in the world, individuals never bragged. They never spoke about how good they were. They didn't need to because everybody else did that for them. The message was clear – Liverpool Football Club is the most important thing, no individual was or ever will be bigger than the club and everybody here must strive to bring silverwear to Anfield every season. Players must have the humility to find ways to improve every season, no matter what they had won the past season, in order to keep Liverpool in their rightful place, perched at the very top of world football. I remember a story my dad told me, about when Liverpool had won the League and the players had reported back for pre-season training. Ronnie Moran walked into the changing rooms with all the players' medals in a box, put them on the treatment table and said, 'Take one if you think you deserve one, but just remember you haven't won anything yet this season.'

There is one dream that I have been able to achieve, a dream that my dad has never been able to fulfil, and the greatest thing any Liverpool fan could ever do. I got to stand on the Kop every week and learn why the Liverpool way was so special. I would stand alongside my fellow reds, always with my friends and Jim, a great man from Scotland, who would stand behind me and sit me on the barrier so I could see – same place every week, by the right-hand pillar, right in the middle of the Kop.

That was where I went after Hillsborough with Dad and Kelly. I don't know why but it was where I wanted to go after witnessing the horrific events of that tragic day unfold in front of my young eyes. I remember standing speechless with Stephen Evans and Brownie, who used to take Stephen and I to the away games. We watched as people tried to climb over the railings at the front, and saw people being lifted from the terracing to the seats above. We had no idea what was happening but we soon realised. I saw dead people for the first time, being carried on advertising boards instead of stretchers, and people taking off their tops to cover the faces of their loved ones. I remember Forest fans singing abusive songs at Liverpool fans, obviously unaware of the seriousness of the situation. I vividly remember one Liverpool fan running the length of the field to confront the whole Forest end only to be stopped by police. It was just after this that I heard my dad's voice come over the speakers in the stadium, asking people to stay calm. I was scared. I wished he could come and get me, and fortunately he did. There were no mobile phones then so I couldn't call him or my mum. I can't tell you how relieved I was when I looked on to the pitch and saw my dad. He had come to find me. As soon as I saw him I ran down and hugged him. He took me and Stephen back to our families who were in the main stand. It sounds strange but we were the lucky ones. Some sons never got to hug their dads again. I never cried on the day of the Hillsborough tragedy. It was on the Kop, in my special place, and in the arms of my father that I felt safe enough to let my emotions out and start the grieving process for my fellow reds. I have never spoken of this before, not even to family, but I suppose I needed to get it off my chest.

I grew up in the corridors of Anfield, I travelled all over the world to watch Liverpool win trophies and spent every day I had off school going to Melwood to watch Liverpool train. I have some great memories and some tragic ones, too, but my greatest memory of my dad's time at Liverpool is being taught how to live the Liverpool way. Bill Shankly created it, Bob Paisley, Ronnie Moran, Joe Fagan, Roy Evans, Tom Saunders and my dad preached the sermon. I was very fortunate to be given the opportunity to learn these values from the great men themselves. I have always tried, and always will try, to live my life the Liverpool way.

Lynsey

Dad isn't the only one who has raised the roof at Anfield by scoring a goal – and I achieved something he never did by bringing a huge cheer from the away fans packed into the Anfield Road end.

It happened like this. After every home match, us kids used to go out to play on the pitch while our dads got changed and went through the whole post-match routine. I remember we used to get into trouble for getting covered in the red dust from the track that surrounded the pitch. On this particular afternoon, Roy Evans's son Stephen had bet me 50p I couldn't score against him. I managed to put the ball past him into the net, to a great 'hurray' from the opposing fans who were being held behind while the Liverpool crowd cleared.

We even made the hallowed Boot Room part of our playground. Paul showed me where they kept the chewing gum for the players and coaches, and taught me how to pinch it. Well, it was Doublemint!

In the late eighties, when Dad was player-manager, I became aware that all the other kids were going round the players' lounge collecting autographs. I decided I had to have my programme signed, which bemused the team somewhat, especially Dad, who inscribed it, 'To my blue-eyed girl'. When I saw the message I was devastated. 'That's not what you write,' I told him. 'You're supposed to say "Best Wishes".'

Lauren

Dad left Liverpool Football Club when I was just three years old, so my memories of the good old days are very sparse. I'm actually a little bit jealous of Kelly, Paul and Lynsey because they tell me that they had a great time. Apparently, I attended my first match when I was only weeks old – arriving five minutes after kick-off, wrapped up inside Mum's coat. She tells me that I slept through the whole match, only to be woken up for food at half-time.

One thing I do remember is being asked by my friends at nursery what my daddy did. I replied, 'He stands in a little box on a Saturday, points and shouts.' It was only once I had watched some of the replays on LFC TV that I realized what a great player Dad must have been. My three-year-old interpretation of his job definitely underestimated his footballing abilities.

However, I did watch Dad play at Anfield more recently. It was a charity match at Anfield a few years ago and Lynsey and I were sitting alongside the Hansens, Thompsons and Whelans, howling with laughter at our fathers' attempts to run. Being used to the pace of Premiership football at Anfield, it was like watching a game in slow motion. I'm sure by their red, sweaty faces that they were trying very hard, and there were moments when we could see touches of their old brilliance, but to us it was hilarious!

CAREER RECORD

The facts and figures of Kenny Dalglish's career at Liverpool FC.

Compiled by John Keith.

1977–78

Dalglish signs for Liverpool in a £440,000 transfer from Celtic on10 August 1977. He is Anfield manager Bob Paisley's replacement for Kevin Keegan, earlier sold to Hamburg for £500,000.

Dalglish makes debut in goalless Charity Shield duel with Manchester United at Wembley three days later and scores on his first League appearance in 1–1 draw at Middlesbrough the following Saturday. He goes on to make 180 consecutive first team appearances spanning three years.

Dalglish wins his 50th Scotland cap on the familiar territory of Anfield in October in the World Cup qualifier against Wales. His header clinches a 2–0 victory and secures Scotland a ticket to the following summer's World Cup finals in Argentina.

He crowns his first season at Liverpool by scoring their European Cup final winner against Bruges at Wembley and also collects runners-up medals in League championship and League Cup and a winners' medal in European Super Cup.

Competition	Appearances	Goals
League	42 (0)	20
FA Cup	1 (0)	1
League Cup	9 (0)	6
European Cup	7 (0)	3
European Super Cup	2 (0)	1
Charity Shield	1 (0)	0
Totals	*62 (0)*	*31*

1978–79

Dalglish plays in all three of Scotland's games in the World Cup finals: a 3–1 defeat by Peru in Cordoba, a 1–1 draw with Iran in Cordoba and a 3–2 win over eventual runners-up Holland in Mendoza in which he scored one of the goals. The tournament also takes Dalglish past Denis Law's 55-cap Scotland appearance record.

Two of the World Cup-winning Argentina team are on the receiving end of a drubbing by Dalglish and his Liverpool colleagues in September. Osvaldo Ardiles and Ricardo Villa are members of the Tottenham side toppled 7–0 at Anfield. Dalglish scores twice in what is regarded as one of Liverpool's finest-ever performances and he and the club go on to lift the championship. They do so with a total of 68 points from 42 games, a record under the two-points-for-a-win system, and concede only 16 goals, also a record. Dalglish scores 21 League goals. During the season he passes the 100th appearance milestone for Liverpool and 50 goals. He is voted Footballer of the Year by the Football Writers' Association.

During the season at international level, Dalglish is reunited with his Celtic manager Jock Stein who succeeds Ally MacLeod in October.

Competition	Appearances	Goals
League	42 (0)	21
FA Cup	7 (0)	4
League Cup	1 (0)	0
European Cup	2 (0)	0
European Super Cup	2 (0)	0
Totals	*54 (0)*	*25*

1979–80

Dalglish opens the curtain on the new season with a goal in Liverpool's 3–1 FA Charity Shield win over Arsenal at Wembley. He completes his third successive ever-present season by contributing 16 goals towards Liverpool's retention of the League championship. Dalglish scores in a four-game record FA Cup semi-final marathon against Arsenal only for Liverpool to lose in the third replay. On the very day of the club's agonising defeat, 1 May, 1980, they make a signing which proves to be of huge significance. Ian Rush, who is to form a legendary partnership with Dalglish, arrives from Chester for £300,000.

Competition	Appearances	Goals
League	42 (0)	16
FA Cup	8 (0)	2
League Cup	7 (0)	4
European Cup	2 (0)	0
Charity Shield	1 (0)	1
Totals	*60 (0)*	*23*

1980–81

Dalglish's long sequence without missing a first-team game since joining Liverpool ends when injury rules him out of the League Cup second-round, first-leg game at Bradford City in August. It ended his 180-game ever-present run. He returns to score twice in the return and in every round to the final when he hits one of the goals in a 2–1 success against West Ham in the Villa Park replay.

In Europe, Dalglish suffers damage to his left ankle and is substituted after only nineminutes in the European Cup semi-final second leg at Bayern Munich. A 1–1 draw takes Liverpool through on the away-goal rule and he is fit for the 1–0 win over Real Madrid in Paris to give Liverpool the trophy for the third time.

Competition	Appearances	Goals
League	34 (0)	8
FA Cup	2 (0)	2
League Cup	8 (0)	7
European Cup	9 (0)	1
Charity Shield	1 (0)	0
Totals	*54 (0)*	*18*

1981–82

Dalglish scores Liverpool's 100th European Cup goal in a 7–0 rout of Finnish club Oulun Palloseura in the first round, second leg at Anfield in September. Liverpool go on to reach the quarter-final but lose on a 2–0 aggregate to CSKA Sofia. Dalglish helps Liverpool retain the League Cup, now called the Milk Cup, with a 3–1 conquest of Tottenham at Wembley. He scores in the 3–1 home League win over Tottenham in May that recaptures the championship.

Dalglish helps Scotland to reach the World Cup finals in Spain in the summer of 1982 and scores in the 5–2 opening win over New Zealand in Malaga. He goes on as a substitute in the 4–1 defeat by Brazil in Seville but misses their final group match when a 2–2 draw with the USSR put out the Scots on goal difference.

Competition	Appearances	Goals
League	42 (0)	13
FA Cup	2 (0)	2
League Cup	10 (0)	5
European Cup	6 (0)	2
World Club Championship	1 (0)	0
Totals	*61 (0)*	*22*

1982–83

Another ever-present League campaign by Dalglish, his fifth in six seasons at Liverpool, helps the club retain the title. He scores 18 goals in the championship triumph.

Dalglish also collects another Milk Cup winners' medal after a 2–1 defeat of Manchester United at Wembley.

In Europe, his absence from the European Cup quarter-final second leg against Widzew Lodz through illness ends his unbroken run of 35 European games, including four Super Cup, since his arrival from Celtic. It was only his 11th absence overall from Liverpool in that time.

Dalglish is named Footballer of the Year for the second time to complete a personal double after his election earlier in the season as the PFA's Player of the Year.

Bob Paisley, the manager who signed Dalglish, retires at the end of the season after an unprecedented haul of 19 trophies in nine seasons. He is succeeded by Joe Fagan.

Competition	Appearances	Goals
League	42 (0)	18
FA Cup	3 (0)	1
Milk Cup	7 (0)	0
European Cup	5 (0)	1
Charity Shield	1 (0)	0
Totals	*58 (0)*	*20*

1983–84

Dalglish helps Liverpool win the treble of League championship, Milk Cup and European Cup, a unique managerial feat by Fagan in his first season in charge.

Dalglish's two goals against Danish side Odense in the first round, second leg at Anfield sets a new European Cup scoring record for a British player of 15, surpassing Denis Law's previous best of 14. It was also Dalglish's 54th European Cup appearance, more than any other British player.

He scores his 100th League goal for Liverpool at Ipswich in November on his 259th appearance. He is the first player in history to complete a League century in both England and Scotland with only two clubs. Neil Martin also scored 100 each side of the border but his goals came for Alloa, Queen of the South, Hibernian, Sunderland, Coventry and Nottingham Forest.

In January, Dalglish suffers a depressed cheekbone fracture in a collision with Manchester United's Kevin Moran at Anfield and is out for two months but returns in March to help Liverpool to their triple success.

Their 15th championship win also completes the first post-war hat-trick and their European Cup triumph comes after a penalty shoot-out against Roma in the Italian club's own Olympic Stadium.

Liverpool's Milk Cup success, achieved by beating Mersey rivals Everton 1–0 in a Maine Road replay, after a goalless draw at Wembley, is the club's fourth consecutive win in the competition, an unprecedented feat in English football.

Competition	Appearances	Goals
League	33 (0)	7
FA Cup	0 (0)	0
Milk Cup	8 (0)	2
European Cup	8 (1)	3
Charity Shield	1 (0)	0
Totals	*50 (1)*	*12*

1984–85

A season that ends in tragedy with the deaths of 39 supporters, mostly Italian, at Liverpool's European Cup final against Juventus in the Heysel stadium, Brussels.

Dalglish makes his 400th senior appearance for Liverpool in a 3–1 defeat at Arsenal in September and the following month he is dropped for the first time by Liverpool when Fagan omits him from the live televised Friday night game at Tottenham, who win 1–0. It is only the 28th game he has missed for the club and he wins an immediate recall. November is a month of mixed fortune for Dalglish. He is sent off for the first time in his career after retaliating in the European Cup return with Benfica in Lisbon's Stadium of Light. He receives a three-game ban but returns in the semi-final against Panathinaikos, making his 50th European appearance for Liverpool in the second leg against the Greeks.

A week after his dismissal in Portugal, Dalglish hits a memorable goal to give Scotland a 3–1 win over Spain at Hampden Park. It was his 30th at international level, equalling Denis Law's record.

In the 1985 New Year Honours List Dalglish is awarded the

MBE for services to football. He receives it at Buckingham Palace the day before his 750th club appearance for Celtic and Liverpool in the 7–0 FA Cup replay win over York City at Anfield in February. Three days later he makes his 300th League appearance for Liverpool in the 2–0 home League win over Stoke City.

The Brussels meeting with Juventus on 29 May is a sad watershed for English football and Liverpool. English clubs are banned from European competitions after the disaster. A Michel Platini penalty gave Juventus a 1–0 victory in a match rendered irrelevant by the tragedy. Less than 24 hours later Dalglish is named as Liverpool's new player-manager in succession to Joe Fagan who informed the club he would be retiring as manager before the events of Heysel.

Competition	Appearances	Goals
League	36 (0)	6
FA Cup	7 (0)	0
Milk Cup	1 (0)	0
Charity Shield	1 (0)	0
World Club Championship	1 (0)	0
European Cup	7 (0)	0
European Super Cup	0 (0)	0
Totals	*53 (0)*	6

1985–86

Sadness for Dalglish early in his first season as player-manager when Jock Stein, his manager at club level with Celtic and international level with Scotland, dies immediately after the World Cup qualifier against Wales at Cardiff's Ninian Park, which ends 1–1 and which Dalglish misses through injury.

Alex Ferguson takes over as Scotland manager and a goalless draw with Australia in Melbourne, a game Dalglish misses through club commitments, ensures qualification for the finals in Mexico.

At club level Dalglish responds magnificently to his new challenge in management by guiding the club to a championship and FA cup Double. He scores the goal at Chelsea in May that clinches the title, becoming the first player-manager to win the championship. A week later he plays in the FA Cup final when a 3–1 win over Everton completes the classic English Double, the first player-manager to achieve the feat. He is named Manager of the Year. During the season he passes the half-century of Cup goals for Liverpool, becoming the first player to score 50 or more in knock-out competitions in England and Scotland.

At a ceremony in March in Glasgow he is made a Freeman of his native city by the Lord Provost, Robert Gray, and two days later Dalglish wins his 100th Scotland cap in the 3–0 win over Romania. Before kick-off he is presented with a solid silver cap, with nine-carat gold braiding, by Franz Beckenbauer, as a gift from the Scottish FA, and Dalglish takes over as captain for the night from his former Liverpool team-mate Graeme Souness.

A Scottish testimonial match for Dalglish at Hampden Park in May between an Alex Ferguson-managed team of home-based players and an Anglo side under the guidance of Tommy Docherty draws a crowd of almost 30,000. Dalglish scores for both sides as Docherty's team run out 5–2 winners.

A knee injury forces Dalglish to withdraw from the squad for Mexico, preventing him becoming the first Briton to play in four World Cup final tournaments after his appearances in West Germany (1974), Argentina (1978) and Spain (1982).

Competition	Appearances	Goals
League	17 (4)	3
FA Cup	6 (0)	1
Milk Cup	2 (0)	1
Screen Sport Super Cup	2 (0)	2
Totals	*27 (4)*	*7*

1986-87

Dalglish's champions and FA Cup winners draw 1–1 with double runners-up Everton at Wembley in the Charity Shield. He goes on as a second-half substitute, with Ian Rush scoring a late equaliser.

Dalglish also makes a substitute appearance against his former club Celtic in the desert clash of the British champions for the Dubai Super Cup. The game finishes 1–1 and Liverpool win 4–2 on penalties.

Liverpool reach another final in the League Cup competition, newly sponsored by Littlewoods. Ian Rush puts Liverpool ahead but two Charlie Nicholas goals give Arsenal a 2–1 victory, ending Liverpool's 144-match unbeaten run in games in which Rush has scored. Dalglish's 72nd-minute introduction as substitute for Paul Walsh sets a new record of 15 Wembley appearances with one club.

Liverpool, who open up a nine-point lead over second-placed Everton on 18 March, finish championship runners-up to their arch rivals who finish with 86 points, nine more than Liverpool.

Dalglish makes his 102nd and final Scotland appearance in the 3–0 win over Luxembourg at Hampden on 12 November. A save by visiting keeper John Van Rijswijck denies him a record-breaking 31st international goal. Andy Roxburgh's succession to Alex Ferguson the previous July makes him the sixth Scotland manager of Dalglish's illustrious career following Tommy Docherty, Willie Ormond, Ally MacLeod, Jock Stein and Ferguson.

Competition	Appearances	Goals
League	12 (6)	6
FA Cup	0 (0)	0
Littlewoods Cup	4 (1)	2
Charity Shield	0 (1)	0
Screen Sport Super Cup	1 (0)	0
Dubai Super Cup	0 (1)	0
Totals	*17 (9)*	*8*

1987–88

The season when Dalglish becomes very much the manager rather than the player, making only two appearances, both as a substitute. But he has the satisfaction of seeing his team storm to Liverpool's 17th championship and their second under his command. A 1–0 home win over Tottenham clinches the title after they equal Leeds United's record of 29 First Division games unbeaten from the start of the season, the run ending at Everton in March.

Liverpool, favourites for another Double, are on the receiving end of one of the all-time upsets when they lose 1–0 to Wimbledon in the FA Cup final after a John Aldridge penalty is saved by Dave Beasant, the first-ever spot-kick failure in an FA Cup final at Wembley and his first in 12 penalties for Liverpool.

Dalglish is named Manager of the Year for the second time.

Competition	Appearances	Goals
Football League	0 (2)	0
FA Cup	0 (0)	0
Littlewoods Cup	0 (0)	0
Totals	*0 (2)*	*0*

1988–89

Another season of appalling tragedy for Liverpool. Their FA Cup semi-final against Nottingham Forest at Hillsborough is abandoned after six minutes following crushing at the Leppings Lane end of the stadium in which 96 supporters die. A fortnight later Liverpool play a Disaster Appeal game at Dalglish's former club Celtic which raises more than £300,000. Dalglish plays at Parkhead on an emotional occasion, his first start for Liverpool since a pre-season friendly in Copenhagen in July 1987, and scores in a 4–0 win.

After long deliberation about their FA Cup future in the aftermath of the Hillsborough disaster, Liverpool continue in the competition and beat Forest 3–1 in the re-staged semi-final at Old Trafford to book an all-Merseyside Wembley meeting with Everton. Ian Rush steps off the substitute's bench to score twice in extra time and give Liverpool a thrilling 3–2 win and surpass Dixie Dean's 19-goal Mersey derby record.

An incredible climax to the season six days later sees Arsenal snatch the championship and deny Liverpool the Double with an injury-time goal from Michael Thomas at Anfield. The London club win 2–0 to go level on points (76) with Liverpool and with an identical goal difference (37). But they are champions on superior number of goals scored (73 to 65).

Competition	Appearances	Goals
League	0 (0)	0
FA Cup	0 (0)	0
Littlewoods Cup	0 (1)	0
Mercantile Credit Trophy	0 (1)	0
Totals	*0 (2)*	*0*

1989–90

Liverpool sweep to their 18th championship, their 10th in 15 seasons and their third of Dalglish's five-season managerial reign. A 2–1 home win over QPR in April secures the title, making Liverpool the first club to be champions in four consecutive decades – 1960s, 1970s, 1980s and 1990s. The championship success sees captain Alan Hansen equal Phil Neal's all-time record of eight title medals as a player. It is also Dalglish's eighth, five as a player and three as player-manager.

The following Tuesday evening, 1 May, Dalglish makes his farewell appearance as a Liverpool player as 72nd-minute substitute for Jan Molby in the 1–0 home win over Derby County. He is involved in the move for Gary Gillespie to score the only goal. At the end, following the championship presentation, he throws his No 14 jersey into the Kop from where his 13-year-old son Paul is watching, wearing Michel Platini's Juventus shirt.

Dalglish is named Manager of the Year for the third time.

Competition	Appearances	Goals
League	0 (1)	0
FA Cup	0 (0)	0
Littlewoods Cup	0 (0)	0
Totals	*0 (1)*	*0*

1990–91

A crowd of 30,461, paying estimated receipts of £150,000, turns out at Anfield to salute Dalglish for his testimonial game between Liverpool and Spanish club Real Sociedad whose team includes former Liverpool star John Aldridge and two other English players in Kevin Richardson and Dalian Atkinson. Dalglish plays for 75 minutes, laying on the passes for Liverpool's first two goals in their 3–1 win, before being replaced by Peter Beardsley. As he walks off the pitch he gives his famous No 7 jersey to 76-year-old wheelchair-bound Eileen Leffler.

The football world is stunned on Friday, 22 February. With Liverpool top of the league and engaged in an FA Cup fifth-round marathon against Everton, Dalglish makes the shock announcement that he is resigning as manager. His last game in charge, less than 48 hours earlier, is the pulsating 4–4 draw with Everton in a Goodison Park replay. Ronnie Moran takes over as acting manager.

Playing Career Record
Liverpool FC

	Appearances	Goals
League	355	118
FA Cup	36	13
LeagueCup (inc. Milk and Littlewoods)	59	27
European Cup	47	10
Charity Shield	7	1
World Club Championship	2	0
European Super Cup	4	1
Mercantile Credit Trophy	1	0
Screen Sport Super Cup	3	2
Dubai Super Cup	1	0
Totals	*515*	*172*

INDEX